STA

WA

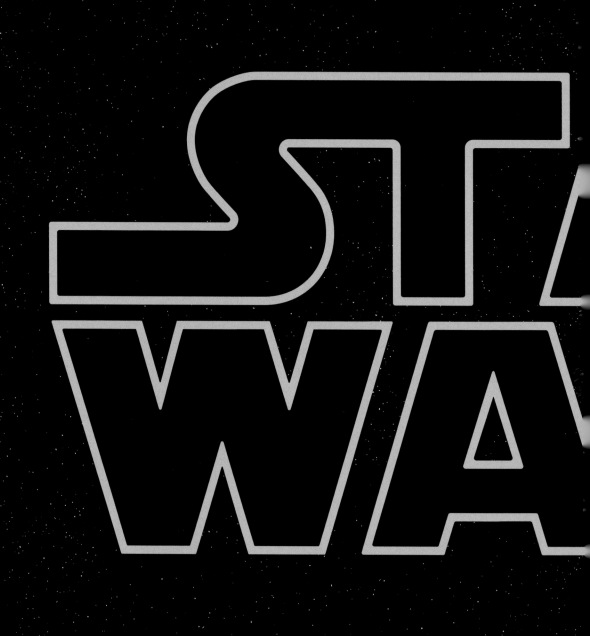

STAR WARS
THE LAST JEDI

GARY WHITTA
Writer

MICHAEL WALSH
with **JOSH HIXON** (#6)
Artists

MIKE SPICER
Colorist

VC'S TRAVIS LANHAM
Letterer

MIKE DEL MUNDO (#1), **KAMOME SHIRAHAMA** (#2), **PHIL NOTO** (#3), **RAHZZAH** (#4),
PAOLO RIVERA (#5) AND **MAHMUD ASRAR & FRANK D'ARMATA** (#6)
Cover Artists

TOM GRONEMAN
WITH **EMILY NEWCOMEN**
Assistant Editors

HEATHER ANTOS, JORDAN D. WHITE
& MARK PANICCIA
Editors

Based on the screenplay by
RIAN JOHNSON

For Lucasfilm:

NICK MARTINO
Assistant Editor

ROBERT SIMPSON
Senior Editor

JENNIFER HEDDLE
Executive Editor

MICHAEL SIGLAIN
Creative Director

JAMES WAUGH, LELAND CHEE, MATT MARTIN
Lucasfilm Story Group

COLLECTION EDITOR: **JENNIFER GRÜNWALD**
ASSISTANT EDITOR: **CAITLIN O'CONNELL**
ASSOCIATE MANAGING EDITOR: **KATERI WOODY**
EDITOR, SPECIAL PROJECTS: **MARK D. BEAZLEY**
VP PRODUCTION & SPECIAL PROJECTS: **JEFF YOUNGQUIST**

SVP PRINT, SALES & MARKETING: **DAVID GABRIEL**
EDITOR IN CHIEF: **C.B. CEBULSKI**
CHIEF CREATIVE OFFICER: **JOE QUESADA**
PRESIDENT: **DAN BUCKLEY**
EXECUTIVE PRODUCER: **ALAN FINE**

DISNEP · LUCASFILM

STAR WARS: THE LAST JEDI ADAPTATION. Contains material originally published in magazine form as STAR WARS: THE LAST JEDI ADAPTATION #1-6. First printing 2018. ISBN 978-1-302-91201-7. Published by MARVEL WORLDWIDE, INC., a subsidiary of MARVEL ENTERTAINMENT, LLC. OFFICE OF PUBLICATION: 135 West 50th Street, New York, NY 10020. STAR WARS and related text and illustrations are trademarks and/or copyrights, in the United States and other countries, of Lucasfilm Ltd. and/or its affiliates. © & TM Lucasfilm Ltd. No similarity between any of the names, characters, persons, and/or institutions in this magazine with those of any living or dead person or institution is intended, and any such similarity which may exist is purely coincidental. Printed in the U.S.A. DAN BUCKLEY, President, Marvel Entertainment; JOHN NEE, Publisher; JOE QUESADA, Chief Creative Officer; TOM BREVOORT, SVP of Publishing; DAVID BOGART, SVP of Business Affairs & Operations, Publishing & Partnership; DAVID GABRIEL, SVP of Sales & Marketing, Publishing; JEFF YOUNGQUIST, VP of Production & Special Projects; DAN CARR, Executive Director of Publishing Technology; ALEX MORALES, Director of Publishing Operations; DAN EDINGTON, Managing Editor; SUSAN CRESPI, Production Manager; STAN LEE, Chairman Emeritus. For information regarding advertising in Marvel Comics or on Marvel.com, please contact Vit DeBellis, Custom Solutions & Integrated Advertising Manager, at vdebellis@marvel.com. For Marvel subscription inquiries, please call 888-511-5480. Manufactured between 8/31/2018 and 10/2/2018 by LSC COMMUNICATIONS INC., KENDALLVILLE, IN, USA.

10 9 8 7 6 5 4 3 2 1

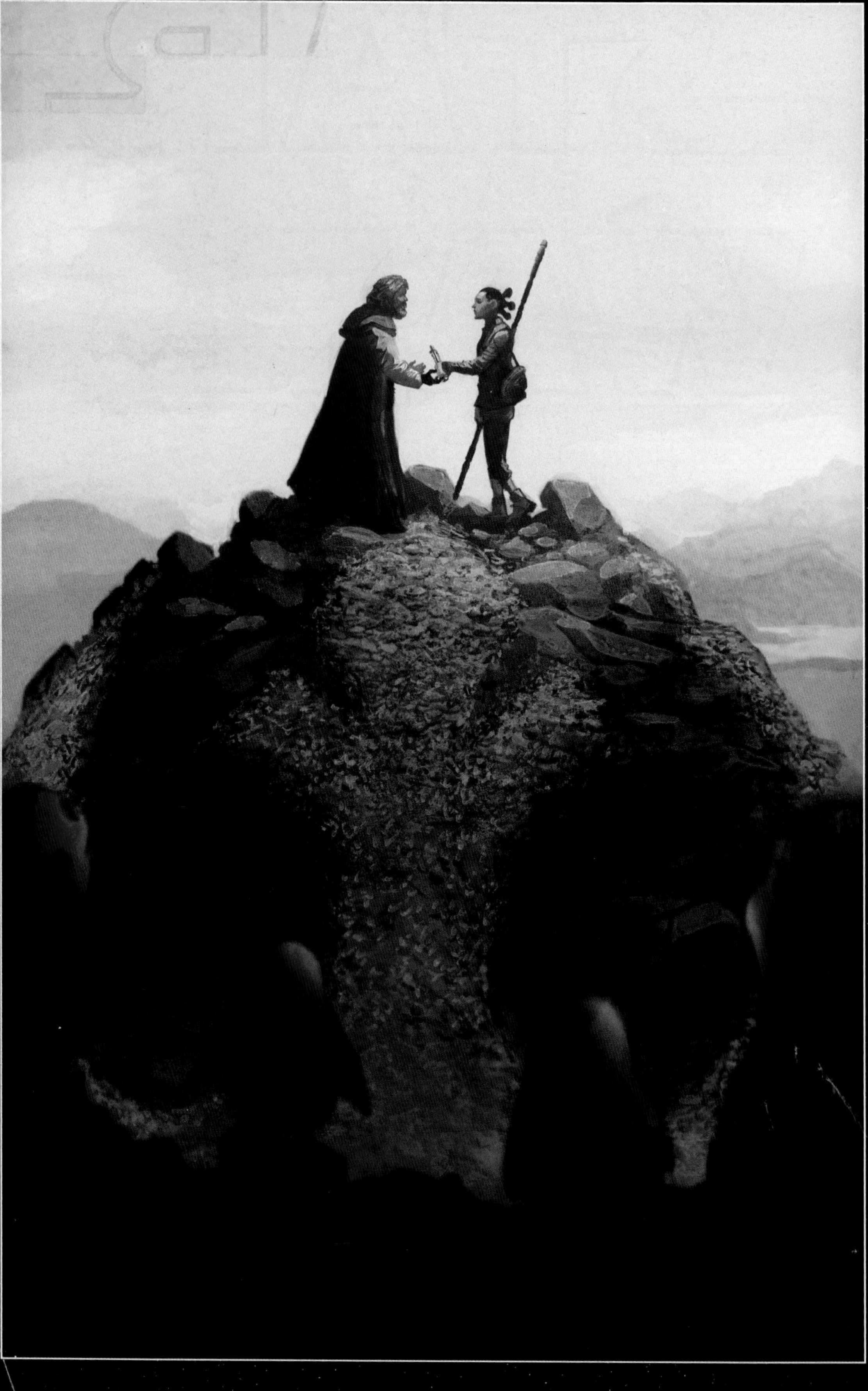

THE LAST JEDI #1

AR

RS

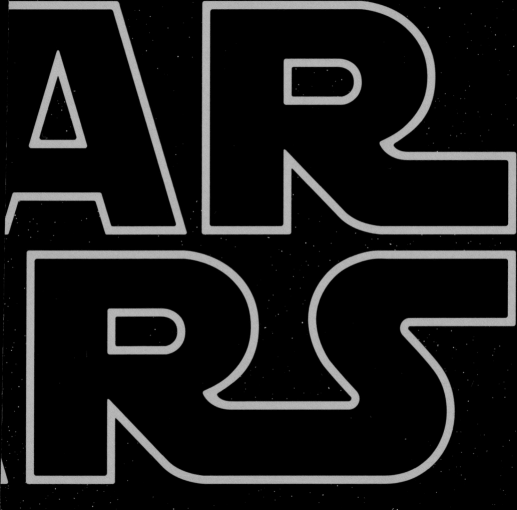

Episode VIII, Part I
THE LAST JEDI

The FIRST ORDER reigns. Having decimated the peaceful Republic, Supreme Leader Snoke now deploys his merciless legions to seize military control of the galaxy.

Only General Leia Organa's band of RESISTANCE fighters stands against the rising tyranny, certain that Jedi Master Luke Skywalker will return and restore a spark of hope to the fight.

But the Resistance has been exposed. As the First Order speeds toward the Rebel base, the brave heroes mount a desperate escape....

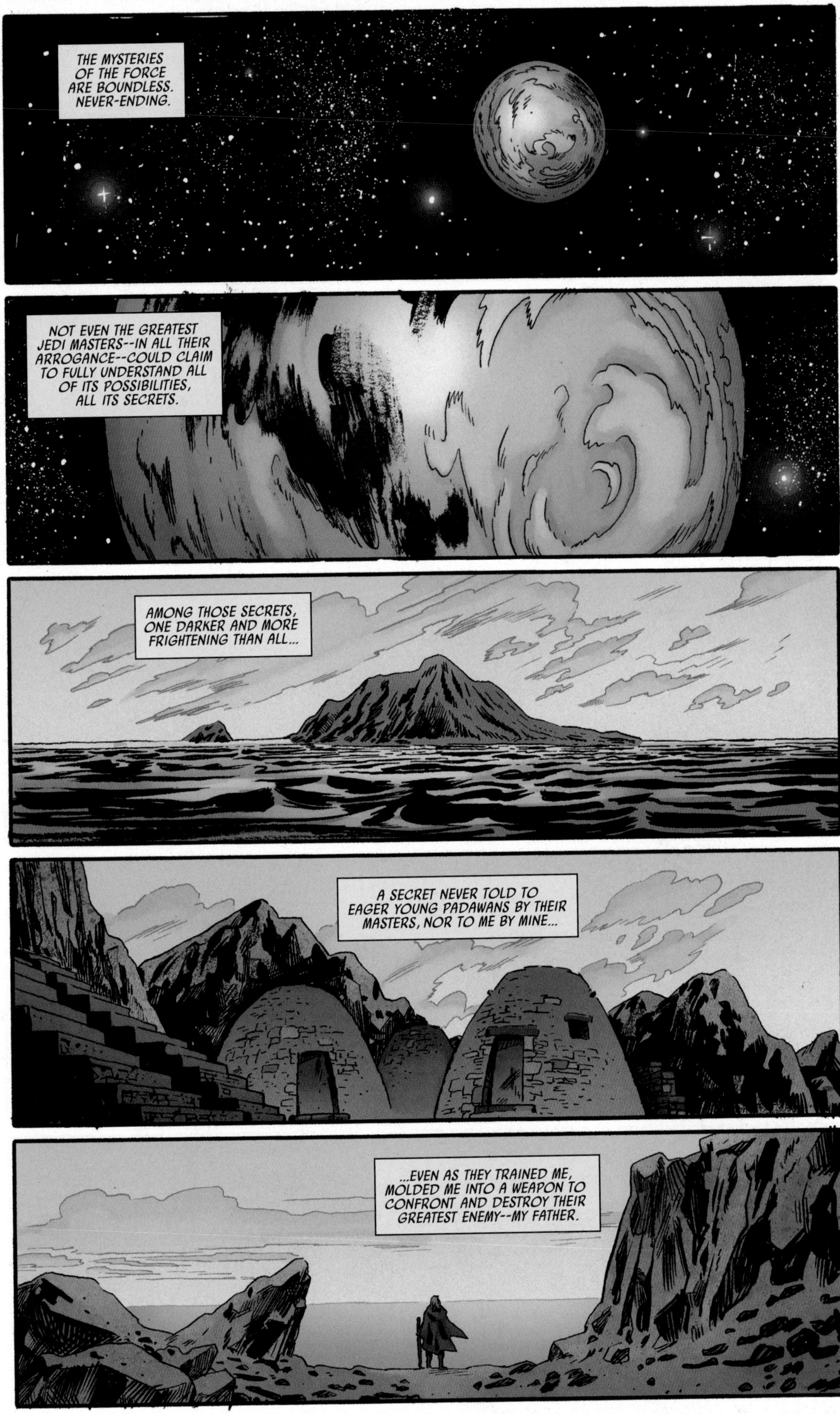
THE MYSTERIES OF THE FORCE ARE BOUNDLESS. NEVER-ENDING.
NOT EVEN THE GREATEST JEDI MASTERS--IN ALL THEIR ARROGANCE--COULD CLAIM TO FULLY UNDERSTAND ALL OF ITS POSSIBILITIES, ALL ITS SECRETS.
AMONG THOSE SECRETS, ONE DARKER AND MORE FRIGHTENING THAN ALL...
A SECRET NEVER TOLD TO EAGER YOUNG PADAWANS BY THEIR MASTERS, NOR TO ME BY MINE...
...EVEN AS THEY TRAINED ME, MOLDED ME INTO A WEAPON TO CONFRONT AND DESTROY THEIR GREATEST ENEMY--MY FATHER.

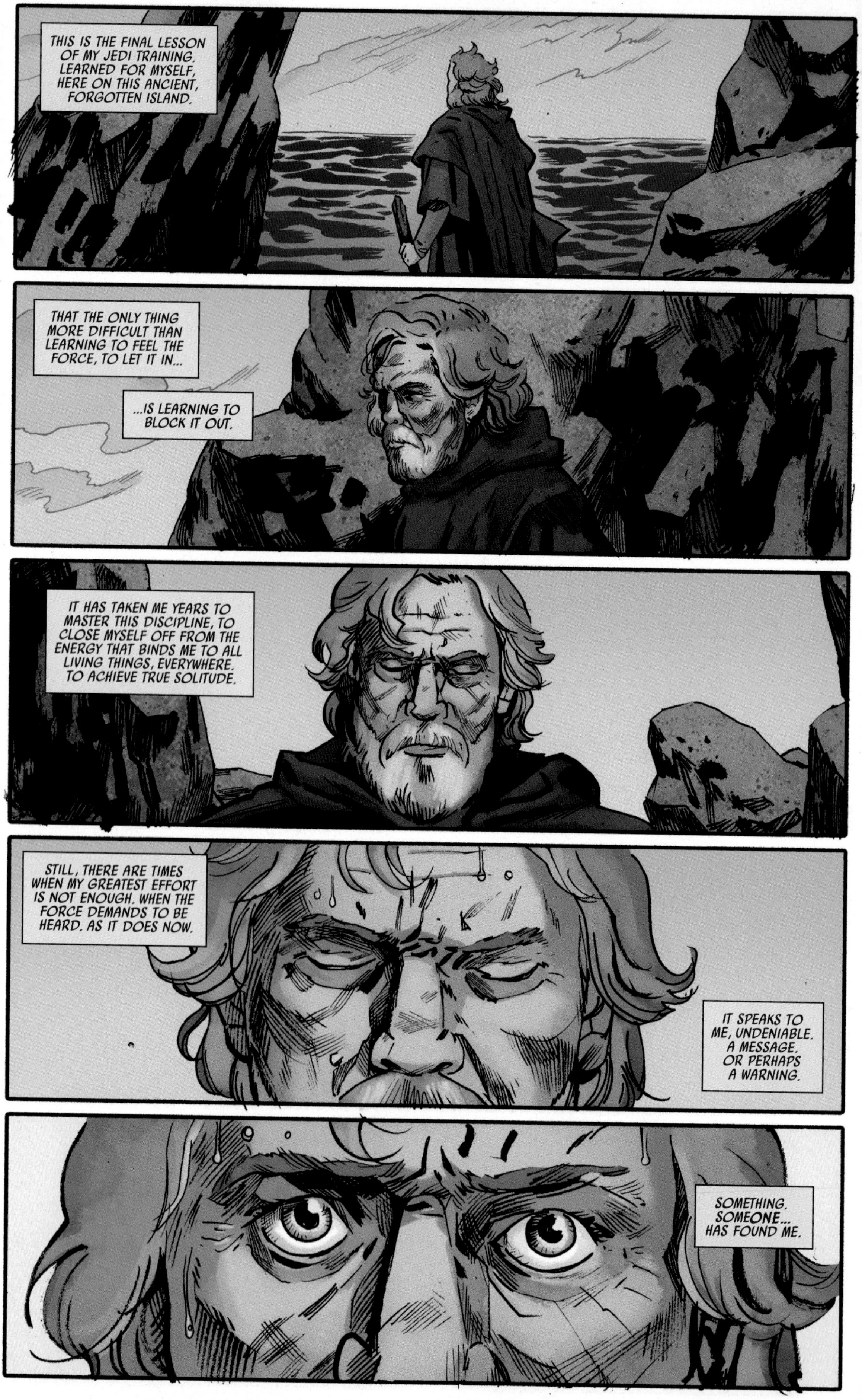
THIS IS THE FINAL LESSON OF MY JEDI TRAINING. LEARNED FOR MYSELF, HERE ON THIS ANCIENT, FORGOTTEN ISLAND.
THAT THE ONLY THING MORE DIFFICULT THAN LEARNING TO FEEL THE FORCE, TO LET IT IN...
...IS LEARNING TO BLOCK IT OUT.
IT HAS TAKEN ME YEARS TO MASTER THIS DISCIPLINE, TO CLOSE MYSELF OFF FROM THE ENERGY THAT BINDS ME TO ALL LIVING THINGS, EVERYWHERE. TO ACHIEVE TRUE SOLITUDE.
STILL, THERE ARE TIMES WHEN MY GREATEST EFFORT IS NOT ENOUGH. WHEN THE FORCE DEMANDS TO BE HEARD. AS IT DOES NOW.
IT SPEAKS TO ME, UNDENIABLE. A MESSAGE. OR PERHAPS A WARNING.
SOMETHING. SOMEONE... HAS FOUND ME.

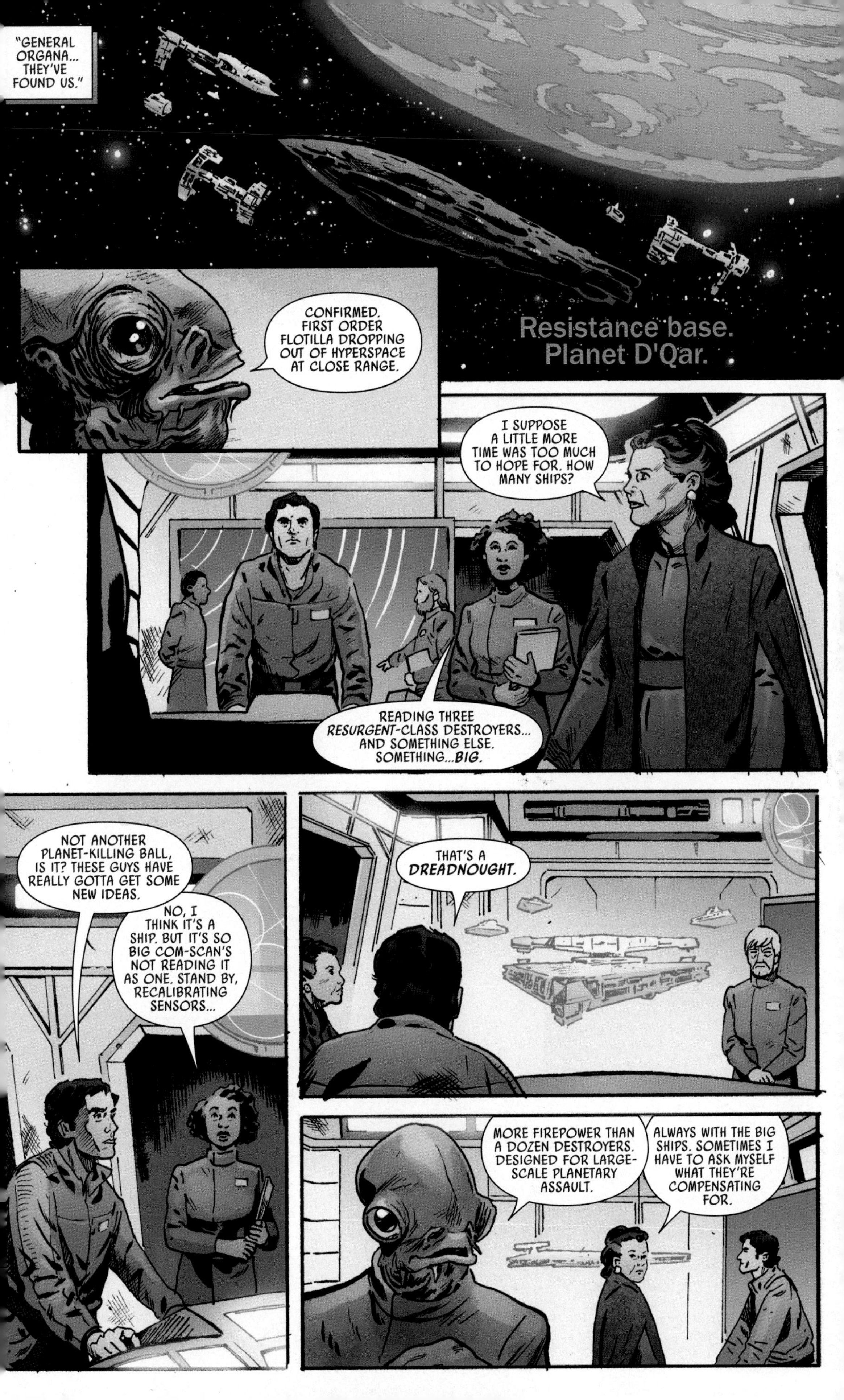
"GENERAL ORGANA... THEY'VE FOUND US."
CONFIRMED. FIRST ORDER FLOTILLA DROPPING OUT OF HYPERSPACE AT CLOSE RANGE.
Resistance base. Planet D'Qar.
I SUPPOSE A LITTLE MORE TIME WAS TOO MUCH TO HOPE FOR. HOW MANY SHIPS?
READING THREE RESURGENT-CLASS DESTROYERS... AND SOMETHING ELSE. SOMETHING...BIG.
NOT ANOTHER PLANET-KILLING BALL, IS IT? THESE GUYS HAVE REALLY GOTTA GET SOME NEW IDEAS.
NO, I THINK IT'S A SHIP. BUT IT'S SO BIG COM-SCAN'S NOT READING IT AS ONE. STAND BY, RECALIBRATING SENSORS...
THAT'S A DREADNOUGHT.
MORE FIREPOWER THAN A DOZEN DESTROYERS. DESIGNED FOR LARGE-SCALE PLANETARY ASSAULT.
ALWAYS WITH THE BIG SHIPS. SOMETIMES I HAVE TO ASK MYSELF WHAT THEY'RE COMPENSATING FOR.

IF THAT THING GETS INTO FIRING RANGE BEFORE THE LAST OF OUR PEOPLE ARE OFF THE SURFACE...

CONNIX, HOW MUCH MORE TIME DO YOU NEED DOWN THERE?

WE SEE IT. WE'LL BUY YOU AS MUCH TIME AS WE CAN.

I NEED OPTIONS.

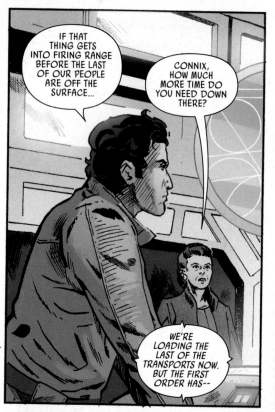

WE'RE LOADING THE LAST OF THE TRANSPORTS NOW. BUT THE FIRST ORDER HAS--

THERE ARE NONE. WE MUST RETREAT INTO HYPERSPACE.

THIS ISN'T MY FIRST EVACUATION, GIAL. I'M NOT LEAVING ANYONE BEHIND.

WHAT I WOULDN'T GIVE FOR ONE GOOD ION CANNON RIGHT NOW.

HOW ABOUT THE NEXT BEST THING?

"WE'VE CAUGHT THEM IN THE MIDDLE OF THEIR EVACUATION..."

...THE ENTIRETY OF THE RESISTANCE, IN ONE FRAGILE BASKET.

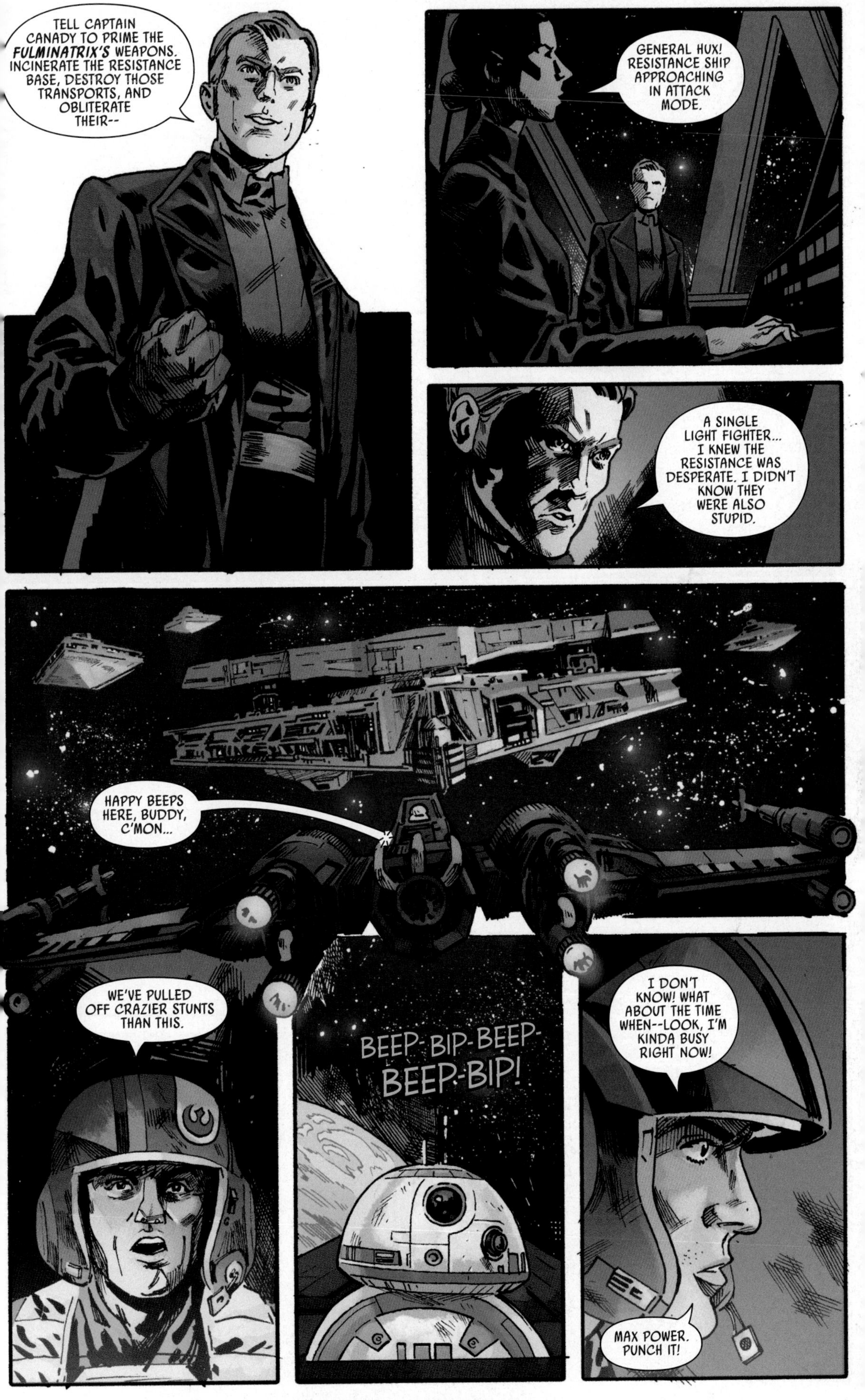
TELL CAPTAIN CANADY TO PRIME THE FULMINATRIX'S WEAPONS. INCINERATE THE RESISTANCE BASE, DESTROY THOSE TRANSPORTS, AND OBLITERATE THEIR--
GENERAL HUX! RESISTANCE SHIP APPROACHING IN ATTACK MODE.
A SINGLE LIGHT FIGHTER... I KNEW THE RESISTANCE WAS DESPERATE. I DIDN'T KNOW THEY WERE ALSO STUPID.
HAPPY BEEPS HERE, BUDDY, C'MON...
WE'VE PULLED OFF CRAZIER STUNTS THAN THIS.
BEEP-BIP-BEEP-BEEP-BIP!
I DON'T KNOW! WHAT ABOUT THE TIME WHEN--LOOK, I'M KINDA BUSY RIGHT NOW!
MAX POWER. PUNCH IT!

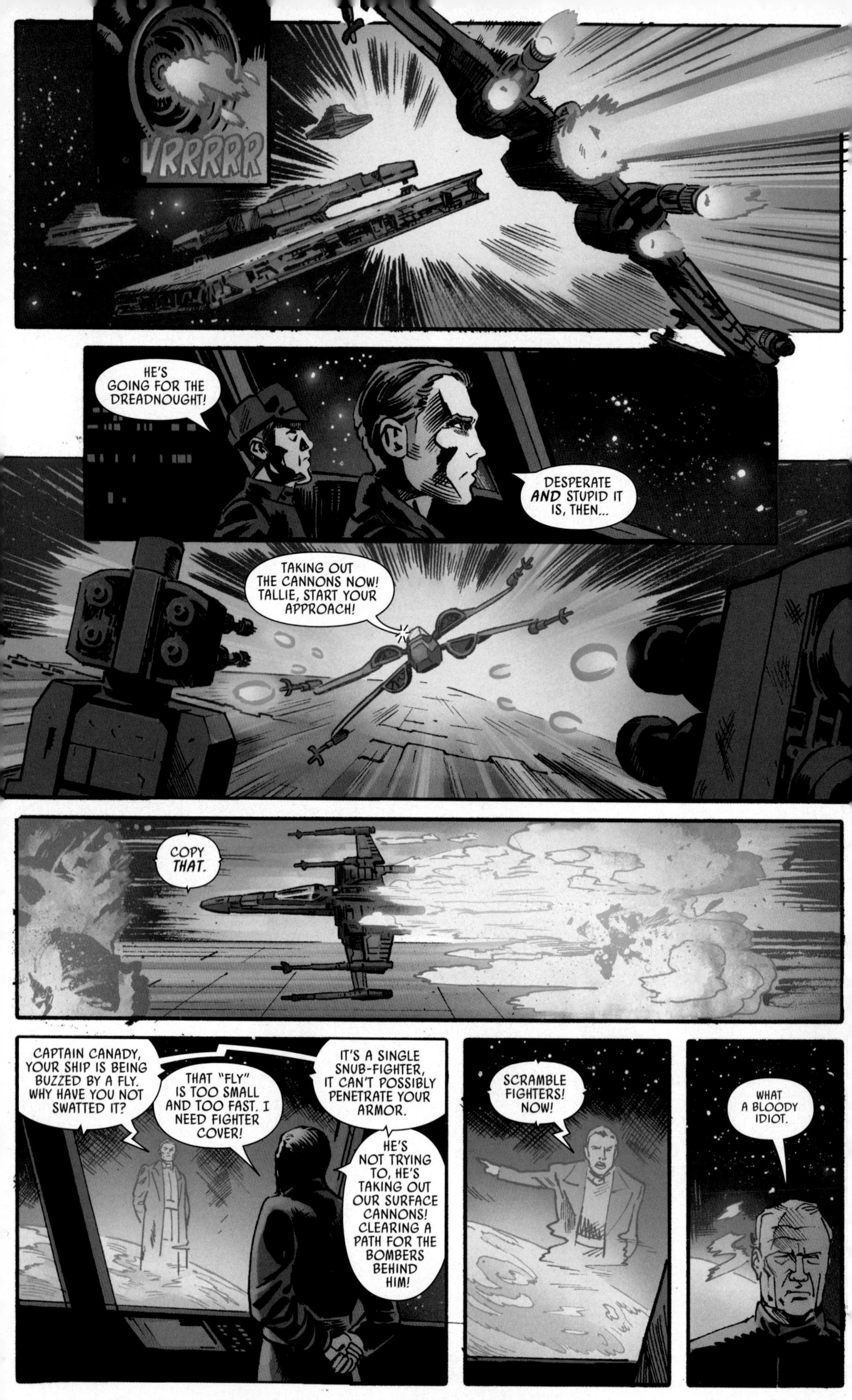
VRRRRR
HE'S GOING FOR THE DREADNOUGHT!
DESPERATE AND STUPID IT IS, THEN...
TAKING OUT THE CANNONS NOW! TALLIE, START YOUR APPROACH!
COPY THAT.
CAPTAIN CANADY, YOUR SHIP IS BEING BUZZED BY A FLY. WHY HAVE YOU NOT SWATTED IT?
THAT "FLY" IS TOO SMALL AND TOO FAST. I NEED FIGHTER COVER!
IT'S A SINGLE SNUB-FIGHTER, IT CAN'T POSSIBLY PENETRATE YOUR ARMOR.
HE'S NOT TRYING TO, HE'S TAKING OUT OUR SURFACE CANNONS! CLEARING A PATH FOR THE BOMBERS BEHIND HIM!
SCRAMBLE FIGHTERS! NOW!
WHAT A BLOODY IDIOT.

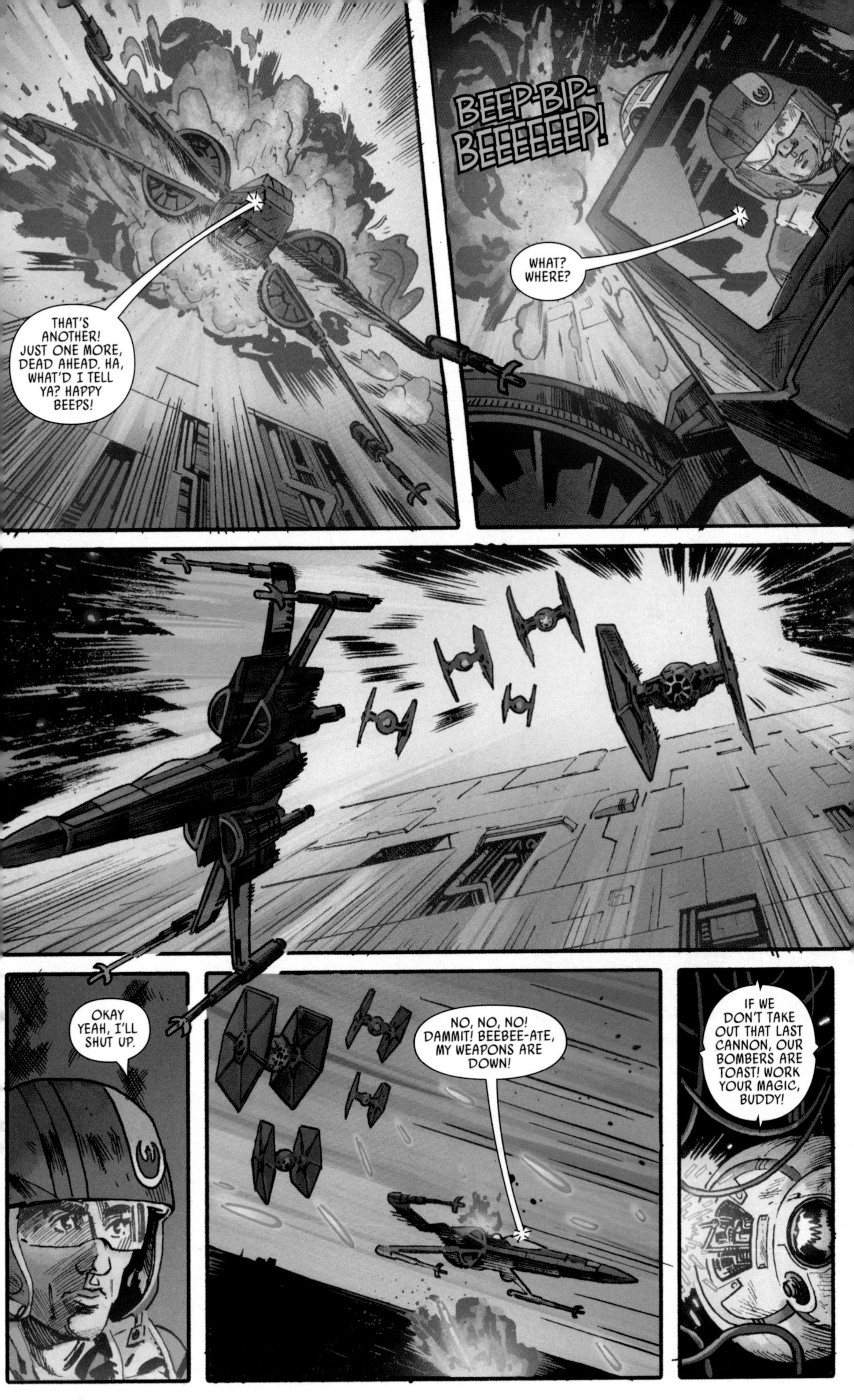
THAT'S ANOTHER! JUST ONE MORE, DEAD AHEAD. HA, WHAT'D I TELL YA? HAPPY BEEPS!
BEEP-BIP-BEEEEEEP!
WHAT? WHERE?
OKAY YEAH, I'LL SHUT UP.
NO, NO, NO! DAMMIT! BEEBEE-ATE, MY WEAPONS ARE DOWN!
IF WE DON'T TAKE OUT THAT LAST CANNON, OUR BOMBERS ARE TOAST! WORK YOUR MAGIC, BUDDY!

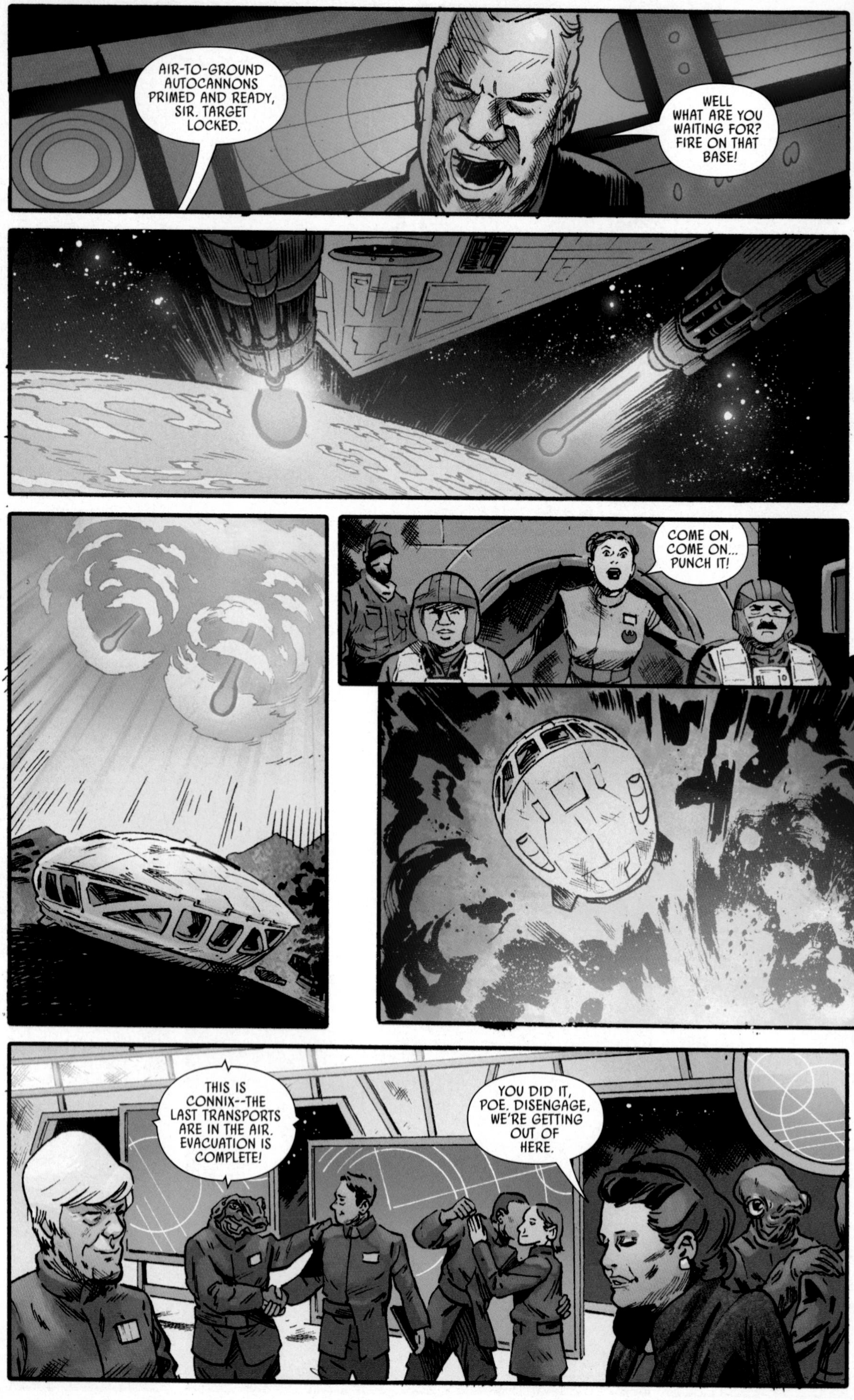
AIR-TO-GROUND AUTOCANNONS PRIMED AND READY, SIR. TARGET LOCKED.
WELL WHAT ARE YOU WAITING FOR? FIRE ON THAT BASE!
COME ON, COME ON... PUNCH IT!
THIS IS CONNIX--THE LAST TRANSPORTS ARE IN THE AIR. EVACUATION IS COMPLETE!
YOU DID IT, POE. DISENGAGE, WE'RE GETTING OUT OF HERE.

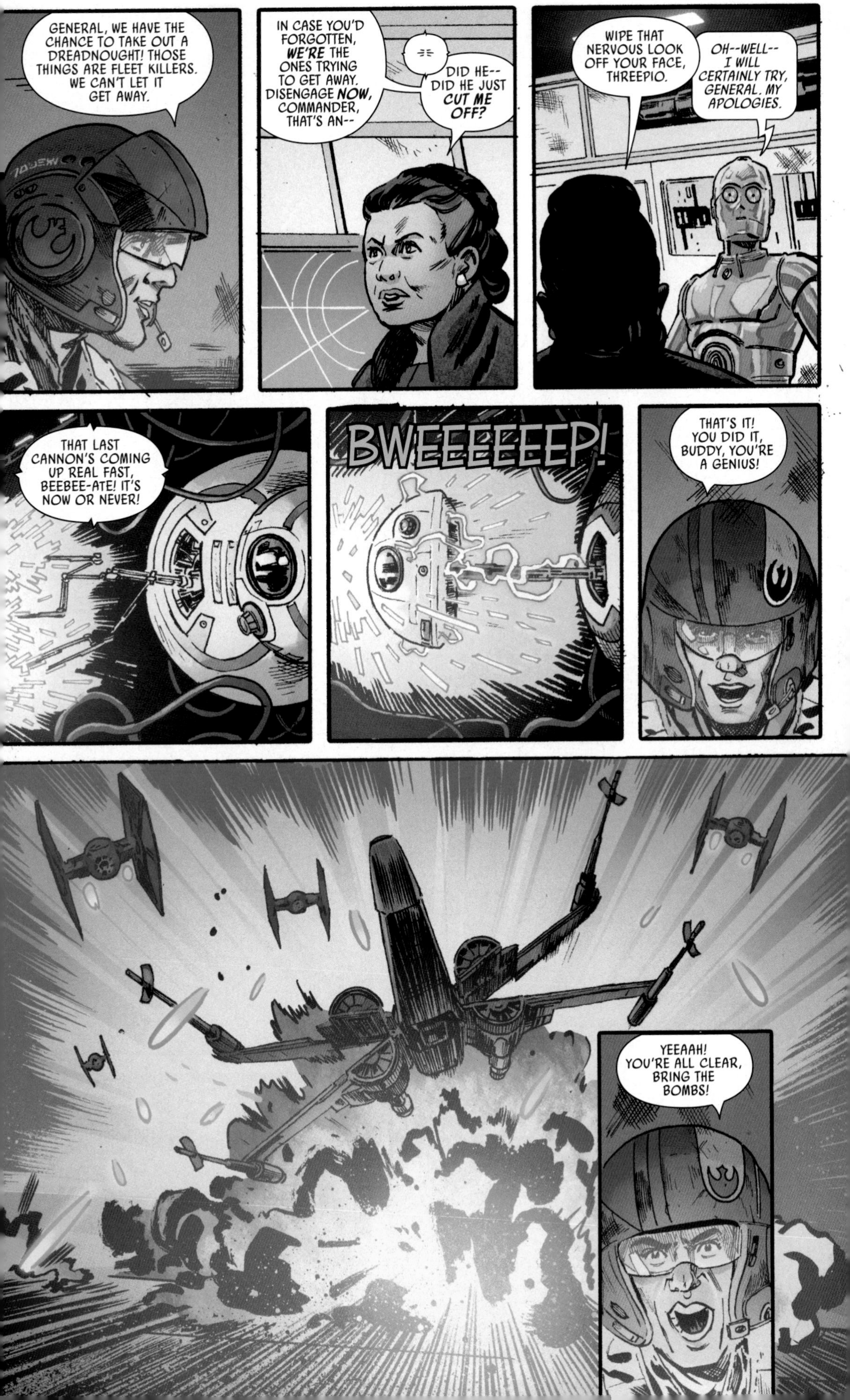

GENERAL, WE HAVE THE CHANCE TO TAKE OUT A DREADNOUGHT! THOSE THINGS ARE FLEET KILLERS. WE CAN'T LET IT GET AWAY.
IN CASE YOU'D FORGOTTEN, WE'RE THE ONES TRYING TO GET AWAY. DISENGAGE NOW, COMMANDER, THAT'S AN--
DID HE--DID HE JUST CUT ME OFF?
WIPE THAT NERVOUS LOOK OFF YOUR FACE, THREEPIO.
OH--WELL--I WILL CERTAINLY TRY, GENERAL. MY APOLOGIES.
THAT LAST CANNON'S COMING UP REAL FAST, BEEBEE-ATE! IT'S NOW OR NEVER!
BWEEEEEEEP!
THAT'S IT! YOU DID IT, BUDDY, YOU'RE A GENIUS!
YEEAAH! YOU'RE ALL CLEAR, BRING THE BOMBS!

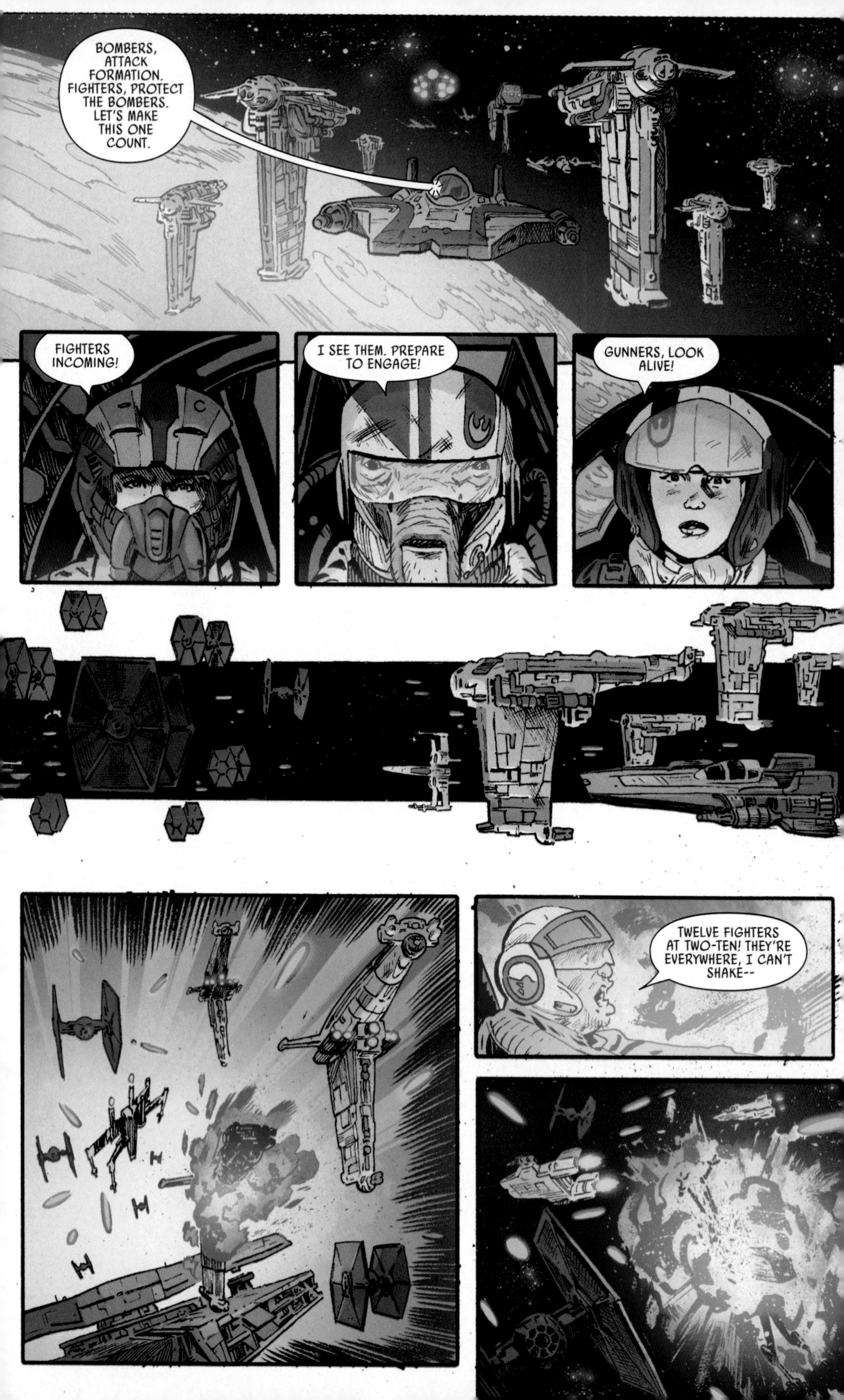
BOMBERS, ATTACK FORMATION. FIGHTERS, PROTECT THE BOMBERS. LET'S MAKE THIS ONE COUNT.
FIGHTERS INCOMING!
I SEE THEM. PREPARE TO ENGAGE!
GUNNERS, LOOK ALIVE!
TWELVE FIGHTERS AT TWO-TEN! THEY'RE EVERYWHERE, I CAN'T SHAKE--

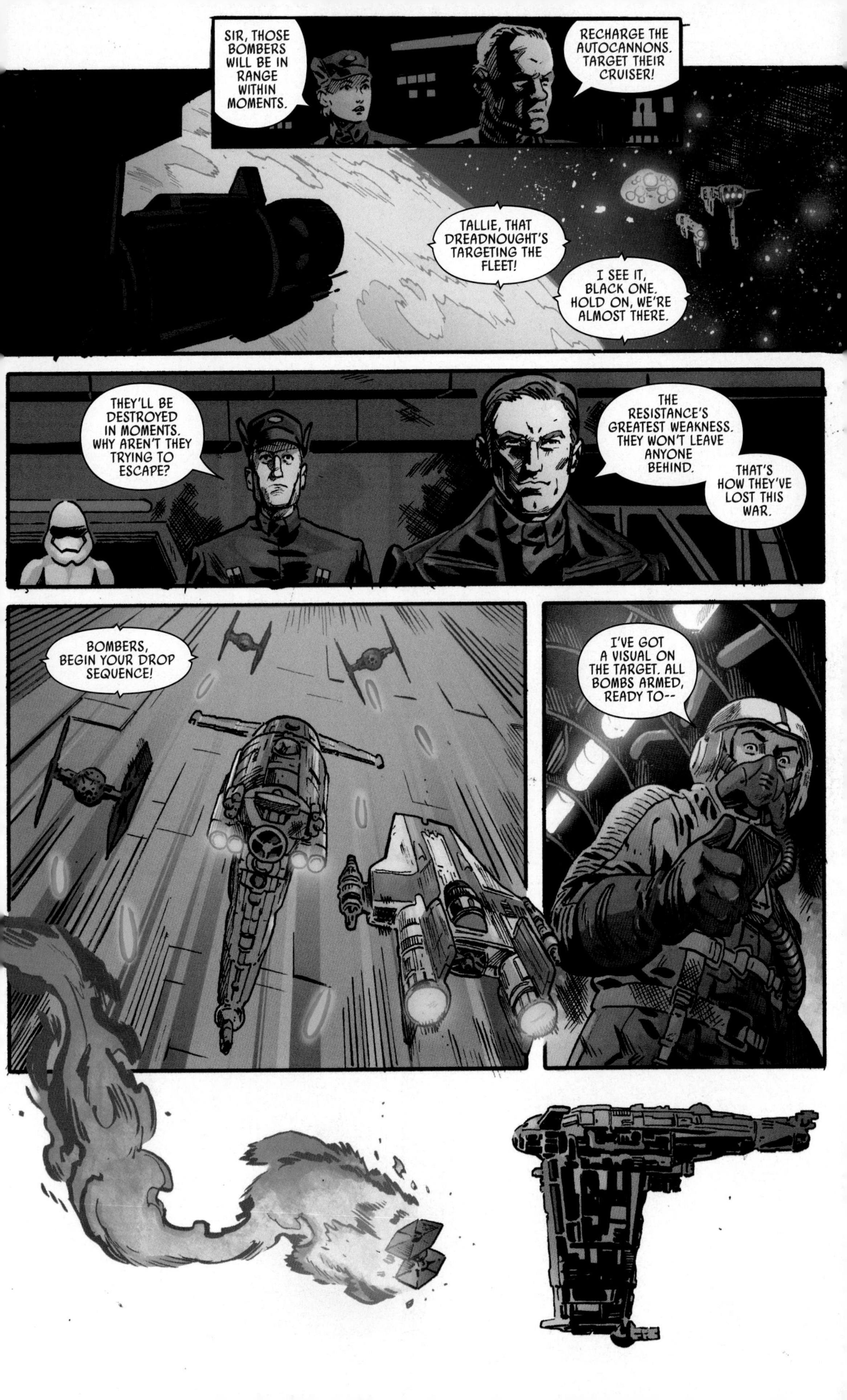
SIR, THOSE BOMBERS WILL BE IN RANGE WITHIN MOMENTS.
RECHARGE THE AUTOCANNONS. TARGET THEIR CRUISER!
TALLIE, THAT DREADNOUGHT'S TARGETING THE FLEET!
I SEE IT, BLACK ONE. HOLD ON, WE'RE ALMOST THERE.
THEY'LL BE DESTROYED IN MOMENTS. WHY AREN'T THEY TRYING TO ESCAPE?
THE RESISTANCE'S GREATEST WEAKNESS. THEY WON'T LEAVE ANYONE BEHIND.
THAT'S HOW THEY'VE LOST THIS WAR.
BOMBERS, BEGIN YOUR DROP SEQUENCE!
I'VE GOT A VISUAL ON THE TARGET. ALL BOMBS ARMED, READY TO--

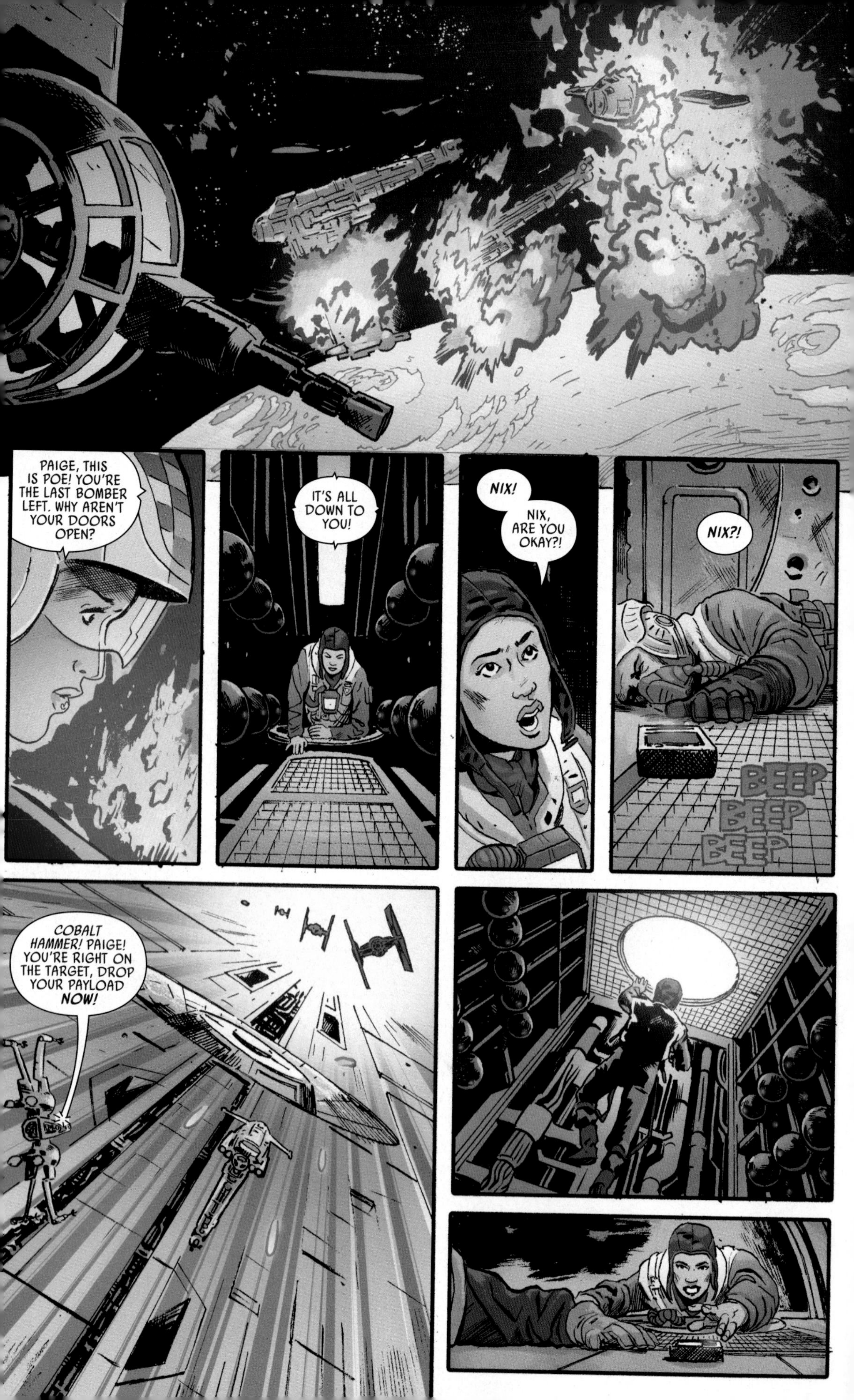
PAIGE, THIS IS POE! YOU'RE THE LAST BOMBER LEFT. WHY AREN'T YOUR DOORS OPEN?
IT'S ALL DOWN TO YOU!
NIX!
NIX, ARE YOU OKAY?!
NIX?!
BEEP
BEEP
BEEP
COBALT HAMMER! PAIGE! YOU'RE RIGHT ON THE TARGET, DROP YOUR PAYLOAD NOW!

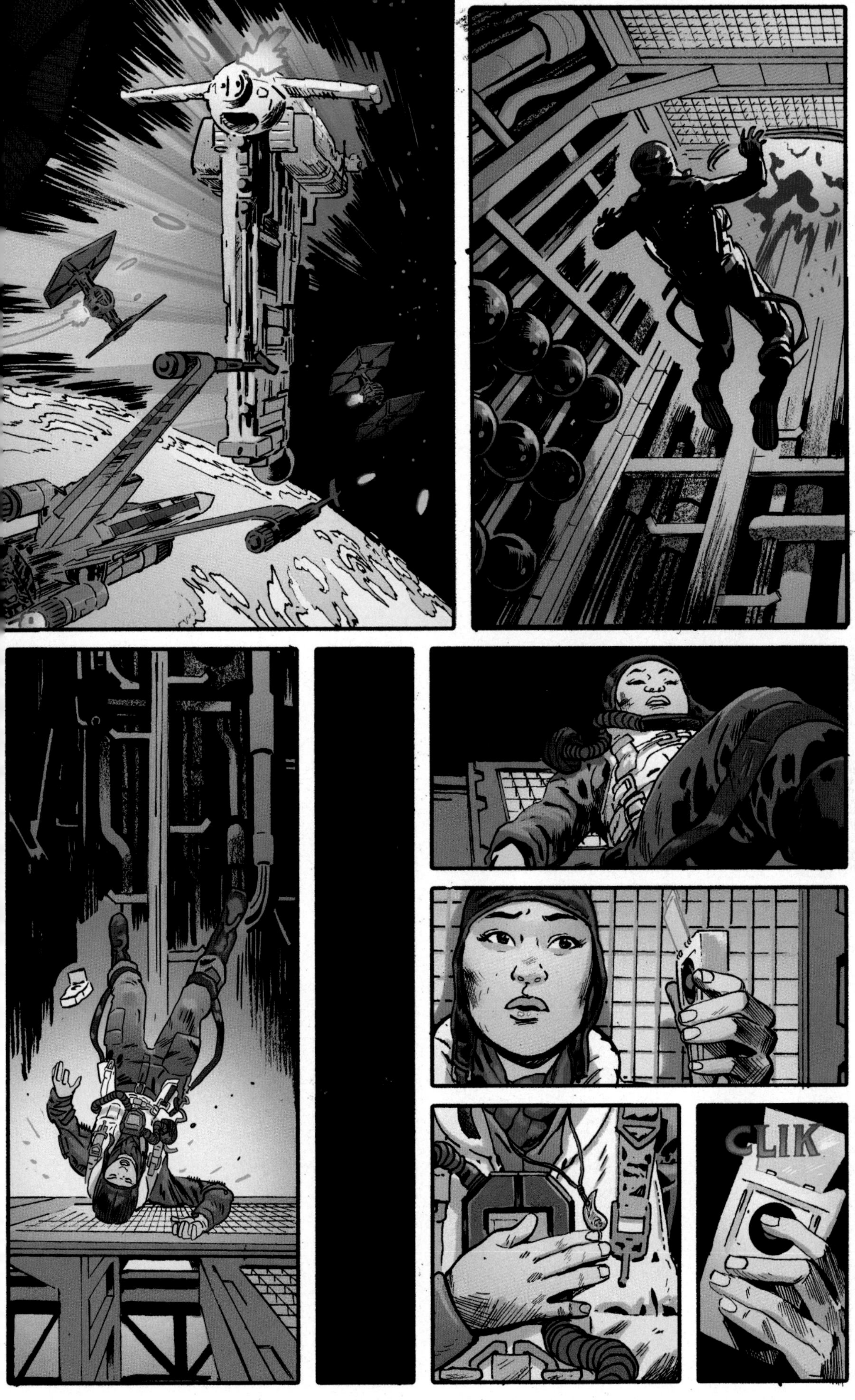
CLIK

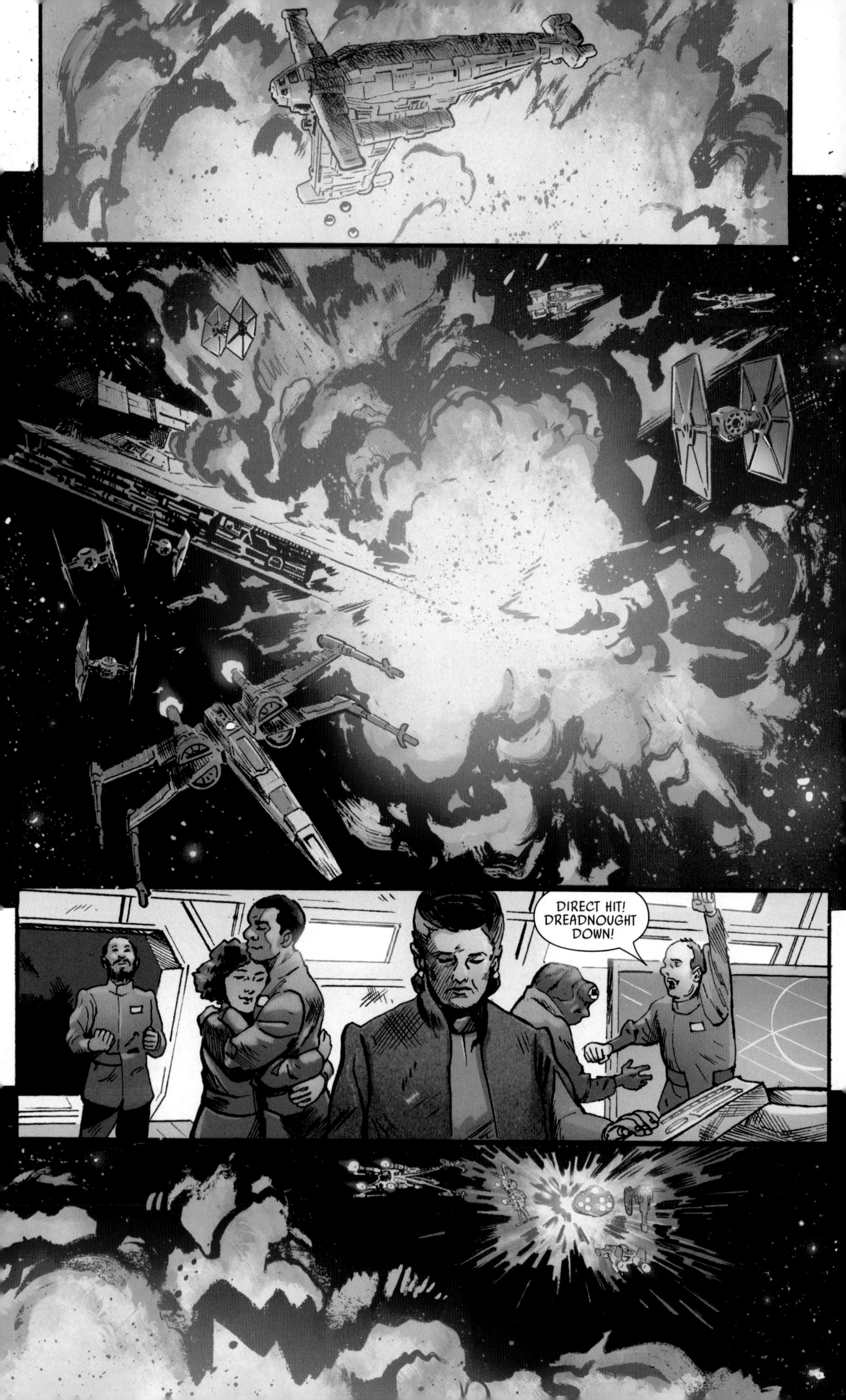
DIRECT HIT! DREADNOUGHT DOWN!

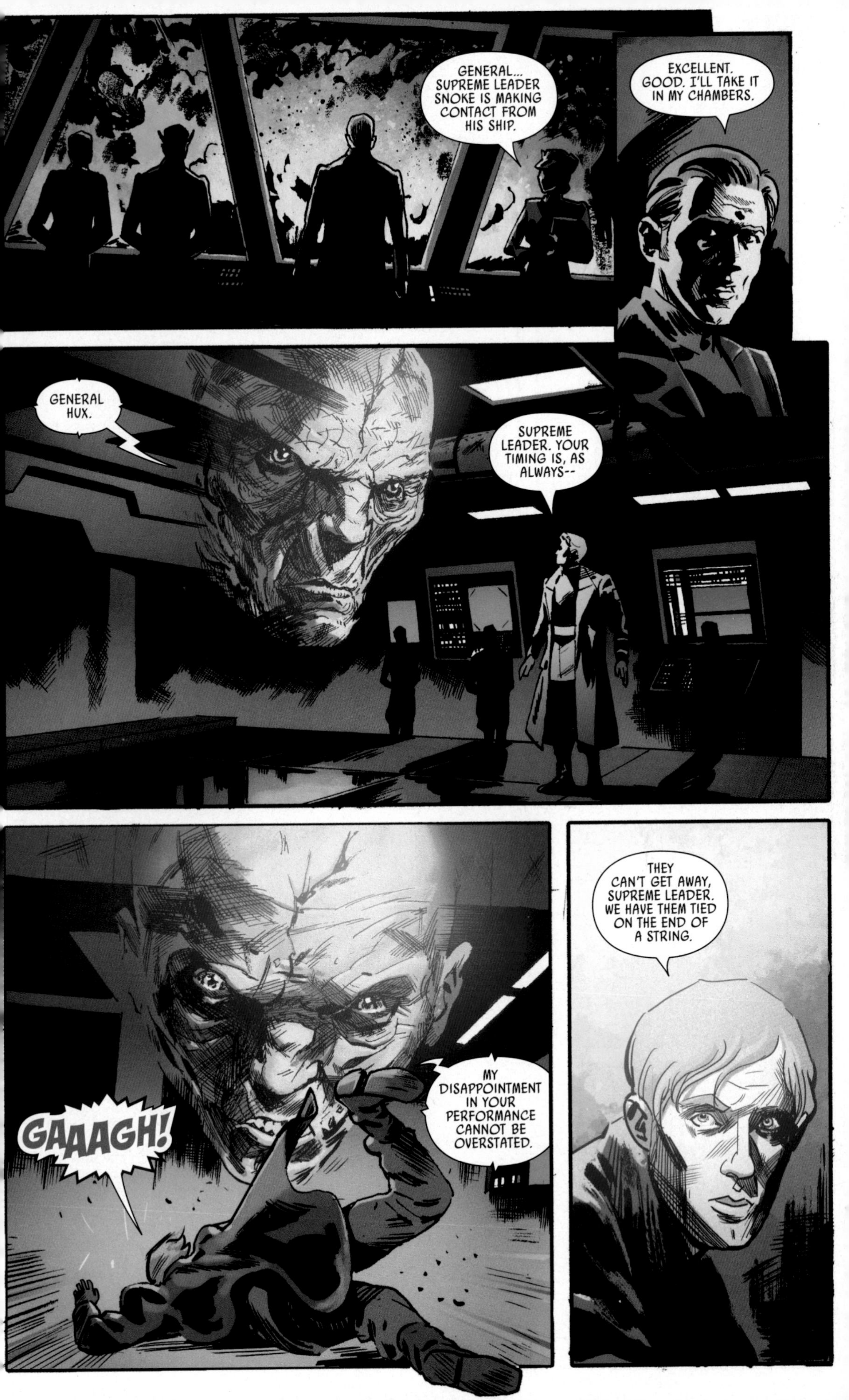
GENERAL... SUPREME LEADER SNOKE IS MAKING CONTACT FROM HIS SHIP.
EXCELLENT. GOOD. I'LL TAKE IT IN MY CHAMBERS.
GENERAL HUX.
SUPREME LEADER. YOUR TIMING IS, AS ALWAYS--
MY DISAPPOINTMENT IN YOUR PERFORMANCE CANNOT BE OVERSTATED.
GAAAGH!
THEY CAN'T GET AWAY, SUPREME LEADER. WE HAVE THEM TIED ON THE END OF A STRING.

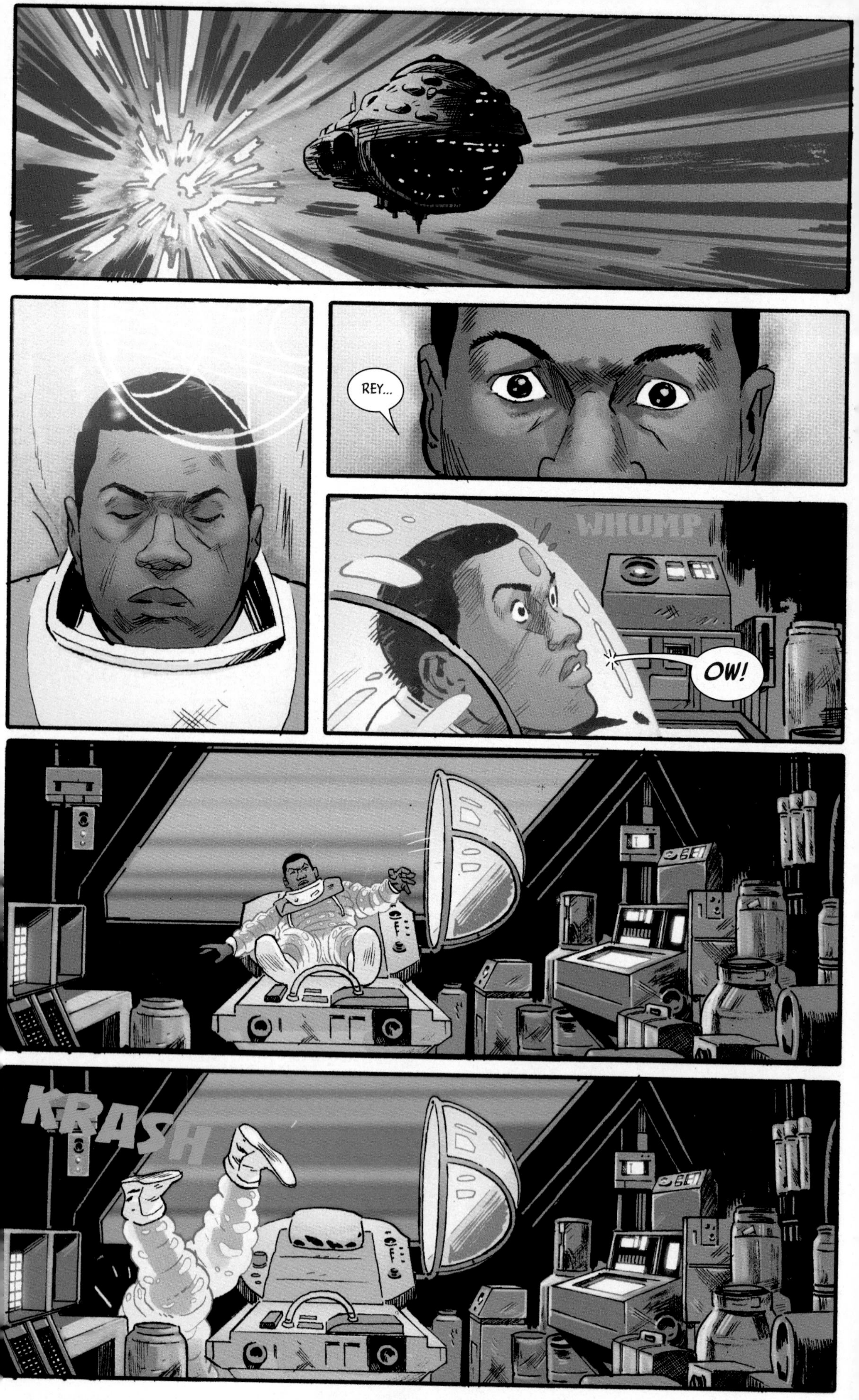
REY...
WHUMP
OW!
KRASH

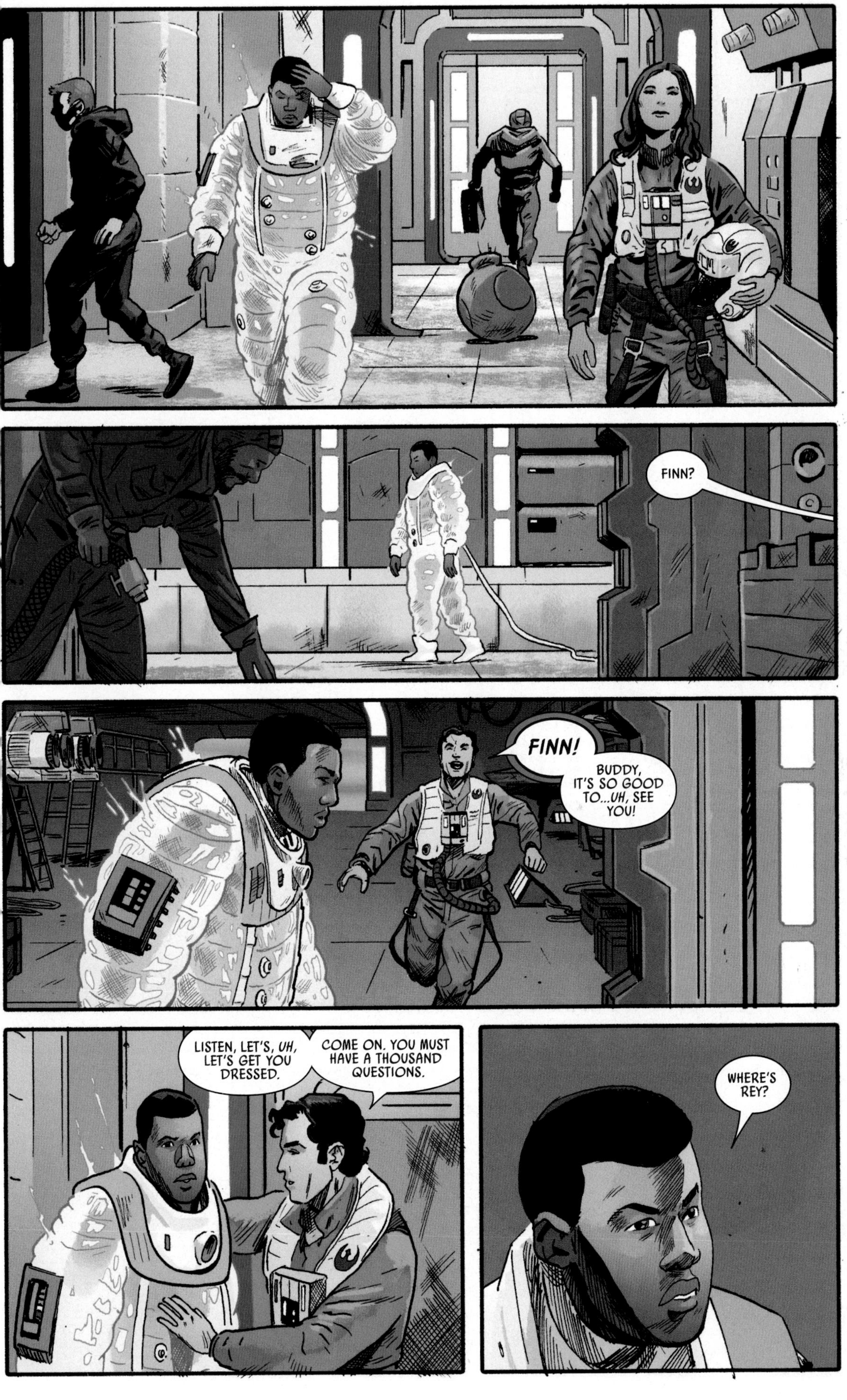
FINN?
FINN!
BUDDY, IT'S SO GOOD TO...UH, SEE YOU!
LISTEN, LET'S, UH, LET'S GET YOU DRESSED.
COME ON. YOU MUST HAVE A THOUSAND QUESTIONS.
WHERE'S REY?

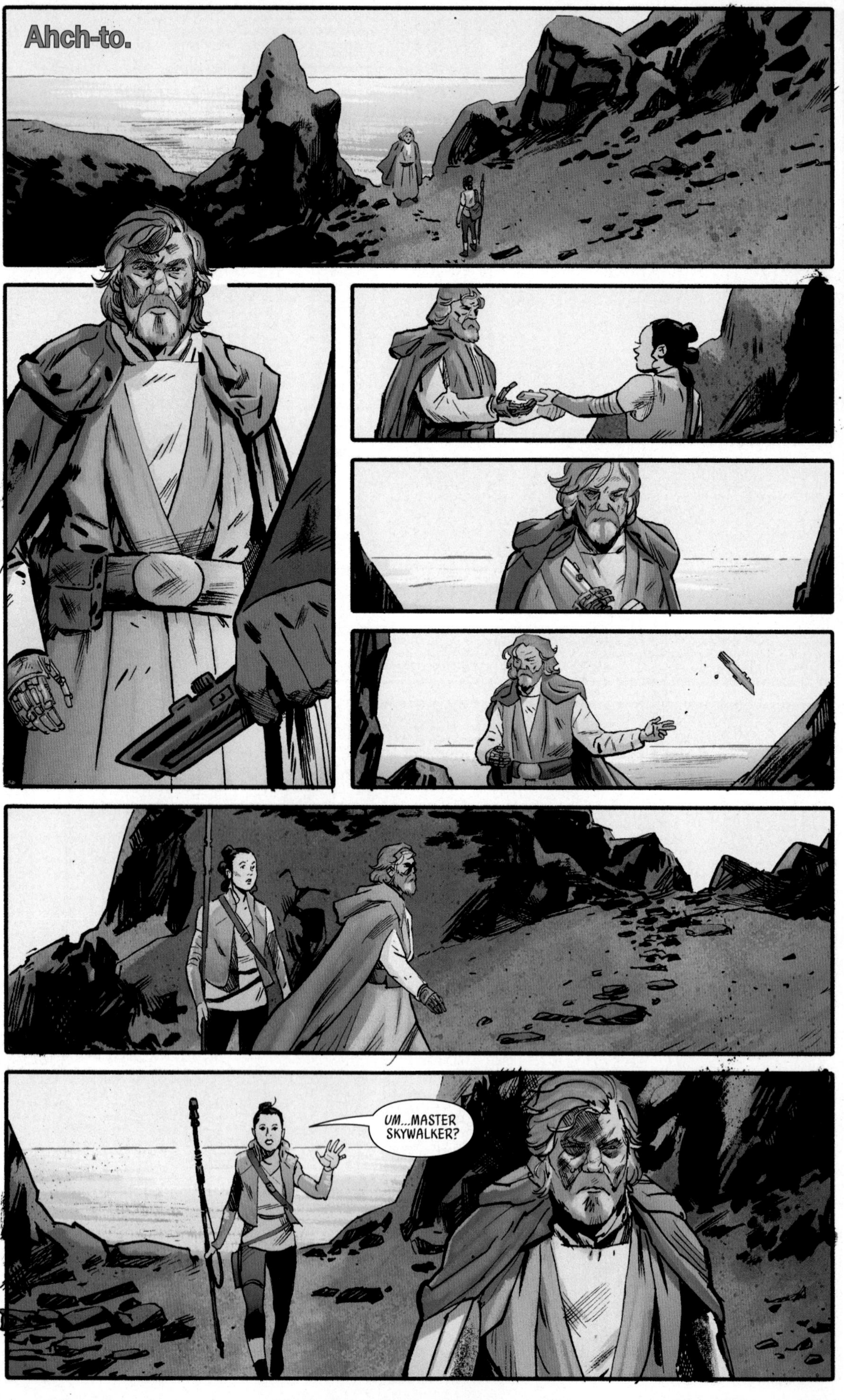
Ahch-to.
UM... MASTER SKYWALKER?

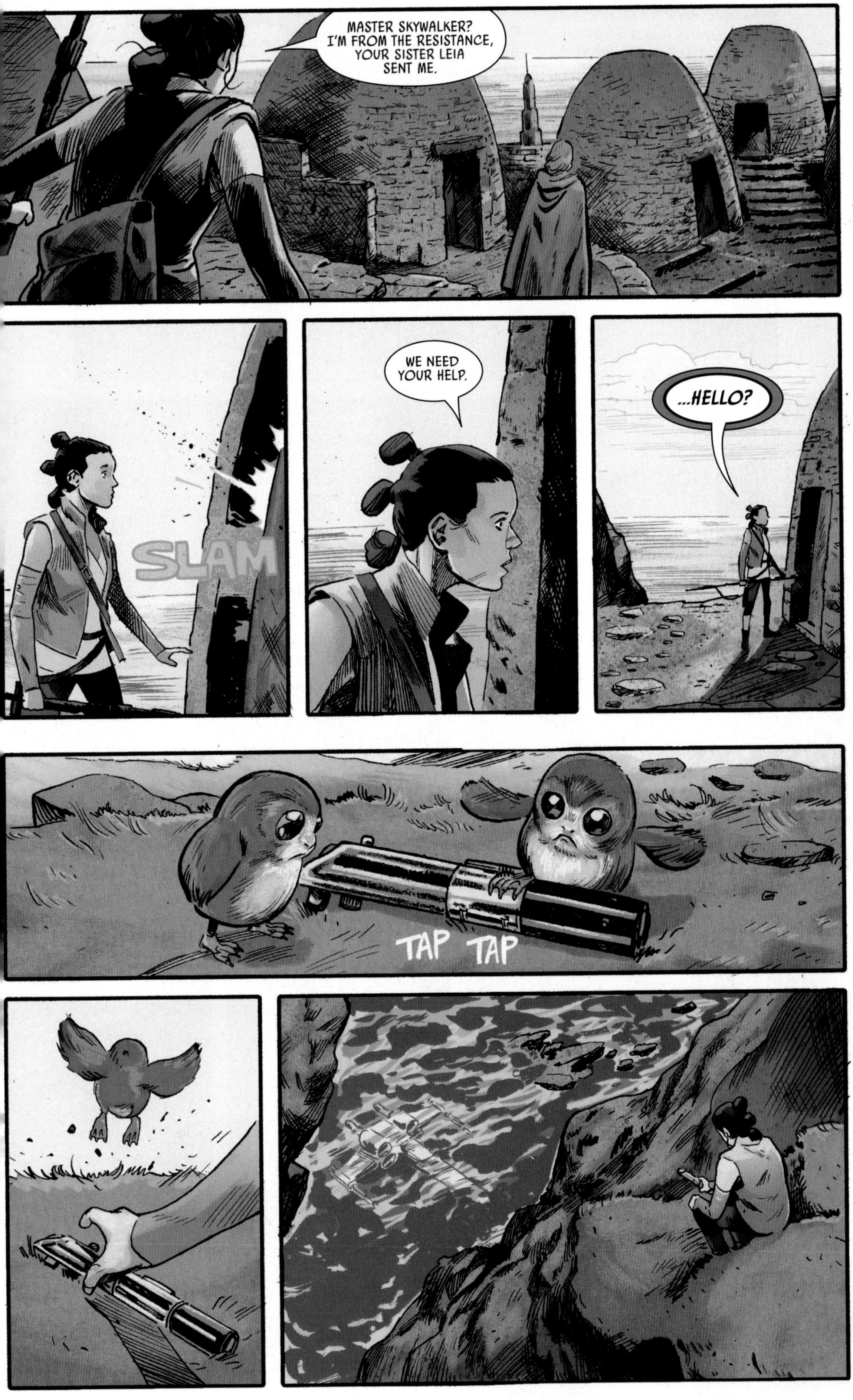
MASTER SKYWALKER? I'M FROM THE RESISTANCE, YOUR SISTER LEIA SENT ME.
SLAM
WE NEED YOUR HELP.
...HELLO?
TAP TAP

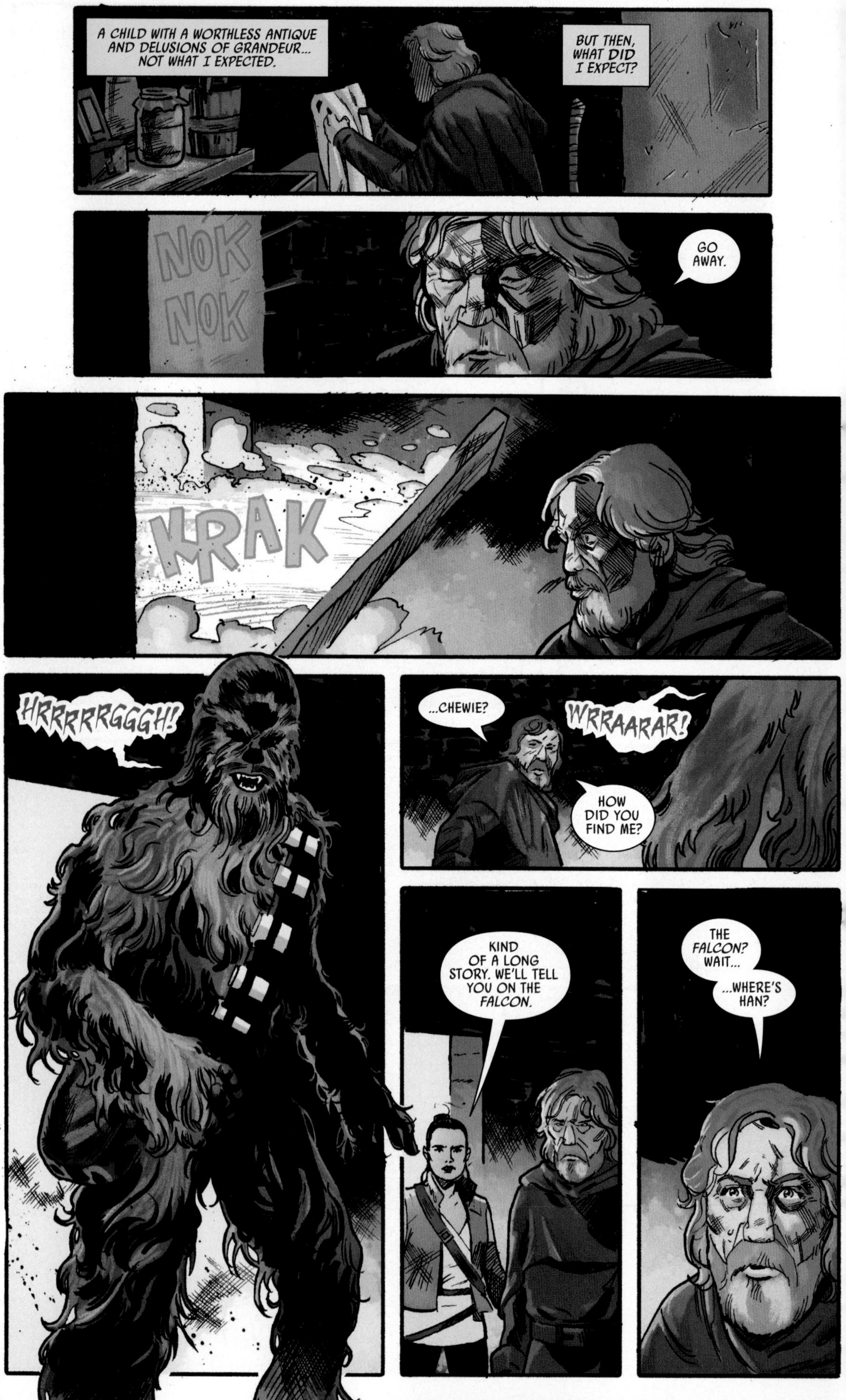

A CHILD WITH A WORTHLESS ANTIQUE AND DELUSIONS OF GRANDEUR... NOT WHAT I EXPECTED.
BUT THEN, WHAT DID I EXPECT?
NOK NOK
GO AWAY.
KRAK
HRRRRRGGGH!
...CHEWIE?
WRRAARAR!
HOW DID YOU FIND ME?
KIND OF A LONG STORY. WE'LL TELL YOU ON THE FALCON.
THE FALCON? WAIT...
...WHERE'S HAN?

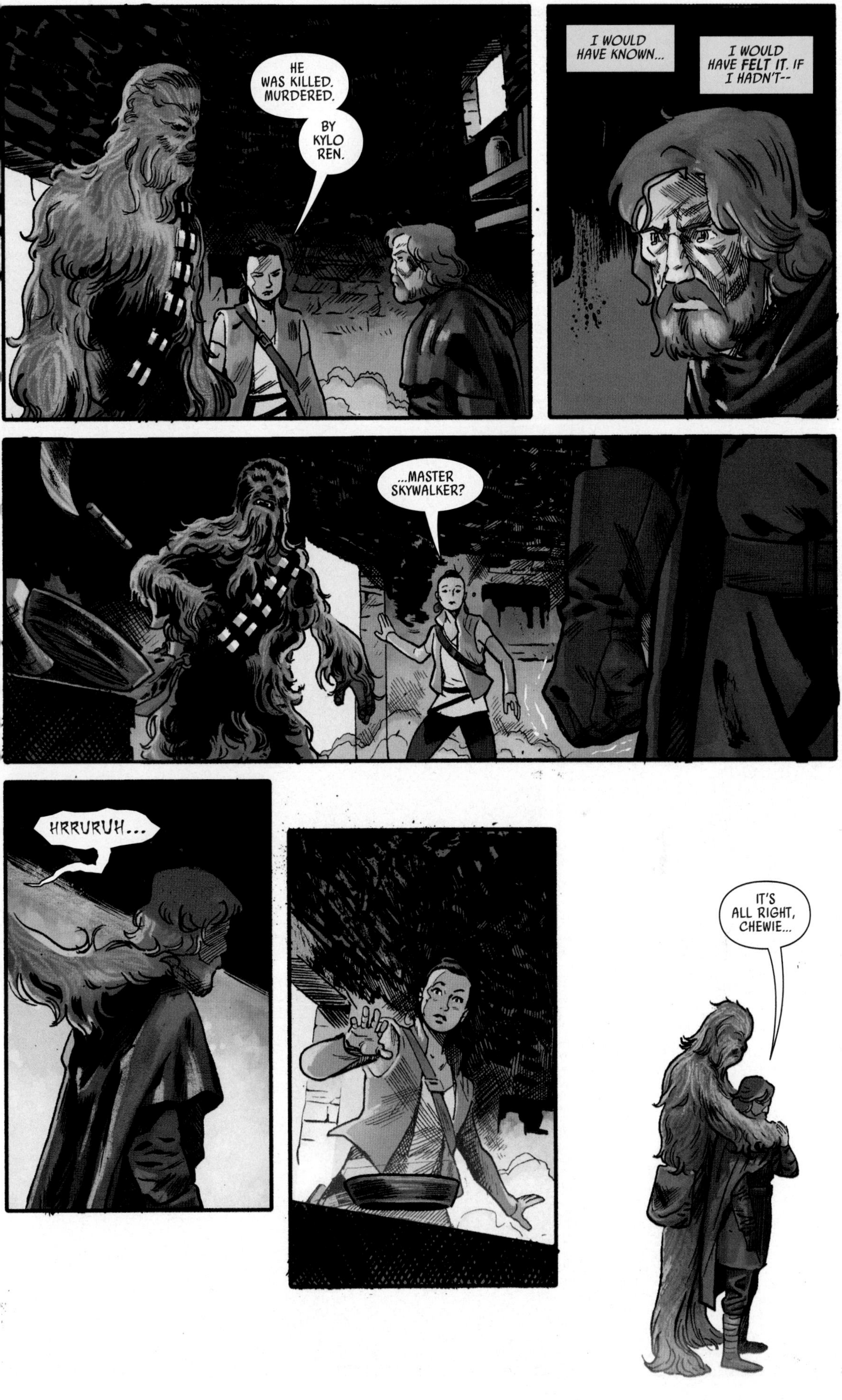
HE WAS KILLED. MURDERED.
BY KYLO REN.
I WOULD HAVE KNOWN...
I WOULD HAVE FELT IT. IF I HADN'T--
...MASTER SKYWALKER?
HRRURUH...
IT'S ALL RIGHT, CHEWIE...

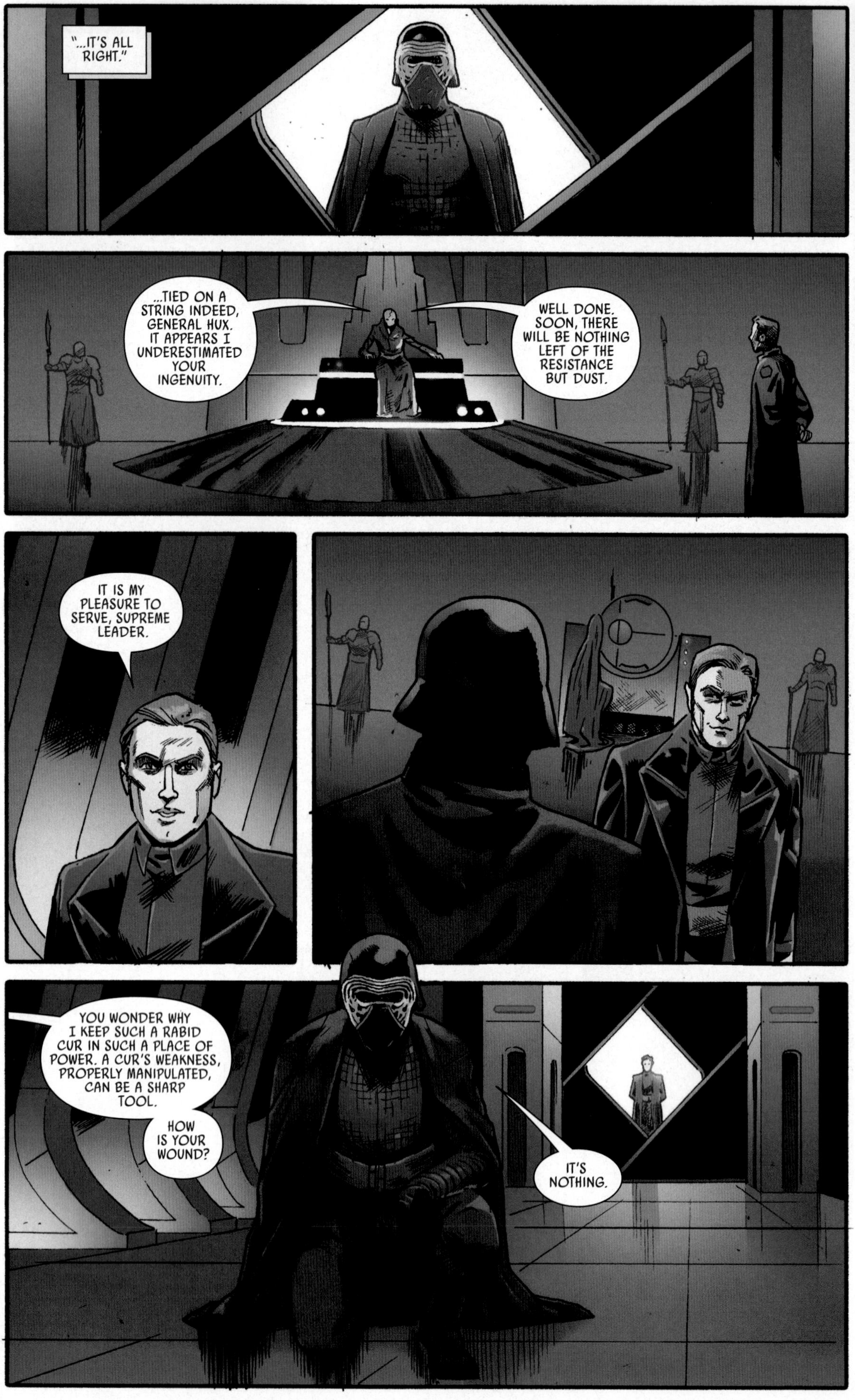
"...IT'S ALL RIGHT."
...TIED ON A STRING INDEED, GENERAL HUX. IT APPEARS I UNDERESTIMATED YOUR INGENUITY.
WELL DONE. SOON, THERE WILL BE NOTHING LEFT OF THE RESISTANCE BUT DUST.
IT IS MY PLEASURE TO SERVE, SUPREME LEADER.
YOU WONDER WHY I KEEP SUCH A RABID CUR IN SUCH A PLACE OF POWER. A CUR'S WEAKNESS, PROPERLY MANIPULATED, CAN BE A SHARP TOOL.
HOW IS YOUR WOUND?
IT'S NOTHING.

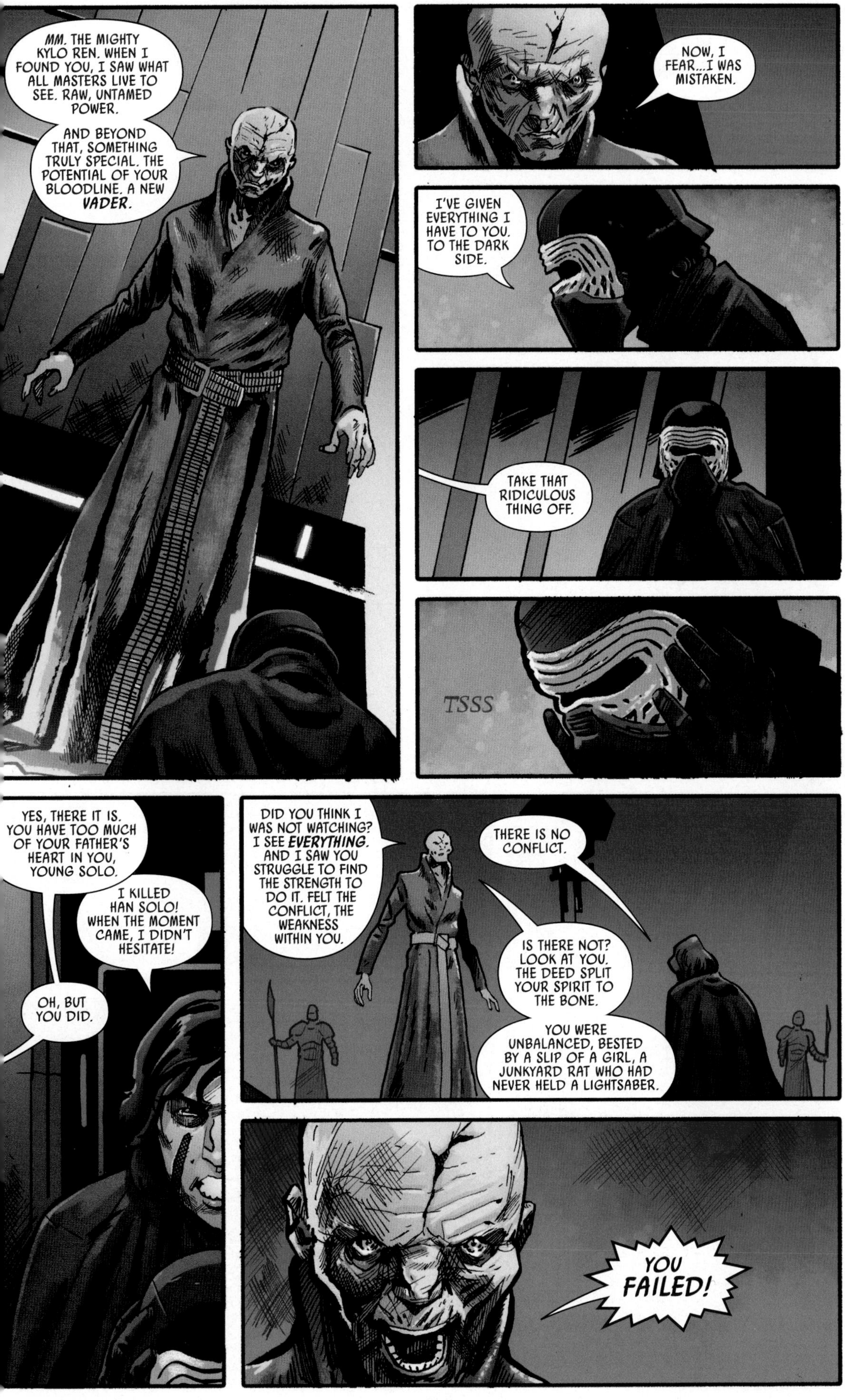

MM. THE MIGHTY KYLO REN. WHEN I FOUND YOU, I SAW WHAT ALL MASTERS LIVE TO SEE. RAW, UNTAMED POWER.
AND BEYOND THAT, SOMETHING TRULY SPECIAL. THE POTENTIAL OF YOUR BLOODLINE. A NEW VADER.
NOW, I FEAR...I WAS MISTAKEN.
I'VE GIVEN EVERYTHING I HAVE TO YOU. TO THE DARK SIDE.
TAKE THAT RIDICULOUS THING OFF.
TSSS
YES, THERE IT IS. YOU HAVE TOO MUCH OF YOUR FATHER'S HEART IN YOU, YOUNG SOLO.
I KILLED HAN SOLO! WHEN THE MOMENT CAME, I DIDN'T HESITATE!
OH, BUT YOU DID.
DID YOU THINK I WAS NOT WATCHING? I SEE EVERYTHING. AND I SAW YOU STRUGGLE TO FIND THE STRENGTH TO DO IT. FELT THE CONFLICT, THE WEAKNESS WITHIN YOU.
THERE IS NO CONFLICT.
IS THERE NOT? LOOK AT YOU. THE DEED SPLIT YOUR SPIRIT TO THE BONE.
YOU WERE UNBALANCED, BESTED BY A SLIP OF A GIRL, A JUNKYARD RAT WHO HAD NEVER HELD A LIGHTSABER.
YOU FAILED!

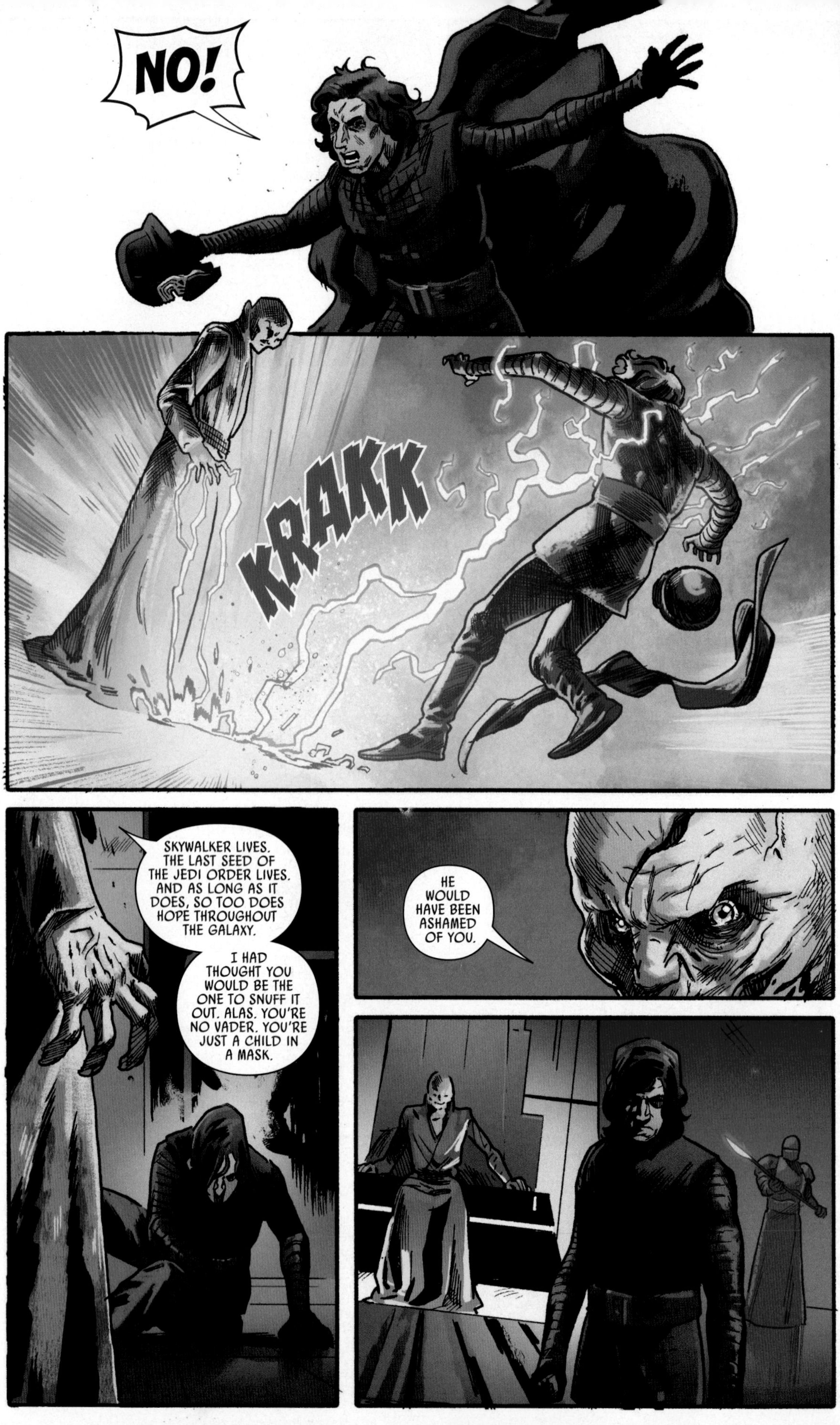
NO!
KRAKK
SKYWALKER LIVES. THE LAST SEED OF THE JEDI ORDER LIVES. AND AS LONG AS IT DOES, SO TOO DOES HOPE THROUGHOUT THE GALAXY.
I HAD THOUGHT YOU WOULD BE THE ONE TO SNUFF IT OUT. ALAS. YOU'RE NO VADER. YOU'RE JUST A CHILD IN A MASK.
HE WOULD HAVE BEEN ASHAMED OF YOU.

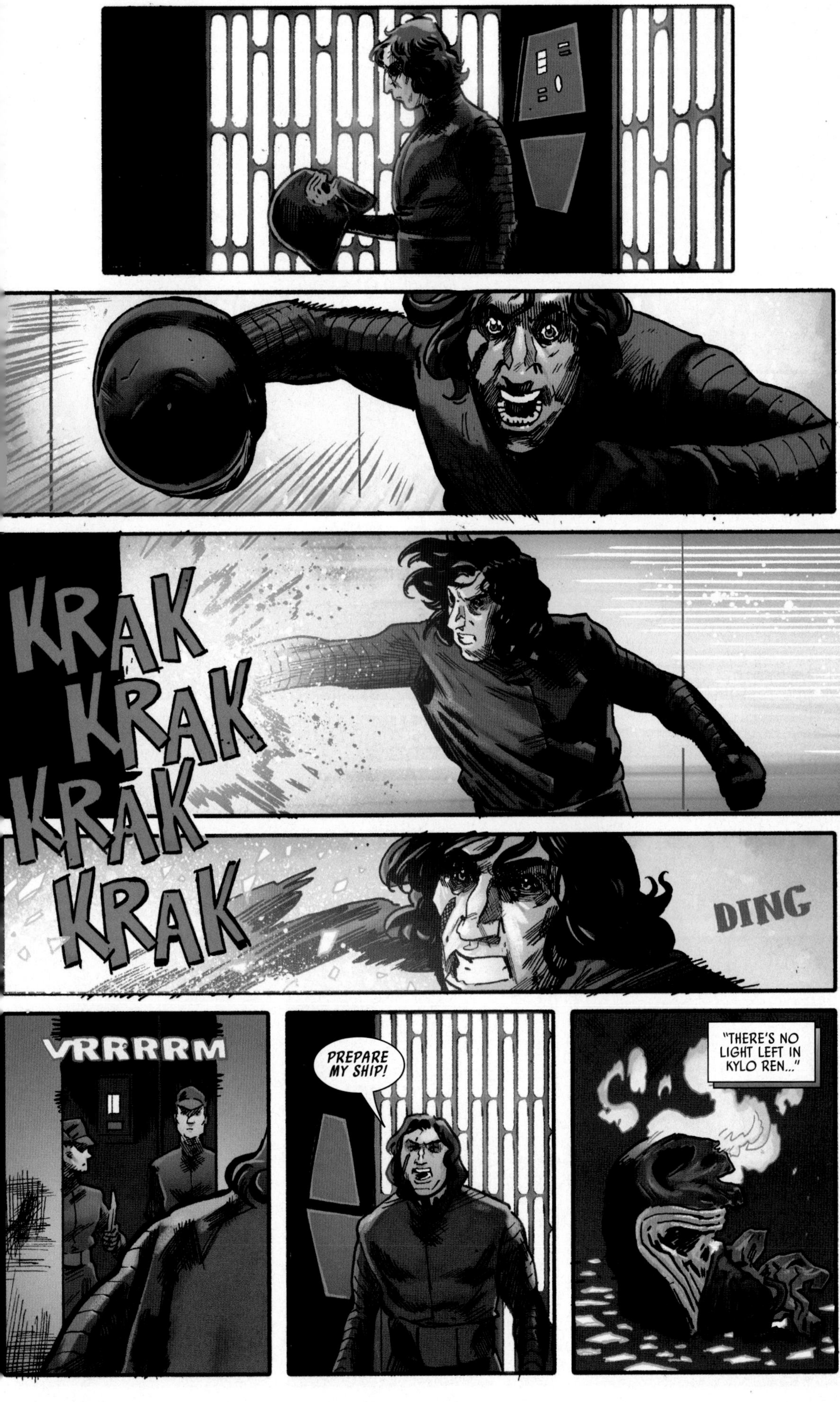
KRAK
KRAK
KRAK
KRAK
DING
VRRRRRM
PREPARE MY SHIP!
"THERE'S NO LIGHT LEFT IN KYLO REN..."

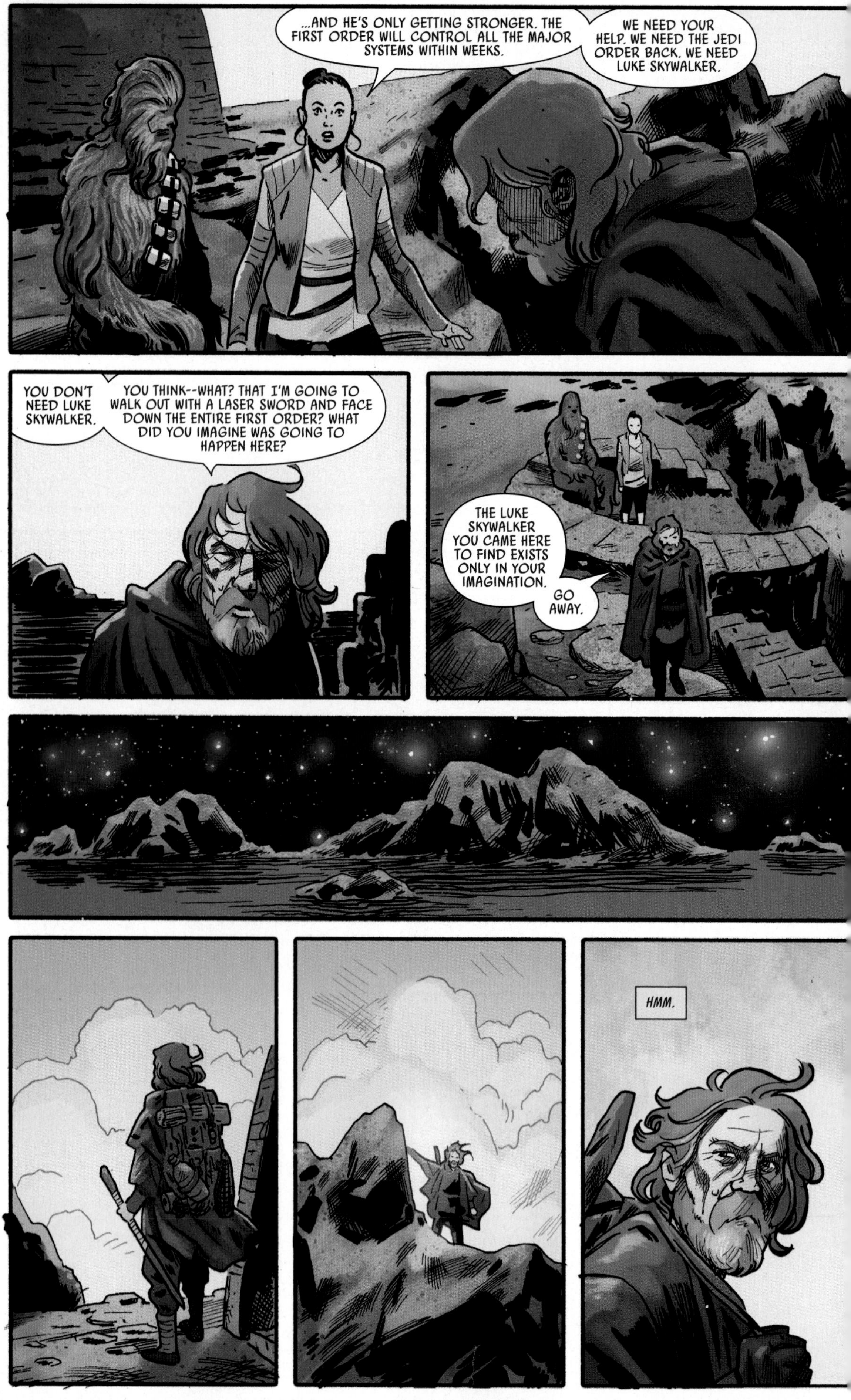
...AND HE'S ONLY GETTING STRONGER. THE FIRST ORDER WILL CONTROL ALL THE MAJOR SYSTEMS WITHIN WEEKS.
WE NEED YOUR HELP. WE NEED THE JEDI ORDER BACK. WE NEED LUKE SKYWALKER.
YOU DON'T NEED LUKE SKYWALKER.
YOU THINK--WHAT? THAT I'M GOING TO WALK OUT WITH A LASER SWORD AND FACE DOWN THE ENTIRE FIRST ORDER? WHAT DID YOU IMAGINE WAS GOING TO HAPPEN HERE?
THE LUKE SKYWALKER YOU CAME HERE TO FIND EXISTS ONLY IN YOUR IMAGINATION.
GO AWAY.
HMM.

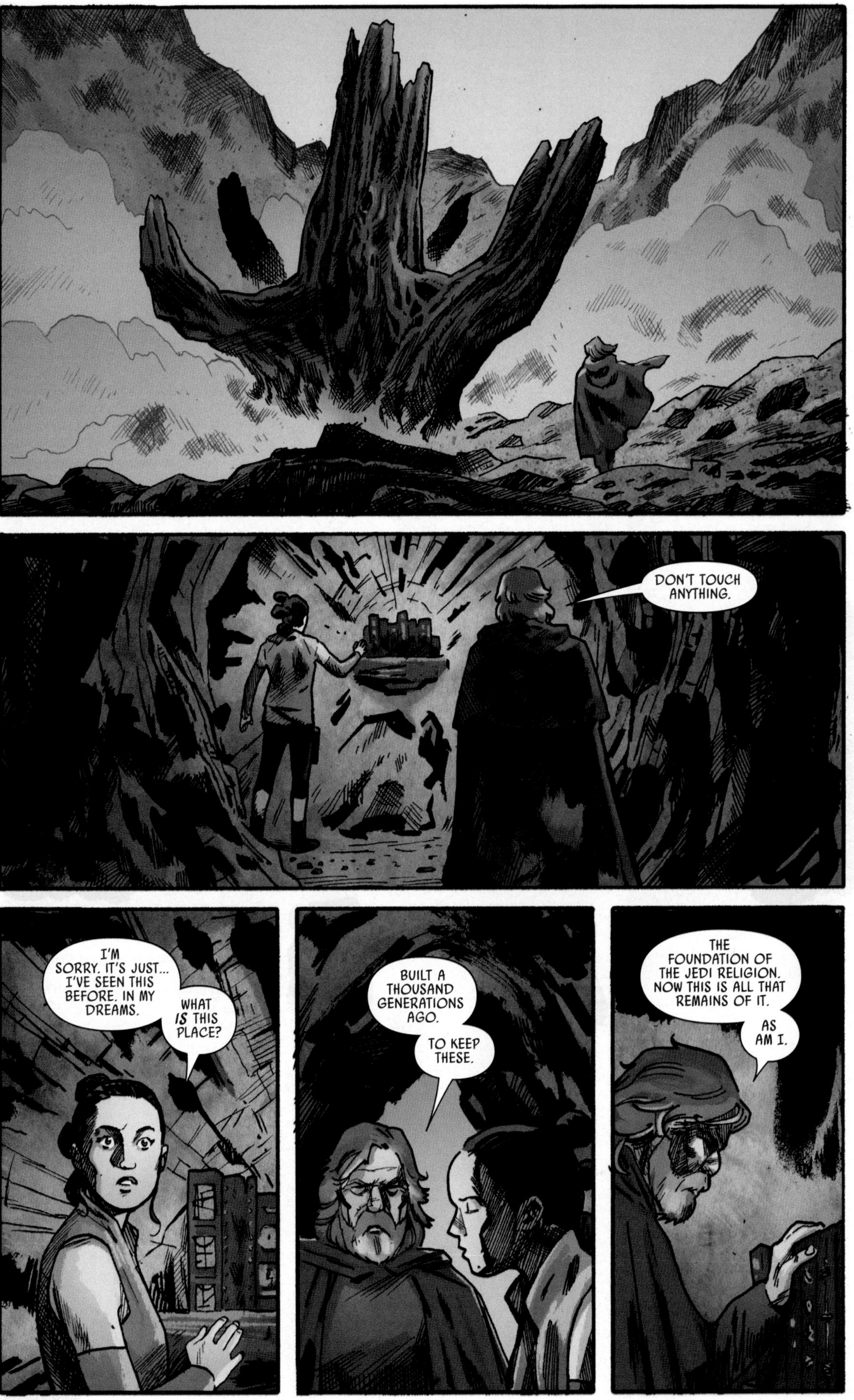
DON'T TOUCH ANYTHING.
I'M SORRY. IT'S JUST... I'VE SEEN THIS BEFORE. IN MY DREAMS.
WHAT *IS* THIS PLACE?
BUILT A THOUSAND GENERATIONS AGO.
TO KEEP THESE.
THE FOUNDATION OF THE JEDI RELIGION. NOW THIS IS ALL THAT REMAINS OF IT.
AS AM I.

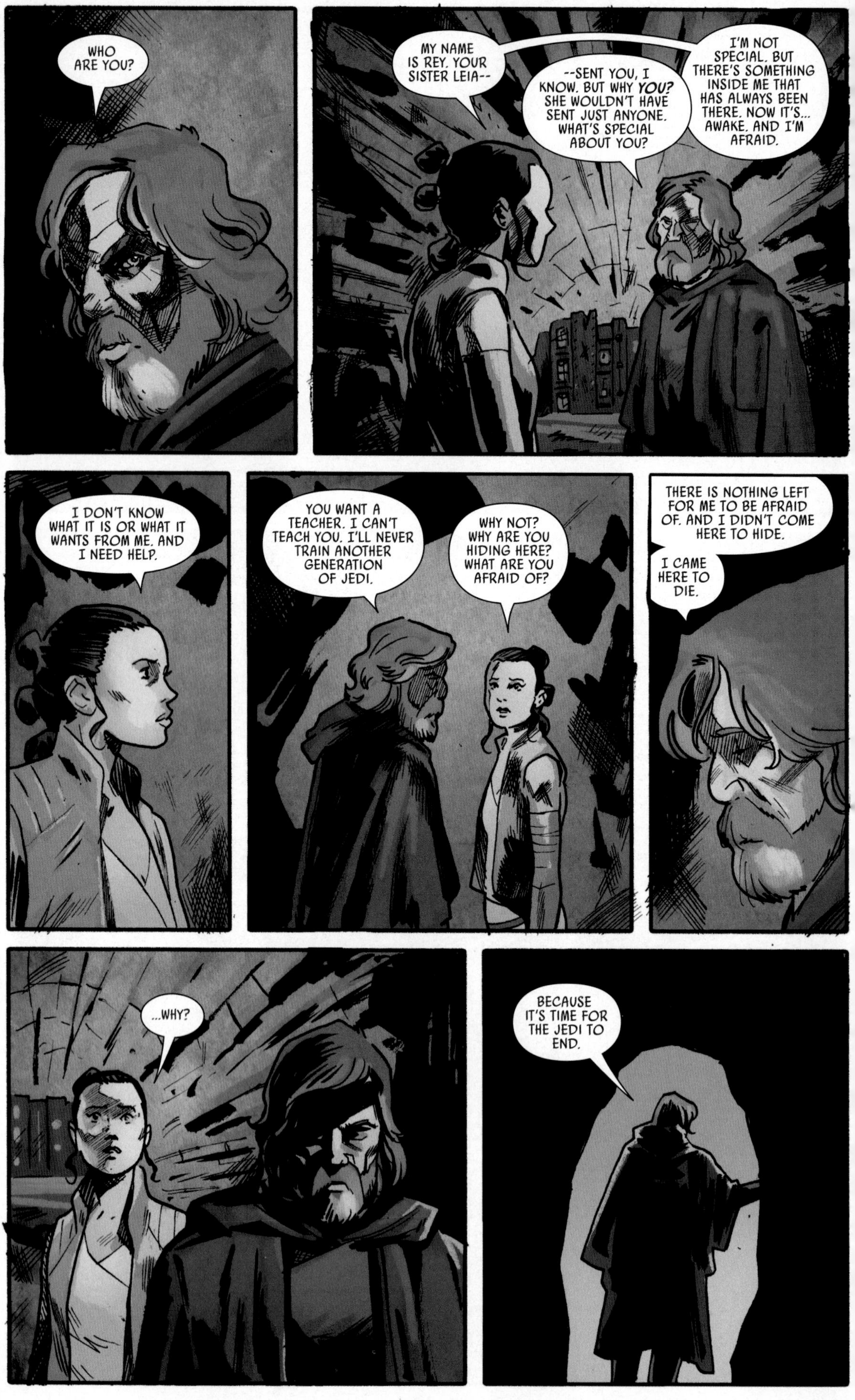
WHO ARE YOU?
MY NAME IS REY. YOUR SISTER LEIA--
--SENT YOU, I KNOW. BUT WHY *YOU?* SHE WOULDN'T HAVE SENT JUST ANYONE. WHAT'S SPECIAL ABOUT YOU?
I'M NOT SPECIAL. BUT THERE'S SOMETHING INSIDE ME THAT HAS ALWAYS BEEN THERE. NOW IT'S... AWAKE. AND I'M AFRAID.
I DON'T KNOW WHAT IT IS OR WHAT IT WANTS FROM ME. AND I NEED HELP.
YOU WANT A TEACHER. I CAN'T TEACH YOU. I'LL NEVER TRAIN ANOTHER GENERATION OF JEDI.
WHY NOT? WHY ARE YOU HIDING HERE? WHAT ARE YOU AFRAID OF?
THERE IS NOTHING LEFT FOR ME TO BE AFRAID OF. AND I DIDN'T COME HERE TO HIDE.
I CAME HERE TO DIE.
...WHY?
BECAUSE IT'S TIME FOR THE JEDI TO END.

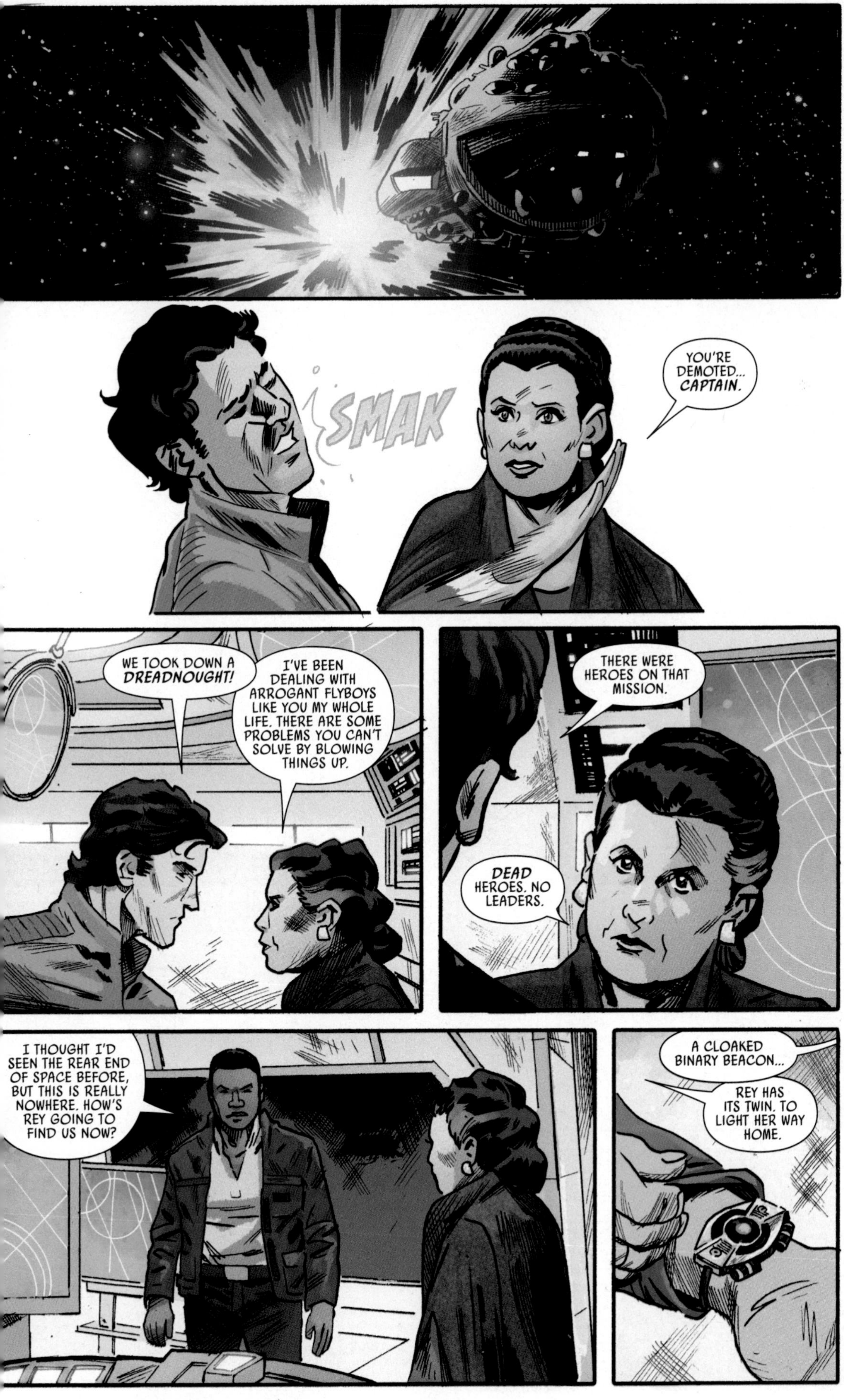
SMAK
YOU'RE DEMOTED... CAPTAIN.
WE TOOK DOWN A DREADNOUGHT!
I'VE BEEN DEALING WITH ARROGANT FLYBOYS LIKE YOU MY WHOLE LIFE. THERE ARE SOME PROBLEMS YOU CAN'T SOLVE BY BLOWING THINGS UP.
THERE WERE HEROES ON THAT MISSION.
DEAD HEROES. NO LEADERS.
I THOUGHT I'D SEEN THE REAR END OF SPACE BEFORE, BUT THIS IS REALLY NOWHERE. HOW'S REY GOING TO FIND US NOW?
A CLOAKED BINARY BEACON...
REY HAS ITS TWIN. TO LIGHT HER WAY HOME.

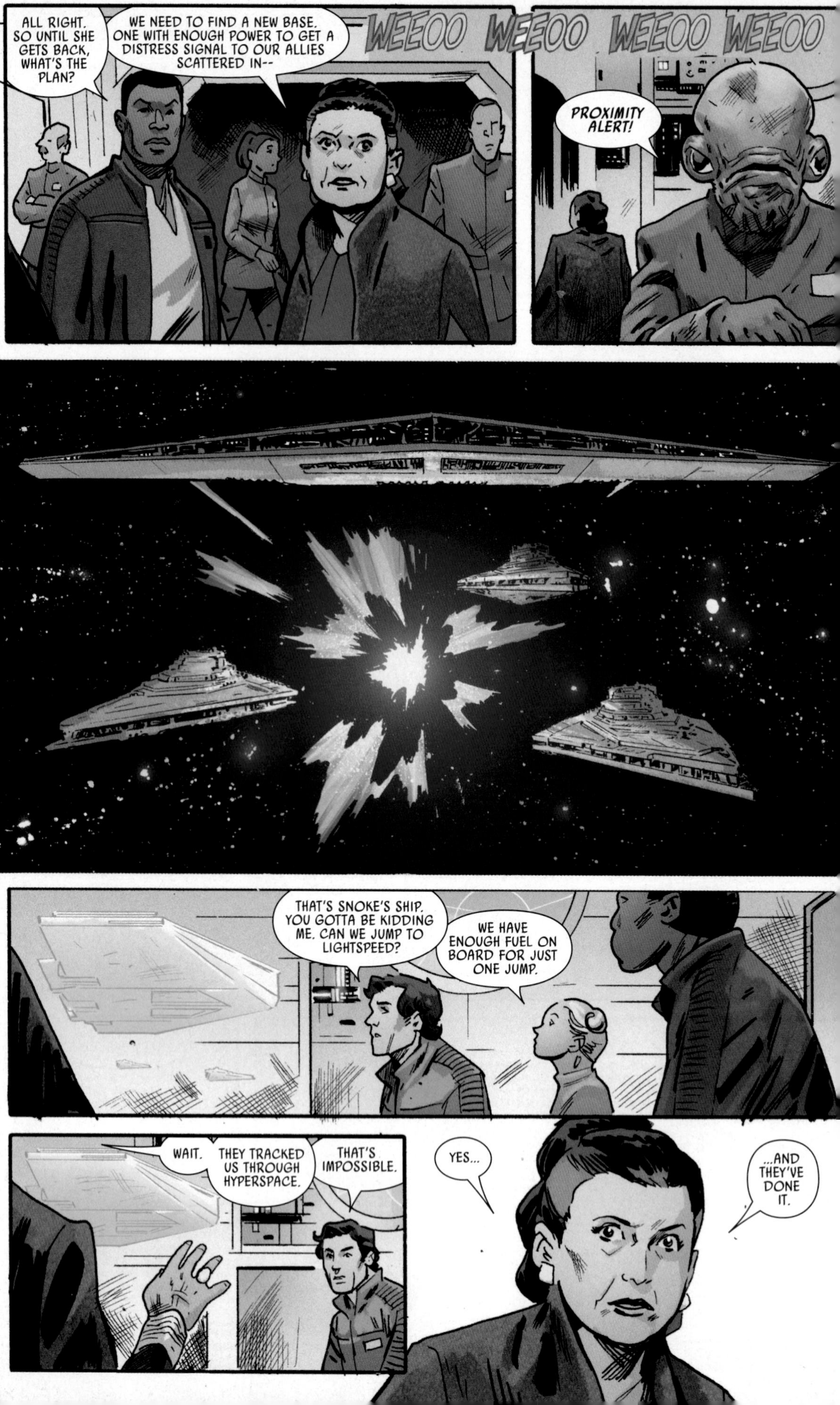

ALL RIGHT. SO UNTIL SHE GETS BACK, WHAT'S THE PLAN?
WE NEED TO FIND A NEW BASE. ONE WITH ENOUGH POWER TO GET A DISTRESS SIGNAL TO OUR ALLIES SCATTERED IN--
WEEOO WEEOO WEEOO WEEOO
PROXIMITY ALERT!
THAT'S SNOKE'S SHIP. YOU GOTTA BE KIDDING ME. CAN WE JUMP TO LIGHTSPEED?
WE HAVE ENOUGH FUEL ON BOARD FOR JUST ONE JUMP.
WAIT.
THEY TRACKED US THROUGH HYPERSPACE.
THAT'S IMPOSSIBLE.
YES...
...AND THEY'VE DONE IT.

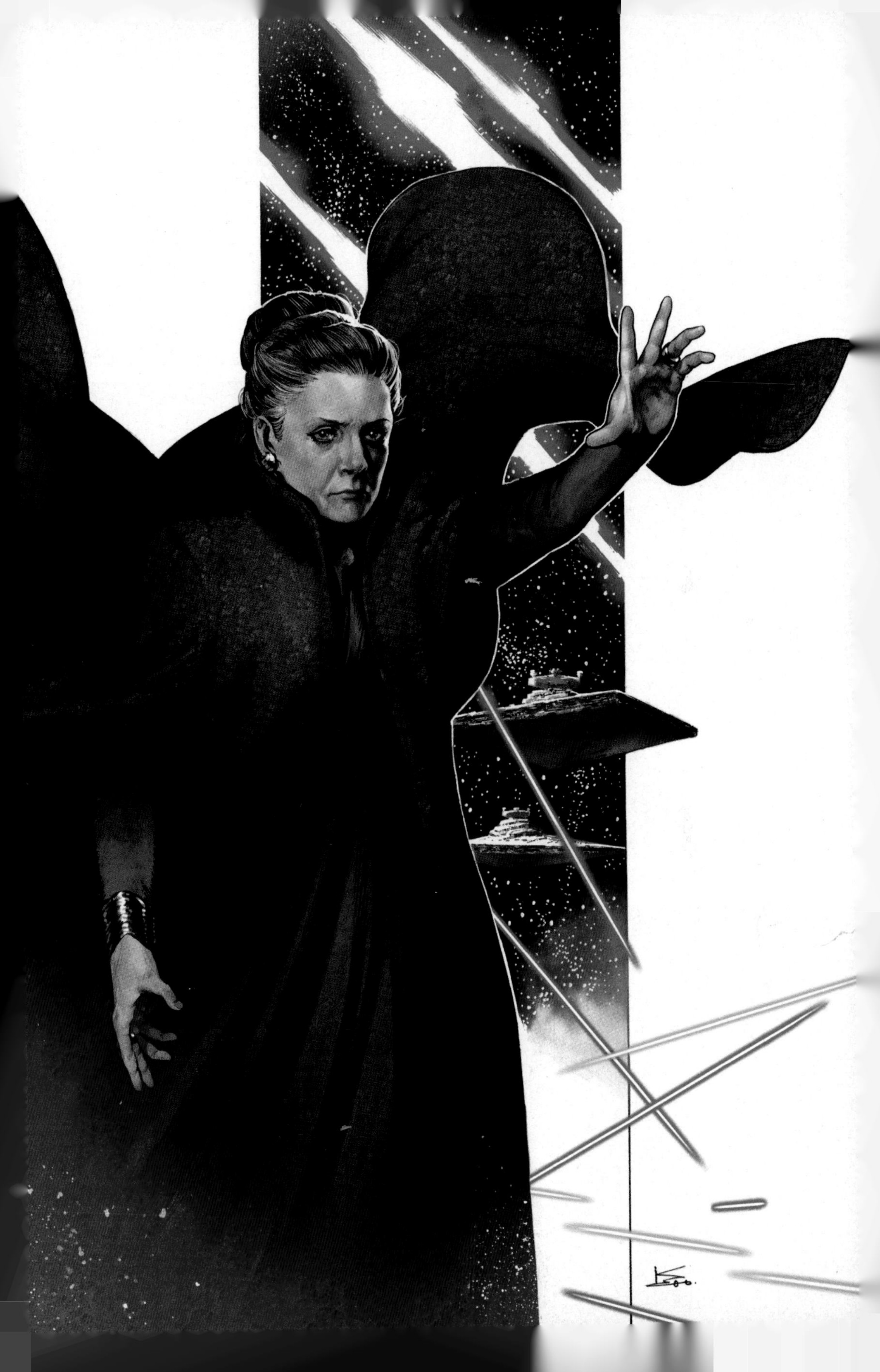

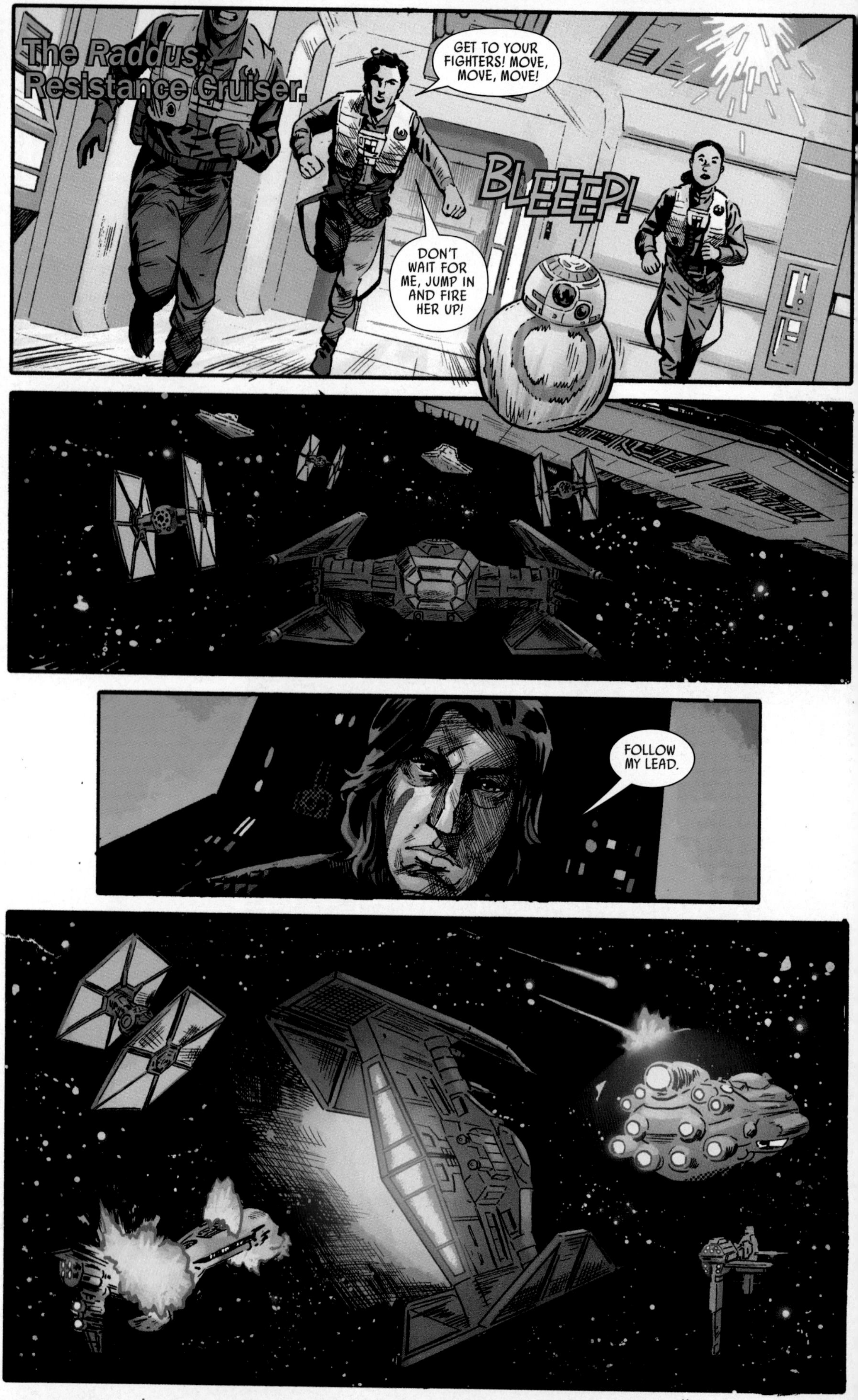
The *Raddus*, Resistance Cruiser.
GET TO YOUR FIGHTERS! MOVE, MOVE, MOVE!
DON'T WAIT FOR ME, JUMP IN AND FIRE HER UP!
BLEEEP!
FOLLOW MY LEAD.

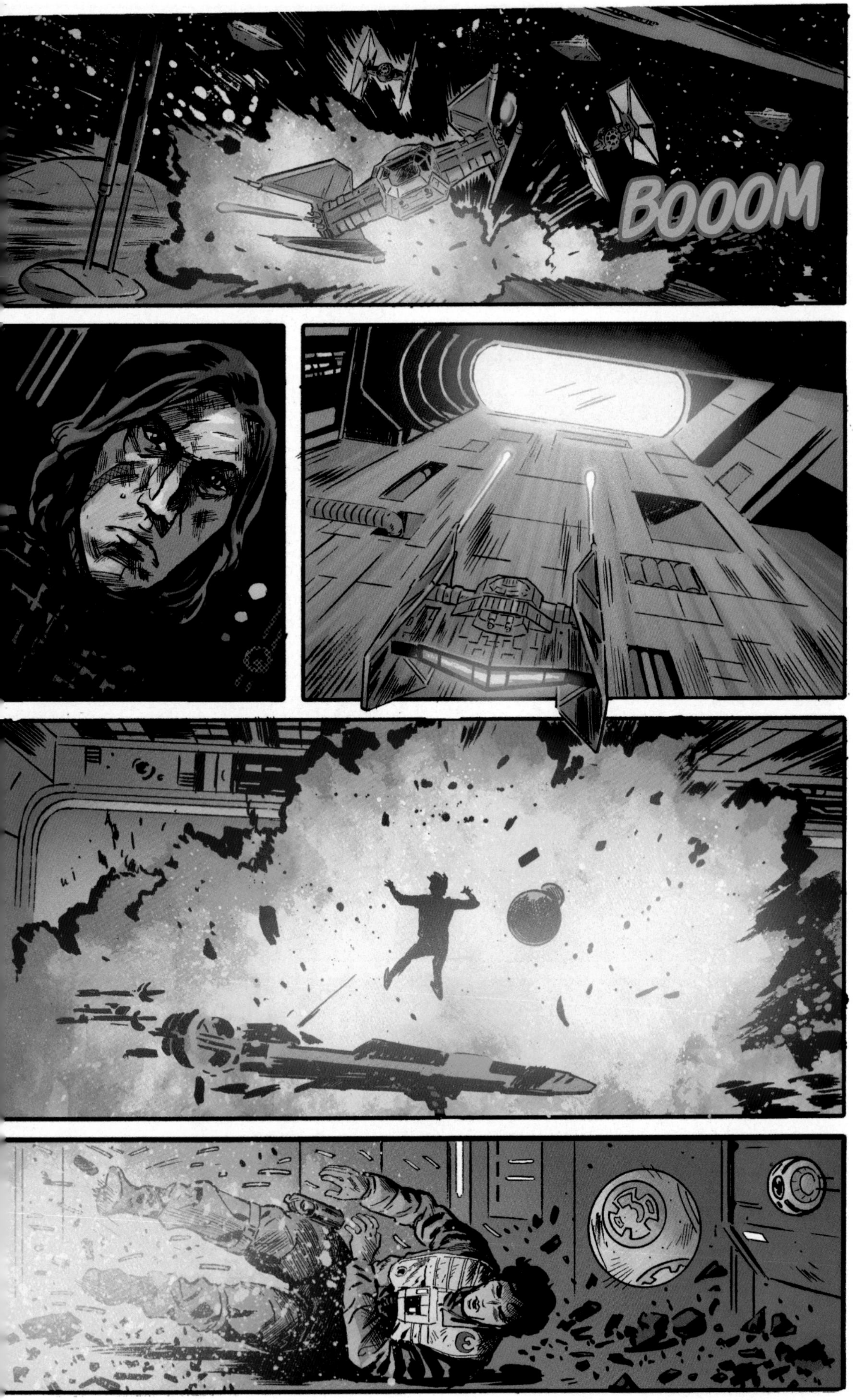
BOOOM

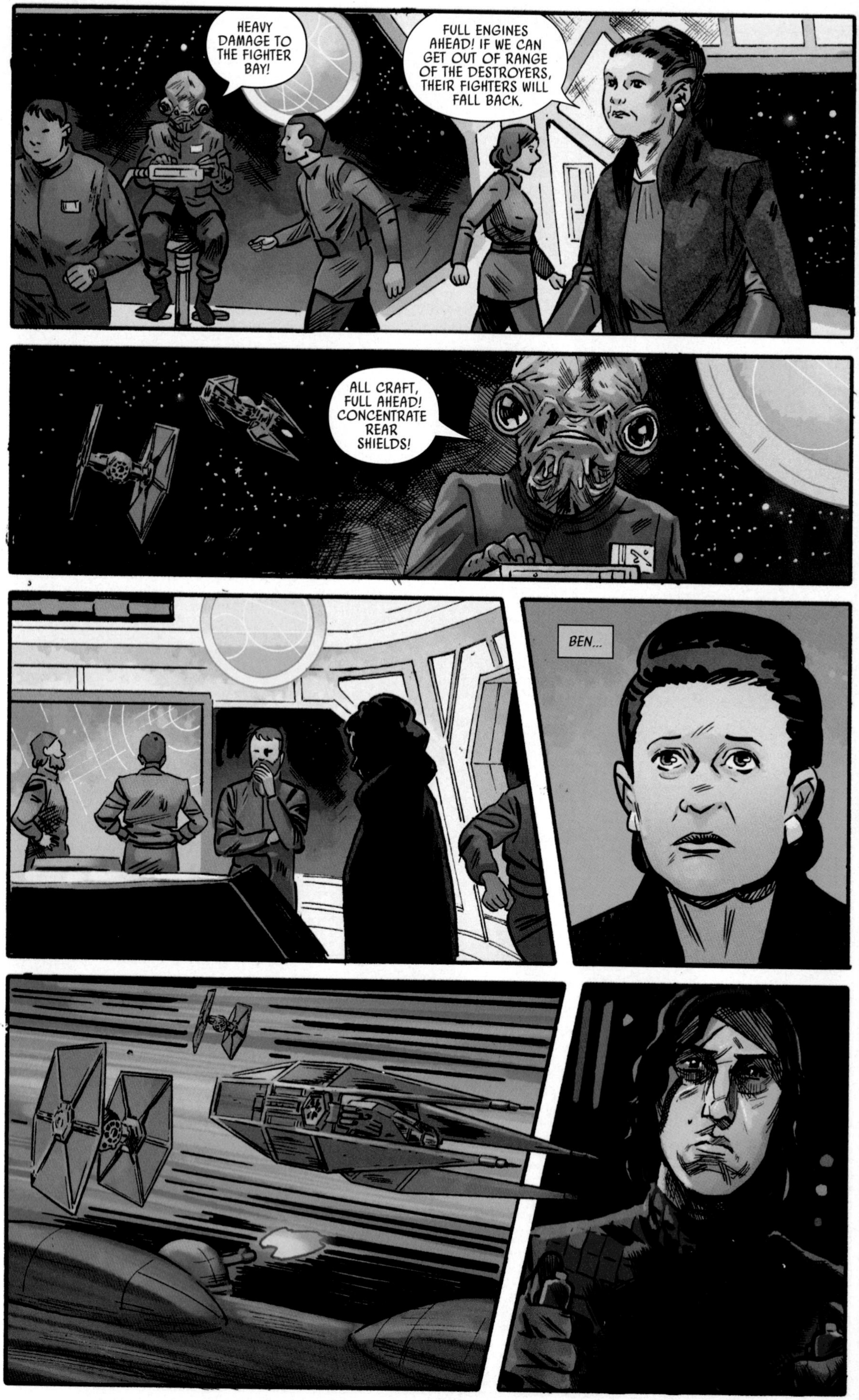
HEAVY DAMAGE TO THE FIGHTER BAY!
FULL ENGINES AHEAD! IF WE CAN GET OUT OF RANGE OF THE DESTROYERS, THEIR FIGHTERS WILL FALL BACK.
ALL CRAFT, FULL AHEAD! CONCENTRATE REAR SHIELDS!
BEN...

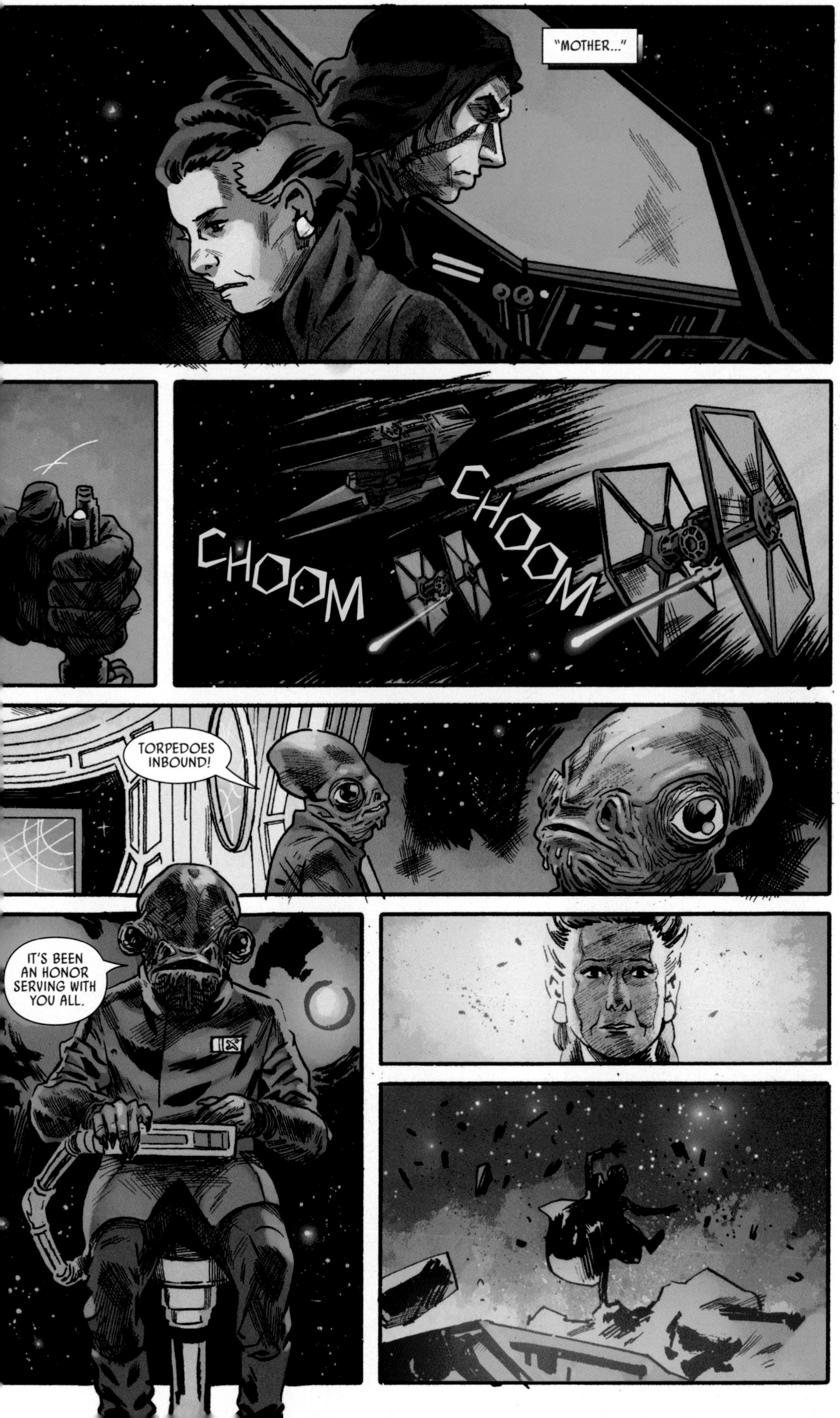
"MOTHER..."
CHOOM
CHOOM
TORPEDOES INBOUND!
IT'S BEEN AN HONOR SERVING WITH YOU ALL.

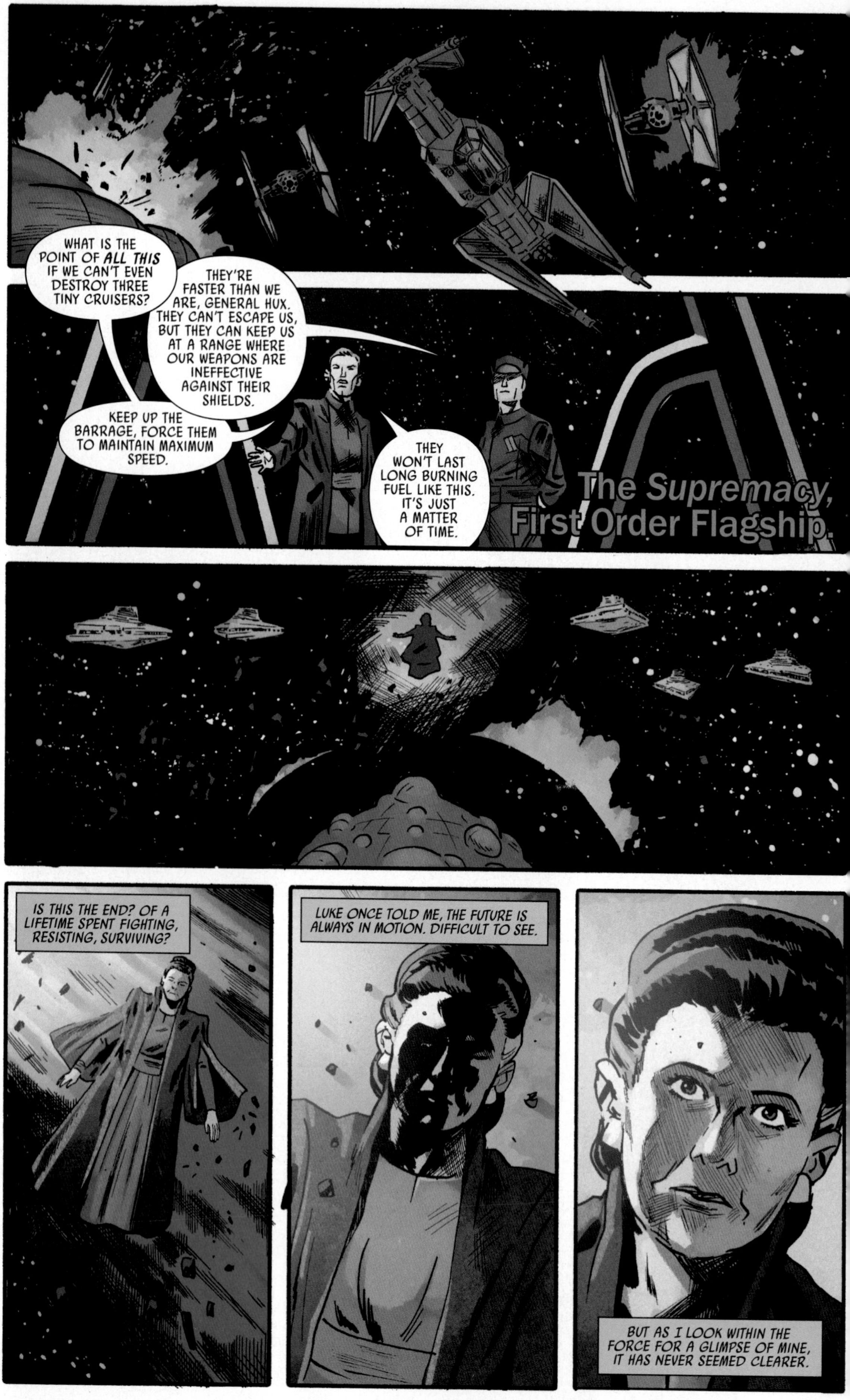

WHAT IS THE POINT OF ALL THIS IF WE CAN'T EVEN DESTROY THREE TINY CRUISERS?
THEY'RE FASTER THAN WE ARE, GENERAL HUX. THEY CAN'T ESCAPE US, BUT THEY CAN KEEP US AT A RANGE WHERE OUR WEAPONS ARE INEFFECTIVE AGAINST THEIR SHIELDS.
KEEP UP THE BARRAGE, FORCE THEM TO MAINTAIN MAXIMUM SPEED.
THEY WON'T LAST LONG BURNING FUEL LIKE THIS. IT'S JUST A MATTER OF TIME.
The Supremacy, First Order Flagship.
IS THIS THE END? OF A LIFETIME SPENT FIGHTING, RESISTING, SURVIVING?
LUKE ONCE TOLD ME, THE FUTURE IS ALWAYS IN MOTION. DIFFICULT TO SEE.
BUT AS I LOOK WITHIN THE FORCE FOR A GLIMPSE OF MINE, IT HAS NEVER SEEMED CLEARER.

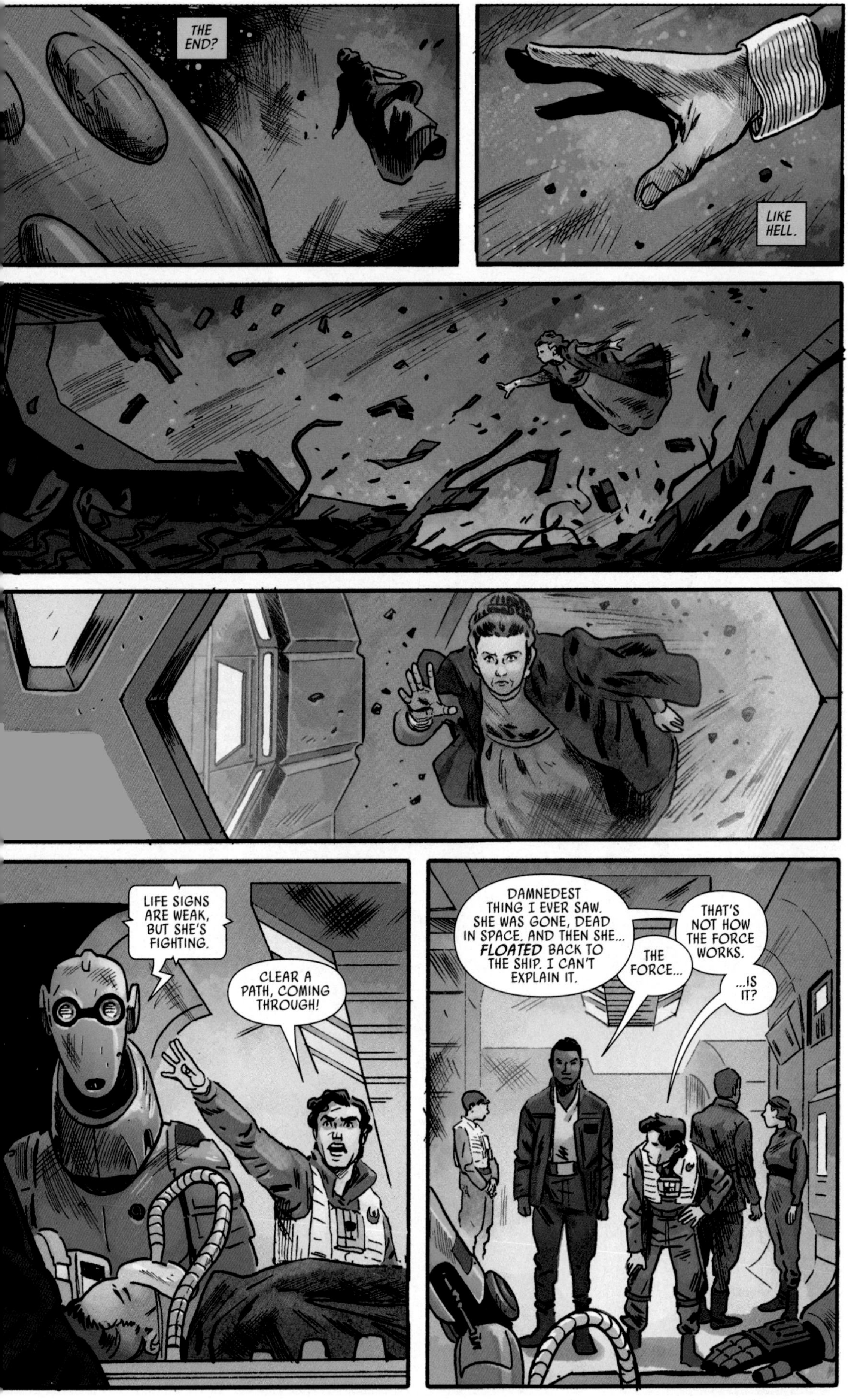
THE END?
LIKE HELL.
LIFE SIGNS ARE WEAK, BUT SHE'S FIGHTING.
CLEAR A PATH, COMING THROUGH!
DAMNEDEST THING I EVER SAW. SHE WAS GONE, DEAD IN SPACE. AND THEN SHE... FLOATED BACK TO THE SHIP. I CAN'T EXPLAIN IT.
THE FORCE...
THAT'S NOT HOW THE FORCE WORKS.
...IS IT?

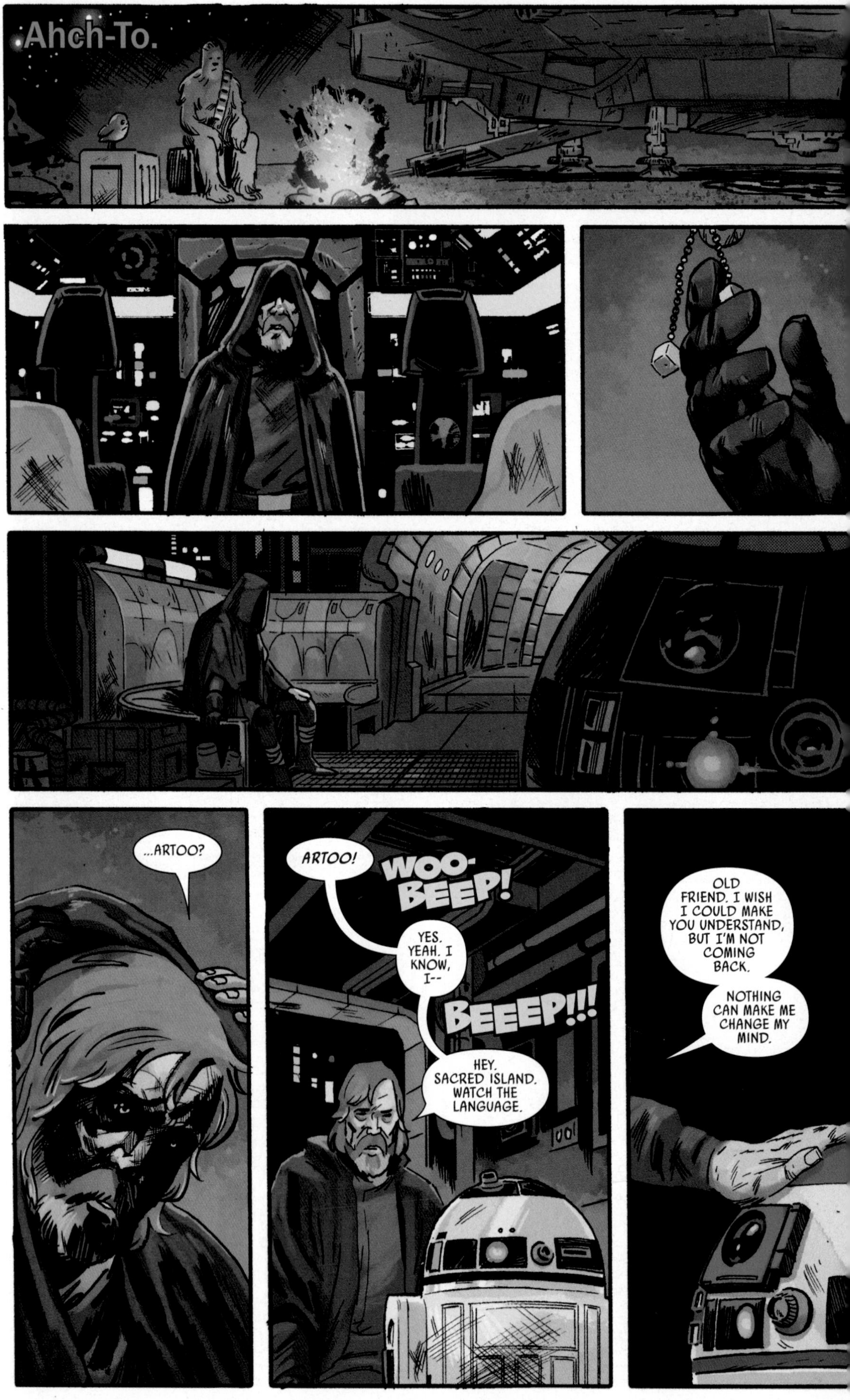

Ahch-To.
...ARTOO?
ARTOO!
WOO-BEEP!
YES. YEAH. I KNOW, I--
BEEEP!!!
HEY. SACRED ISLAND. WATCH THE LANGUAGE.
OLD FRIEND. I WISH I COULD MAKE YOU UNDERSTAND, BUT I'M NOT COMING BACK.
NOTHING CAN MAKE ME CHANGE MY MIND.

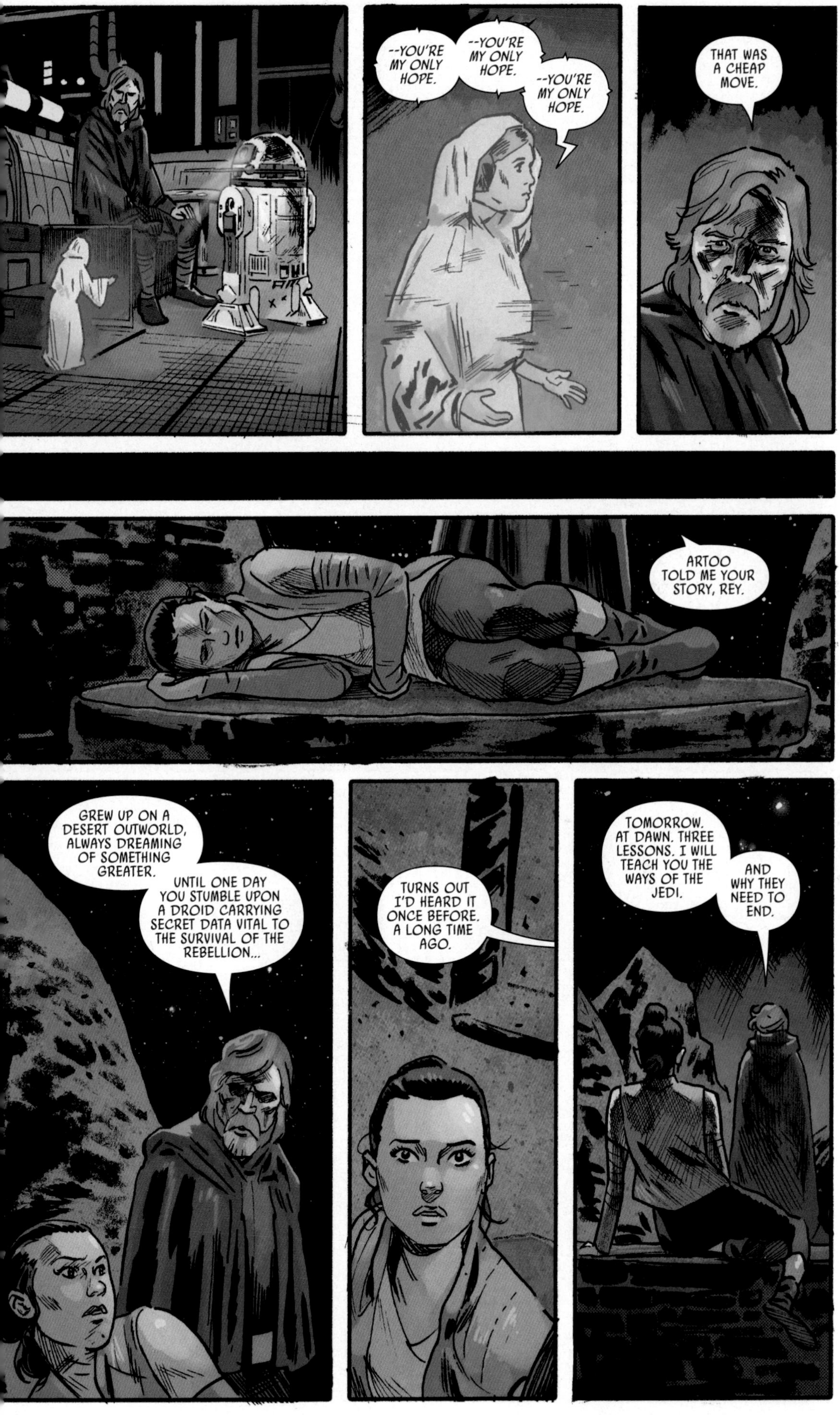
--YOU'RE MY ONLY HOPE.
--YOU'RE MY ONLY HOPE.
--YOU'RE MY ONLY HOPE.
THAT WAS A CHEAP MOVE.
ARTOO TOLD ME YOUR STORY, REY.
GREW UP ON A DESERT OUTWORLD, ALWAYS DREAMING OF SOMETHING GREATER.
UNTIL ONE DAY YOU STUMBLE UPON A DROID CARRYING SECRET DATA VITAL TO THE SURVIVAL OF THE REBELLION...
TURNS OUT I'D HEARD IT ONCE BEFORE. A LONG TIME AGO.
TOMORROW. AT DAWN. THREE LESSONS. I WILL TEACH YOU THE WAYS OF THE JEDI.
AND WHY THEY NEED TO END.

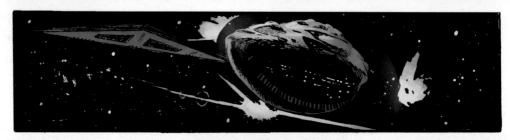

GENERAL ORGANA... LEIA...IS UNCONSCIOUS BUT RECOVERING. IF SHE WERE HERE, SHE'D SAY SAVE YOUR SORROW FOR AFTER THE FIGHT.

TO THAT END, THE CHAIN OF COMMAND IS CLEAR AS TO WHO SHOULD TAKE HER PLACE.

VICE-ADMIRAL HOLDO, OF THE CRUISER *NINKA*.

FOUR HUNDRED OF US ON THREE SHIPS. WE'RE THE VERY LAST OF THE RESISTANCE, BUT WE ARE NOT ALONE.

IN EVERY CORNER OF THE GALAXY, THE DOWNTRODDEN AND THE OPPRESSED KNOW OUR SYMBOL AND FIND HOPE IN IT. WE ARE THE SPARK THAT WILL LIGHT THE FIRE THAT WILL RESTORE THE REPUBLIC.

THAT SPARK, THIS RESISTANCE, MUST SURVIVE. THAT IS OUR MISSION. NOW, TO YOUR STATIONS. AND MAY THE FORCE BE WITH US.

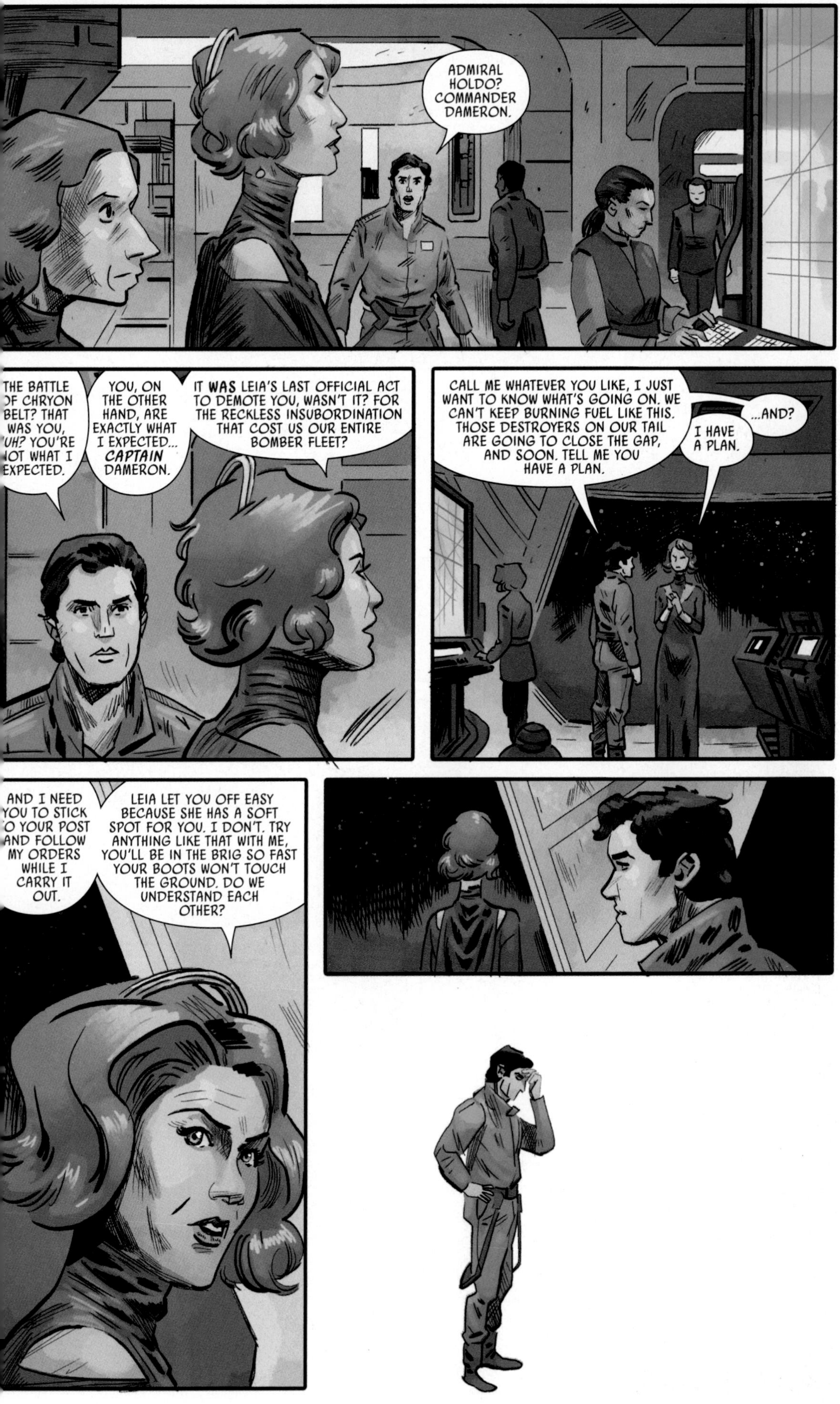

ADMIRAL HOLDO? COMMANDER DAMERON.
THE BATTLE)F CHRYON BELT? THAT WAS YOU, 'UH? YOU'RE IOT WHAT I EXPECTED.
YOU, ON THE OTHER HAND, ARE EXACTLY WHAT I EXPECTED... CAPTAIN DAMERON.
IT WAS LEIA'S LAST OFFICIAL ACT TO DEMOTE YOU, WASN'T IT? FOR THE RECKLESS INSUBORDINATION THAT COST US OUR ENTIRE BOMBER FLEET?
CALL ME WHATEVER YOU LIKE, I JUST WANT TO KNOW WHAT'S GOING ON. WE CAN'T KEEP BURNING FUEL LIKE THIS. THOSE DESTROYERS ON OUR TAIL ARE GOING TO CLOSE THE GAP, AND SOON. TELL ME YOU HAVE A PLAN.
I HAVE A PLAN.
...AND?
AND I NEED YOU TO STICK 'O YOUR POST AND FOLLOW MY ORDERS WHILE I CARRY IT OUT.
LEIA LET YOU OFF EASY BECAUSE SHE HAS A SOFT SPOT FOR YOU. I DON'T. TRY ANYTHING LIKE THAT WITH ME, YOU'LL BE IN THE BRIG SO FAST YOUR BOOTS WON'T TOUCH THE GROUND. DO WE UNDERSTAND EACH OTHER?

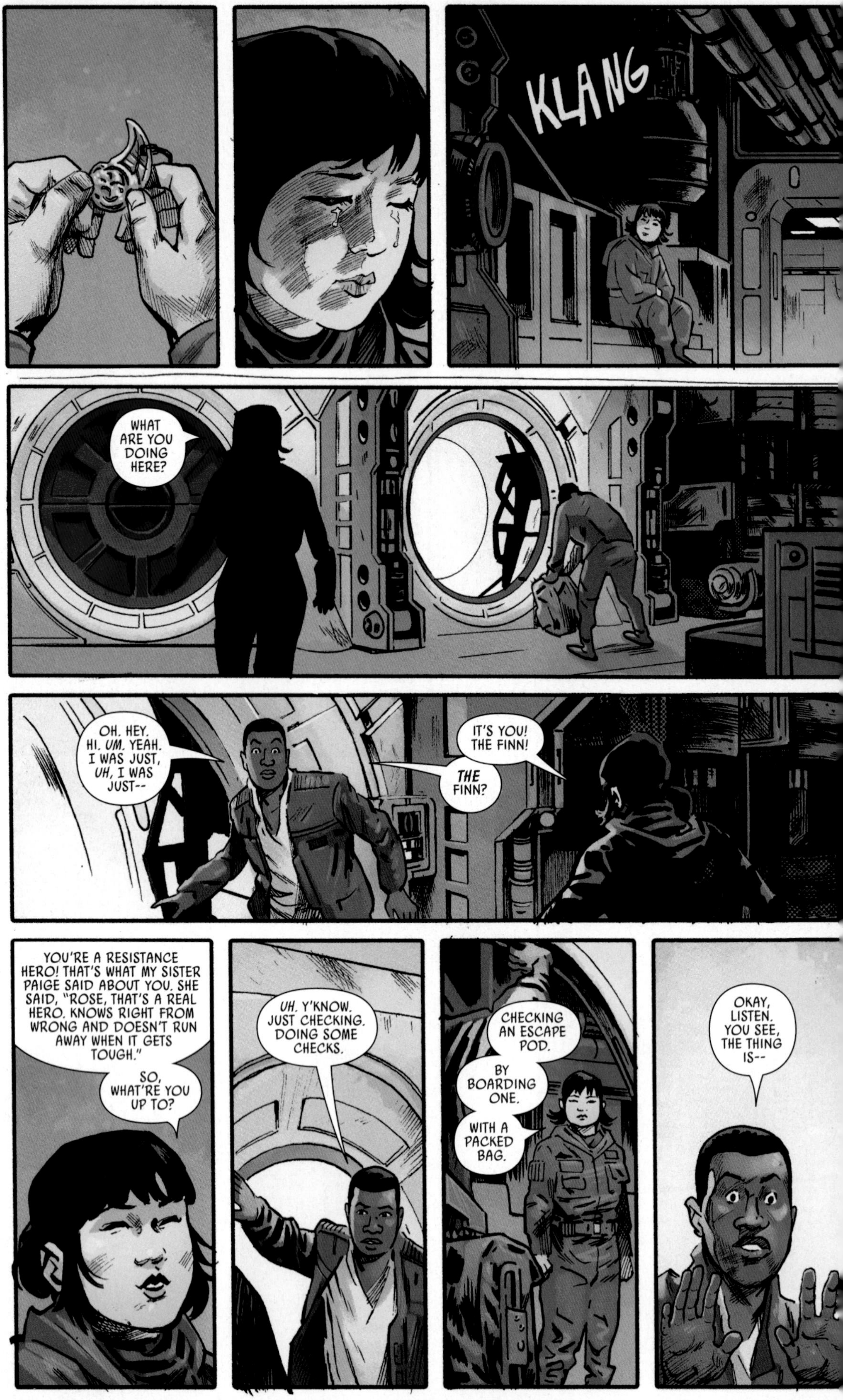
KLANG
WHAT ARE YOU DOING HERE?
OH. HEY. HI. UM. YEAH. I WAS JUST, UH, I WAS JUST--
IT'S YOU! THE FINN!
THE FINN?
YOU'RE A RESISTANCE HERO! THAT'S WHAT MY SISTER PAIGE SAID ABOUT YOU. SHE SAID, "ROSE, THAT'S A REAL HERO. KNOWS RIGHT FROM WRONG AND DOESN'T RUN AWAY WHEN IT GETS TOUGH."
SO, WHAT'RE YOU UP TO?
UH. Y'KNOW. JUST CHECKING. DOING SOME CHECKS.
CHECKING AN ESCAPE POD.
BY BOARDING ONE.
WITH A PACKED BAG.
OKAY, LISTEN. YOU SEE, THE THING IS--

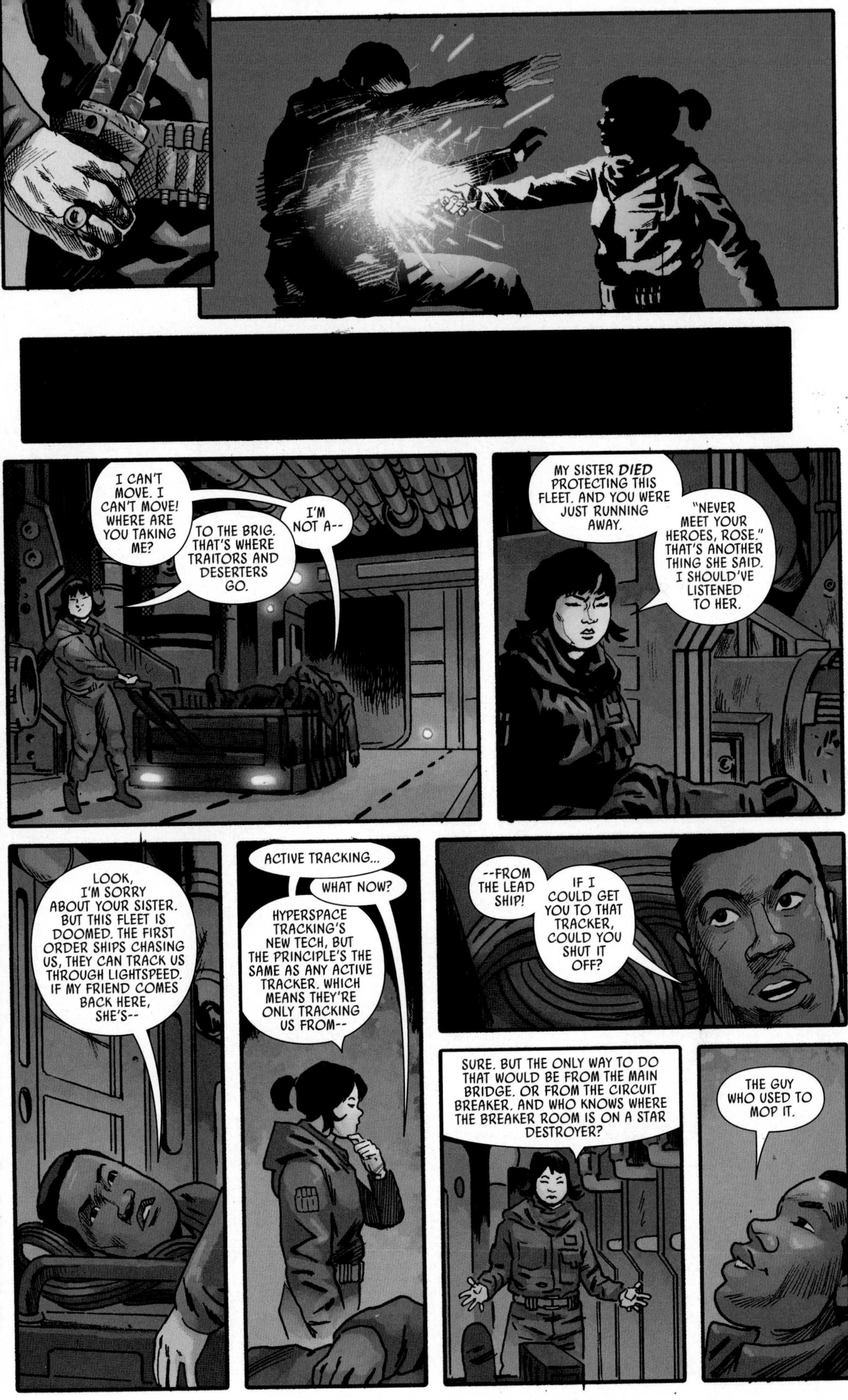
I CAN'T MOVE. I CAN'T MOVE! WHERE ARE YOU TAKING ME?
TO THE BRIG. THAT'S WHERE TRAITORS AND DESERTERS GO.
I'M NOT A--
MY SISTER *DIED* PROTECTING THIS FLEET. AND YOU WERE JUST RUNNING AWAY.
"NEVER MEET YOUR HEROES, ROSE." THAT'S ANOTHER THING SHE SAID. I SHOULD'VE LISTENED TO HER.
LOOK, I'M SORRY ABOUT YOUR SISTER. BUT THIS FLEET IS DOOMED. THE FIRST ORDER SHIPS CHASING US, THEY CAN TRACK US THROUGH LIGHTSPEED. IF MY FRIEND COMES BACK HERE, SHE'S--
ACTIVE TRACKING...
WHAT NOW?
HYPERSPACE TRACKING'S NEW TECH, BUT THE PRINCIPLE'S THE SAME AS ANY ACTIVE TRACKER. WHICH MEANS THEY'RE ONLY TRACKING US FROM--
--FROM THE LEAD SHIP!
IF I COULD GET YOU TO THAT TRACKER, COULD YOU SHUT IT OFF?
SURE. BUT THE ONLY WAY TO DO THAT WOULD BE FROM THE MAIN BRIDGE. OR FROM THE CIRCUIT BREAKER. AND WHO KNOWS WHERE THE BREAKER ROOM IS ON A STAR DESTROYER?
THE GUY WHO USED TO MOP IT.

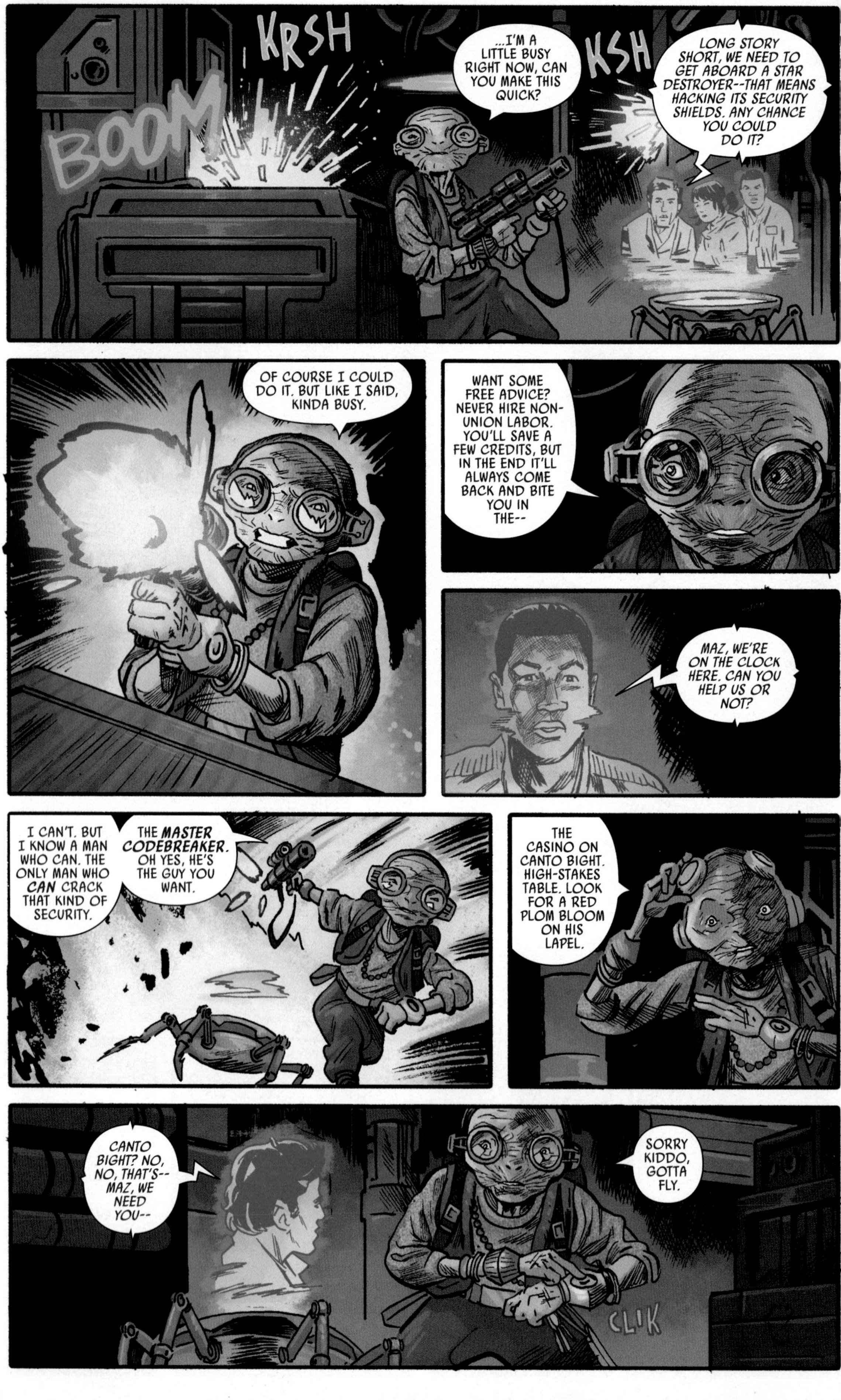
KRSH
BOOM
...I'M A LITTLE BUSY RIGHT NOW, CAN YOU MAKE THIS QUICK?
KSH
LONG STORY SHORT, WE NEED TO GET ABOARD A STAR DESTROYER--THAT MEANS HACKING ITS SECURITY SHIELDS. ANY CHANCE YOU COULD DO IT?
OF COURSE I COULD DO IT. BUT LIKE I SAID, KINDA BUSY.
WANT SOME FREE ADVICE? NEVER HIRE NON-UNION LABOR. YOU'LL SAVE A FEW CREDITS, BUT IN THE END IT'LL ALWAYS COME BACK AND BITE YOU IN THE--
MAZ, WE'RE ON THE CLOCK HERE. CAN YOU HELP US OR NOT?
I CAN'T. BUT I KNOW A MAN WHO CAN. THE ONLY MAN WHO CAN CRACK THAT KIND OF SECURITY.
THE MASTER CODEBREAKER. OH YES, HE'S THE GUY YOU WANT.
THE CASINO ON CANTO BIGHT. HIGH-STAKES TABLE. LOOK FOR A RED PLOM BLOOM ON HIS LAPEL.
CANTO BIGHT? NO, NO, THAT'S-- MAZ, WE NEED YOU--
SORRY KIDDO, GOTTA FLY.
CLIK

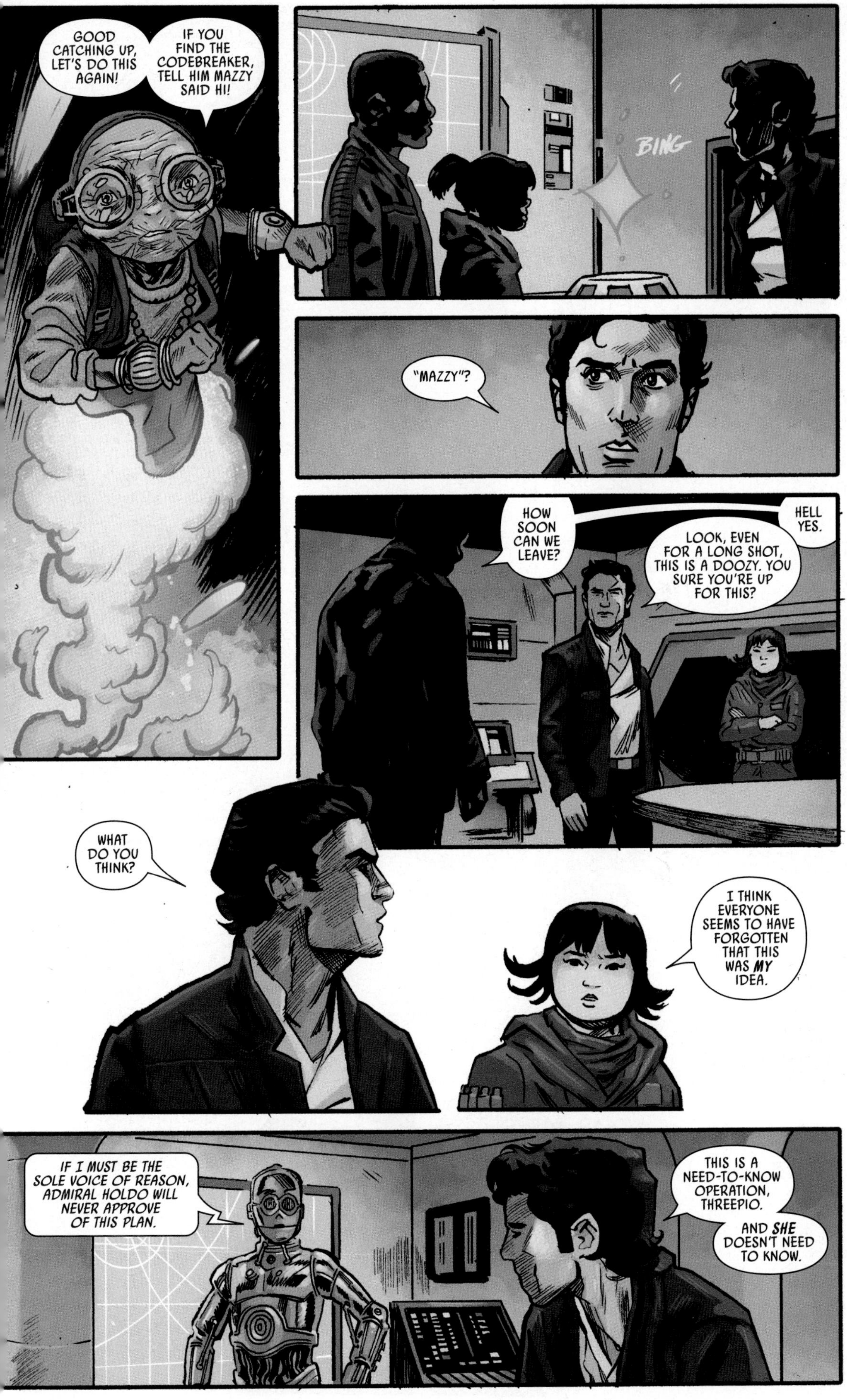

GOOD CATCHING UP, LET'S DO THIS AGAIN!
IF YOU FIND THE CODEBREAKER, TELL HIM MAZZY SAID HI!
BING
"MAZZY"?
HOW SOON CAN WE LEAVE?
HELL YES.
LOOK, EVEN FOR A LONG SHOT, THIS IS A DOOZY. YOU SURE YOU'RE UP FOR THIS?
WHAT DO YOU THINK?
I THINK EVERYONE SEEMS TO HAVE FORGOTTEN THAT THIS WAS *MY* IDEA.
IF I MUST BE THE SOLE VOICE OF REASON, ADMIRAL HOLDO WILL NEVER APPROVE OF THIS PLAN.
THIS IS A NEED-TO-KNOW OPERATION, THREEPIO.
AND *SHE* DOESN'T NEED TO KNOW.

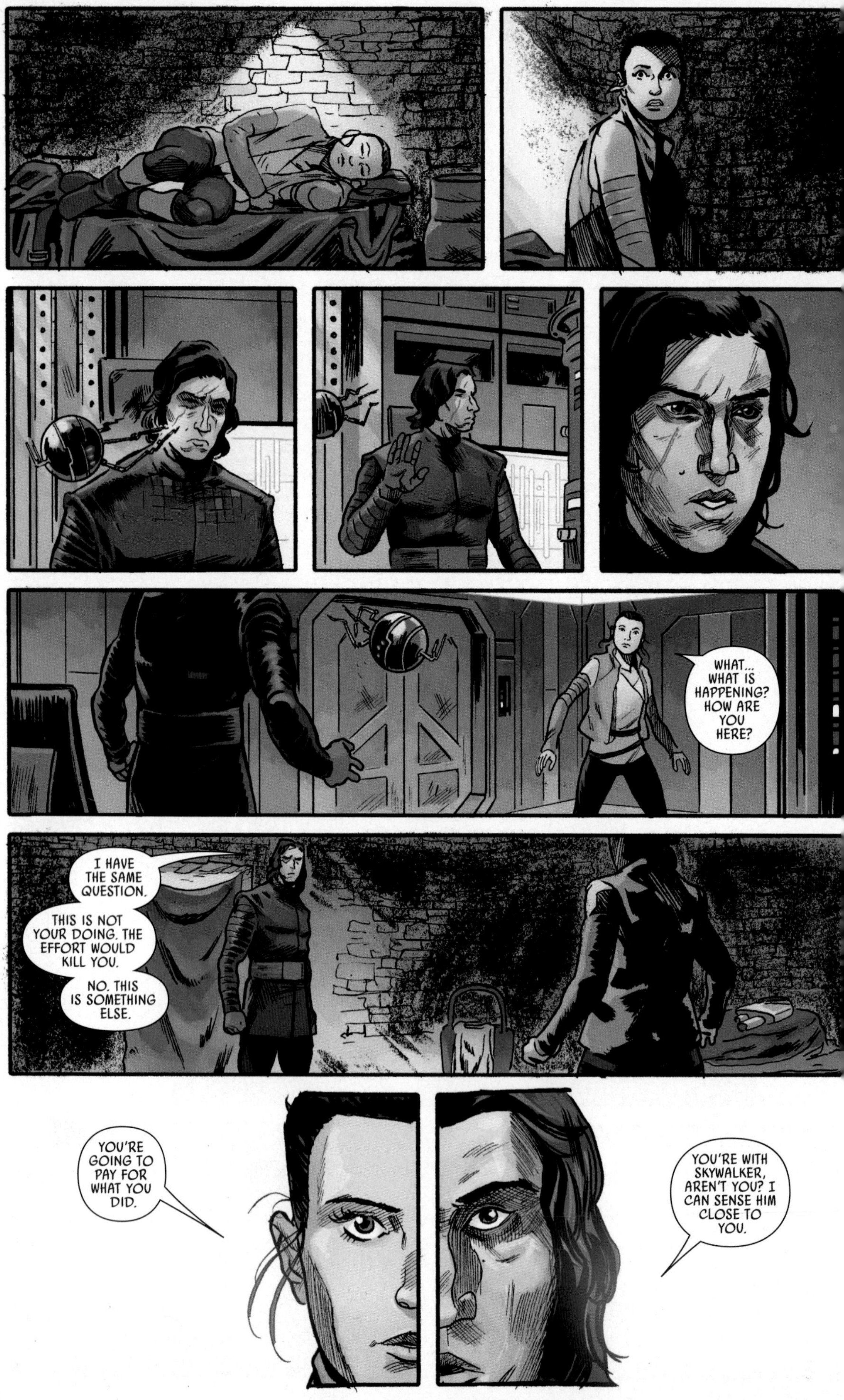
WHAT... WHAT IS HAPPENING? HOW ARE YOU HERE?
I HAVE THE SAME QUESTION.
THIS IS NOT YOUR DOING. THE EFFORT WOULD KILL YOU.
NO. THIS IS SOMETHING ELSE.
YOU'RE GOING TO PAY FOR WHAT YOU DID.
YOU'RE WITH SKYWALKER, AREN'T YOU? I CAN SENSE HIM CLOSE TO YOU.

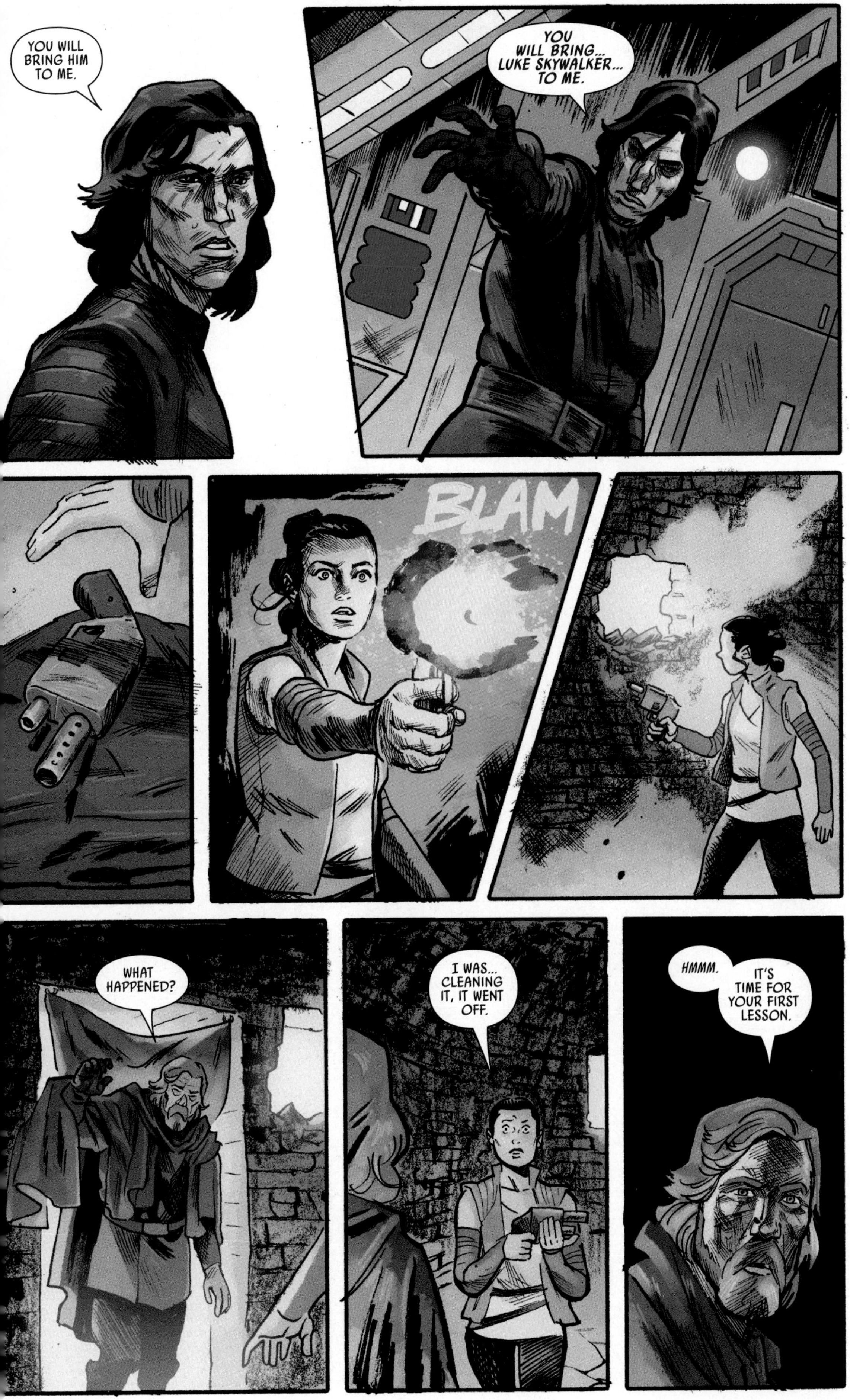
YOU WILL BRING HIM TO ME.
YOU WILL BRING... LUKE SKYWALKER... TO ME.
BLAM
WHAT HAPPENED?
I WAS... CLEANING IT, IT WENT OFF.
HMMM.
IT'S TIME FOR YOUR FIRST LESSON.

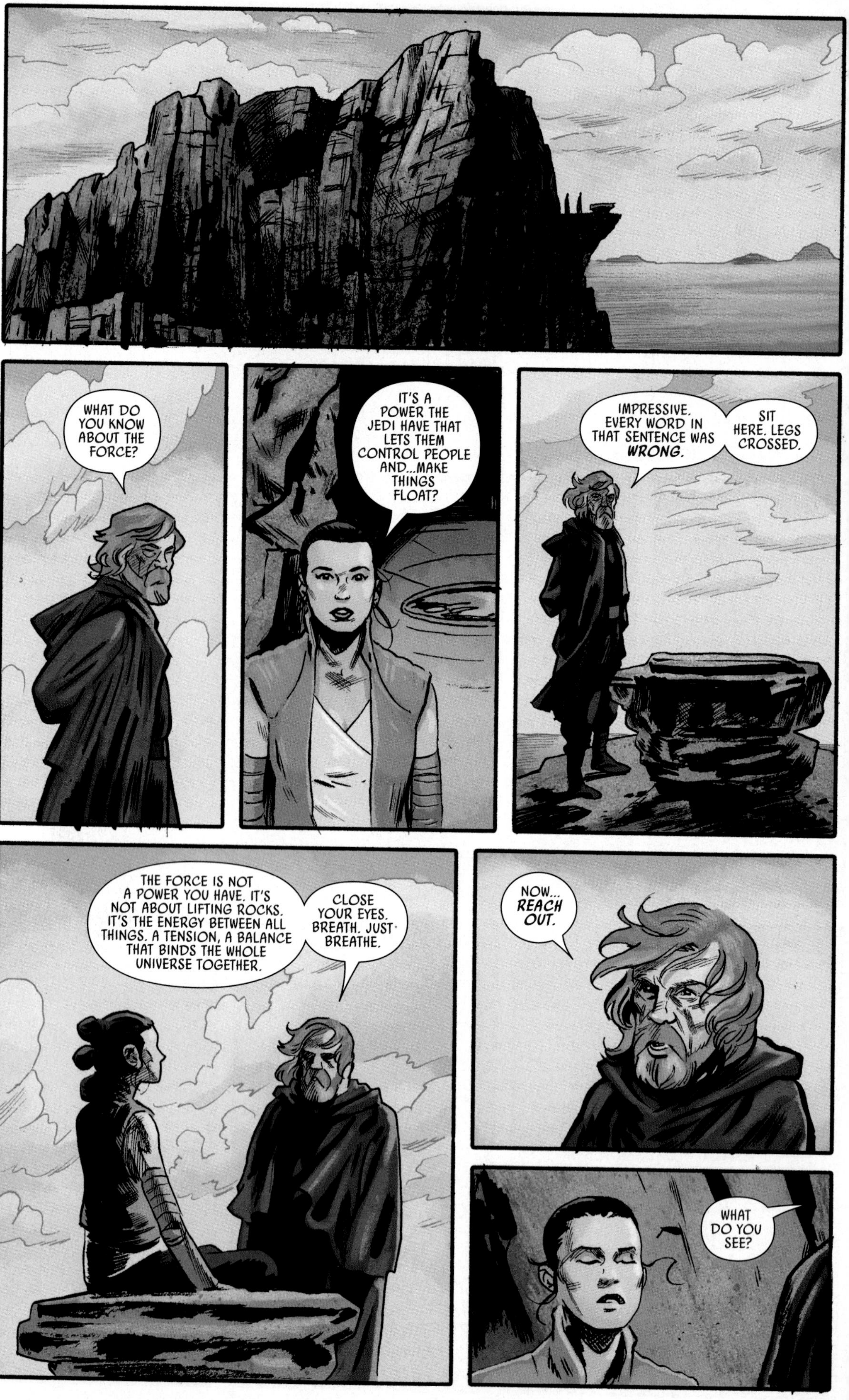
WHAT DO YOU KNOW ABOUT THE FORCE?
IT'S A POWER THE JEDI HAVE THAT LETS THEM CONTROL PEOPLE AND...MAKE THINGS FLOAT?
IMPRESSIVE. EVERY WORD IN THAT SENTENCE WAS WRONG.
SIT HERE. LEGS CROSSED.
THE FORCE IS NOT A POWER YOU HAVE. IT'S NOT ABOUT LIFTING ROCKS. IT'S THE ENERGY BETWEEN ALL THINGS. A TENSION, A BALANCE THAT BINDS THE WHOLE UNIVERSE TOGETHER.
CLOSE YOUR EYES. BREATH. JUST BREATHE.
NOW... REACH OUT.
WHAT DO YOU SEE?

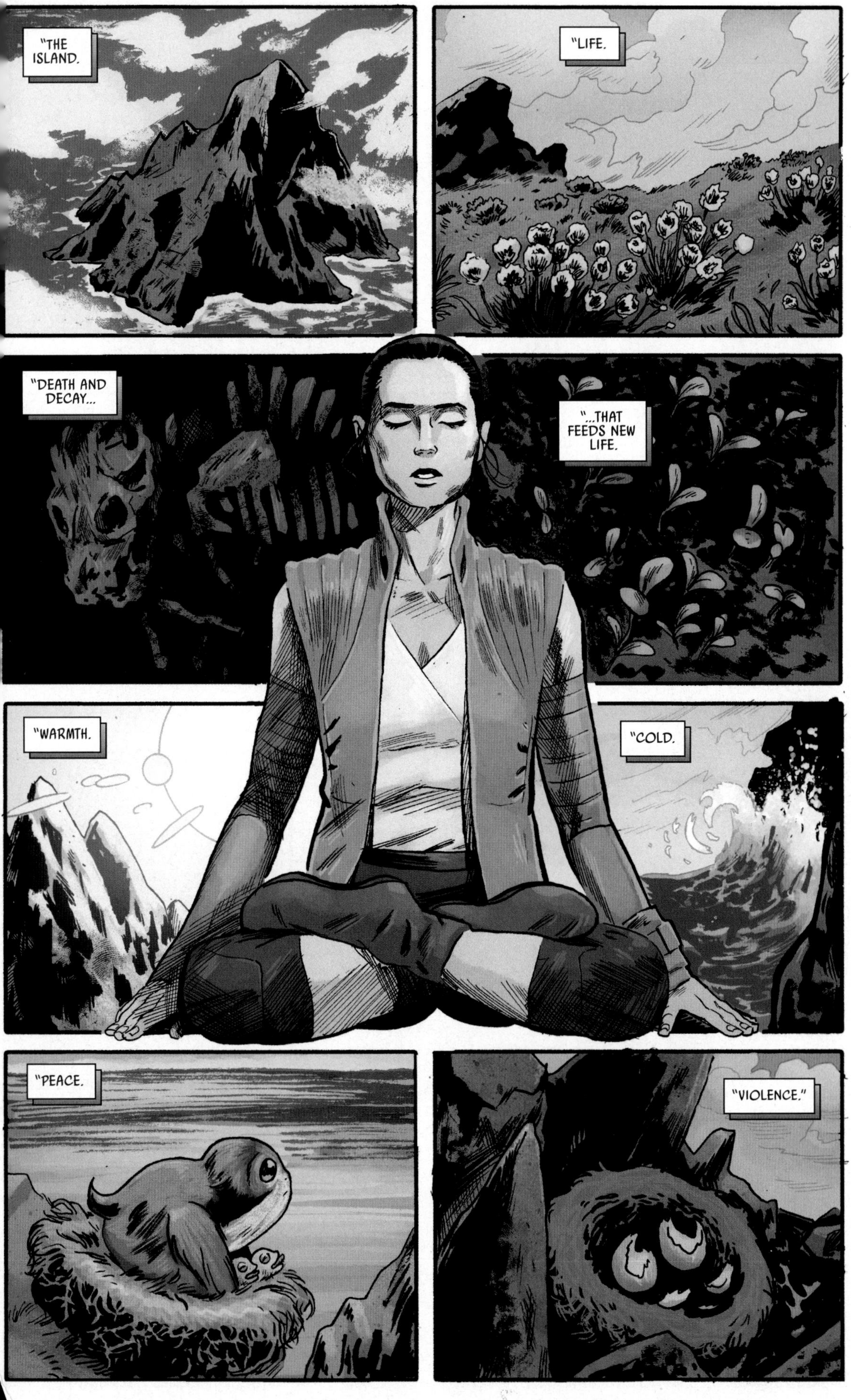
"THE ISLAND.
"LIFE.
"DEATH AND DECAY...
"...THAT FEEDS NEW LIFE.
"WARMTH.
"COLD.
"PEACE.
"VIOLENCE."

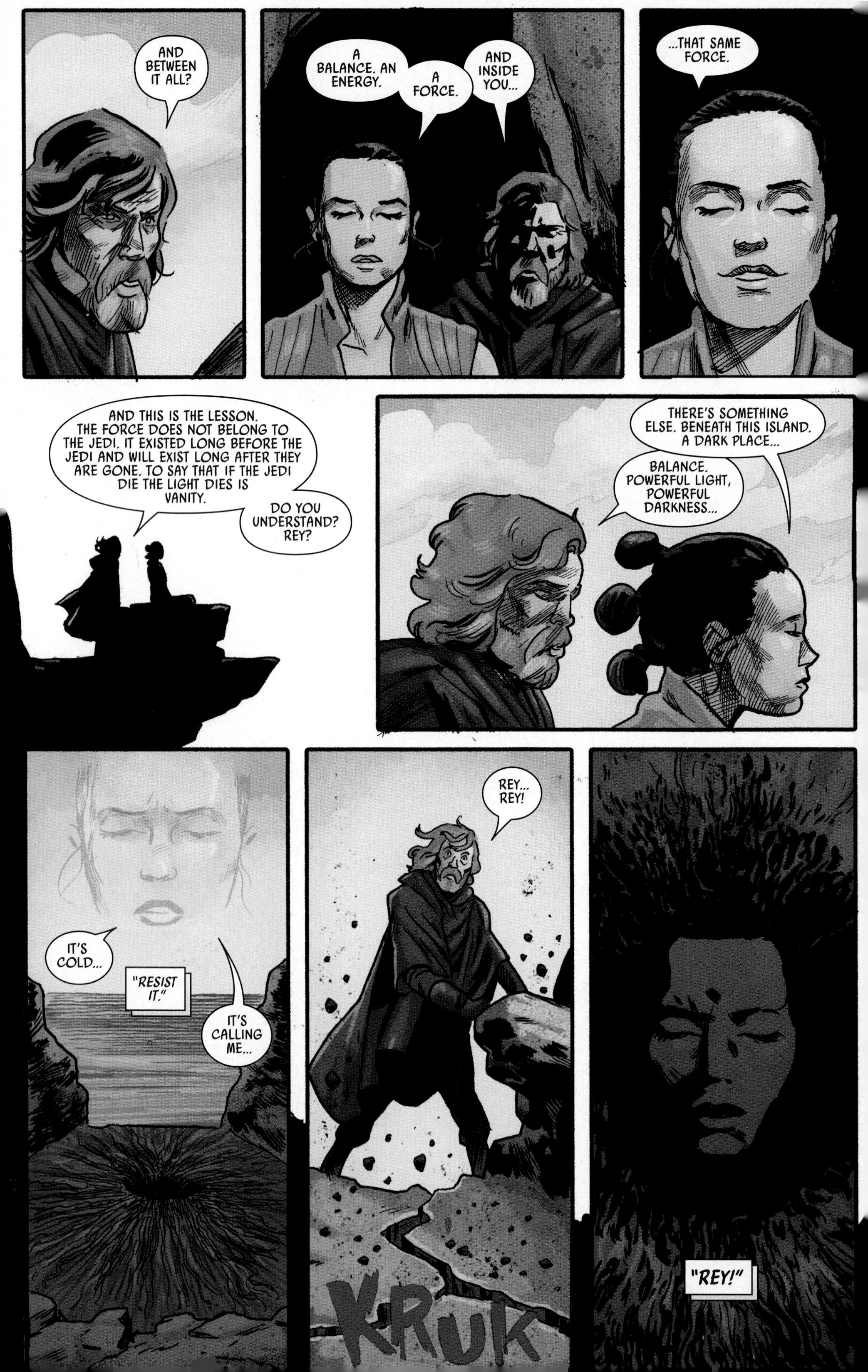
AND BETWEEN IT ALL?
A BALANCE. AN ENERGY.
A FORCE.
AND INSIDE YOU...
...THAT SAME FORCE.
AND THIS IS THE LESSON. THE FORCE DOES NOT BELONG TO THE JEDI. IT EXISTED LONG BEFORE THE JEDI AND WILL EXIST LONG AFTER THEY ARE GONE. TO SAY THAT IF THE JEDI DIE THE LIGHT DIES IS VANITY.
DO YOU UNDERSTAND? REY?
THERE'S SOMETHING ELSE. BENEATH THIS ISLAND. A DARK PLACE...
BALANCE. POWERFUL LIGHT, POWERFUL DARKNESS...
IT'S COLD...
"RESIST IT."
IT'S CALLING ME...
REY... REY!
KRUK
"REY!"

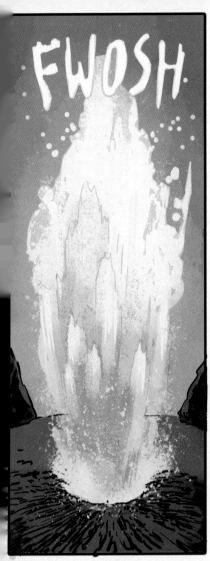

FWOSH

YOU WENT STRAIGHT TO THE DARK.

IT WAS TRYING TO SHOW ME SOMETHING.

IT OFFERED YOU SOMETHING YOU NEEDED AND YOU DIDN'T EVEN TRY TO STOP YOURSELF.

YOU WEREN'T THERE. I DIDN'T SENSE YOU. *NOTHING* FROM YOU.

YOU'VE CLOSED YOURSELF OFF FROM THE FORCE.

WAIT. WHERE ARE YOU GOING?

I'VE SEEN THIS RAW STRENGTH ONLY ONCE BEFORE-- IN BEN SOLO. IT DIDN'T SCARE ME ENOUGH THEN--

--IT DOES NOW.

NOT JUST BEN. I SEE SO MUCH OF MYSELF IN HER.

MAYBE THAT'S WHAT I'M MOST AFRAID OF.

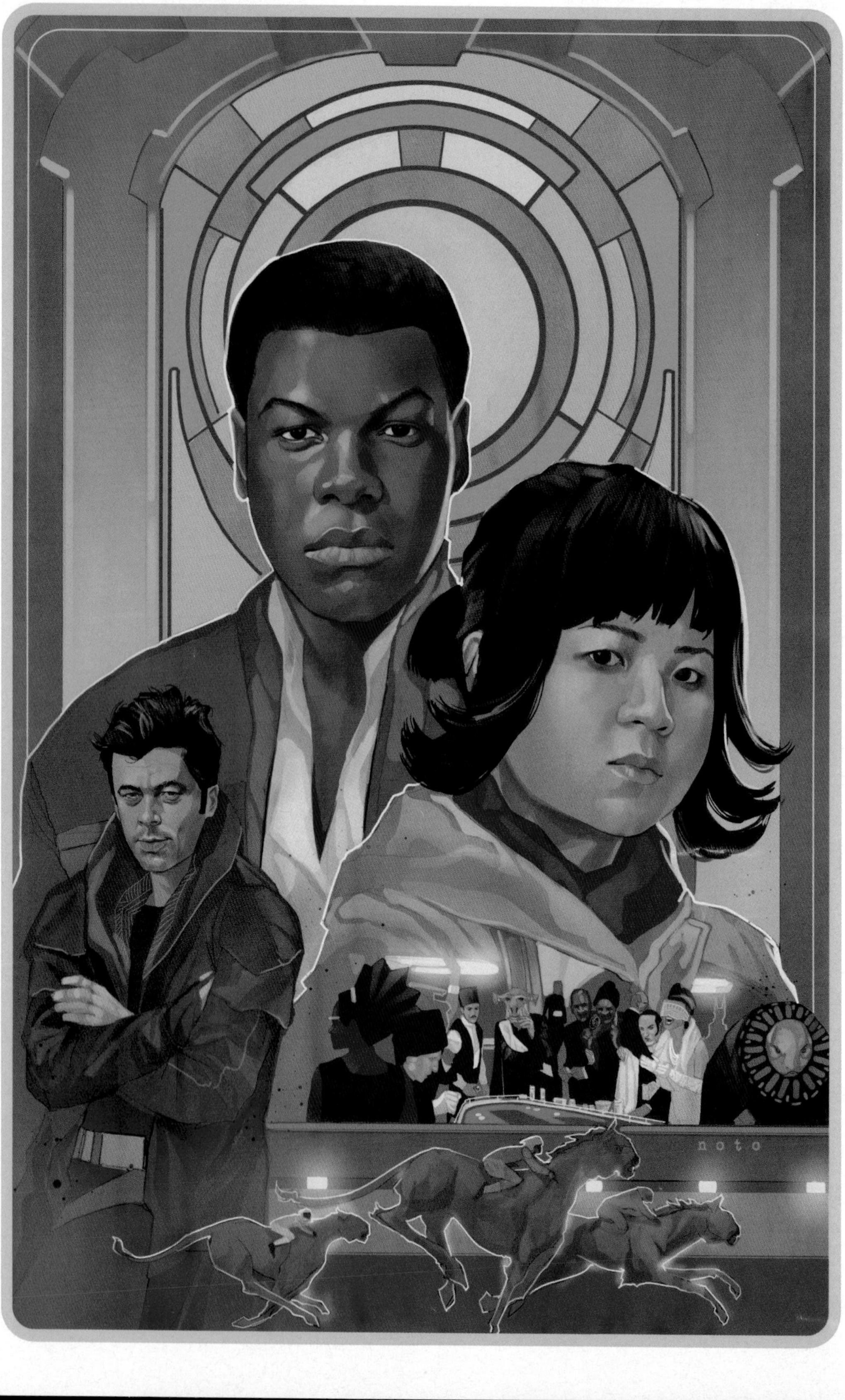
noto

THE LAST JEDI #3

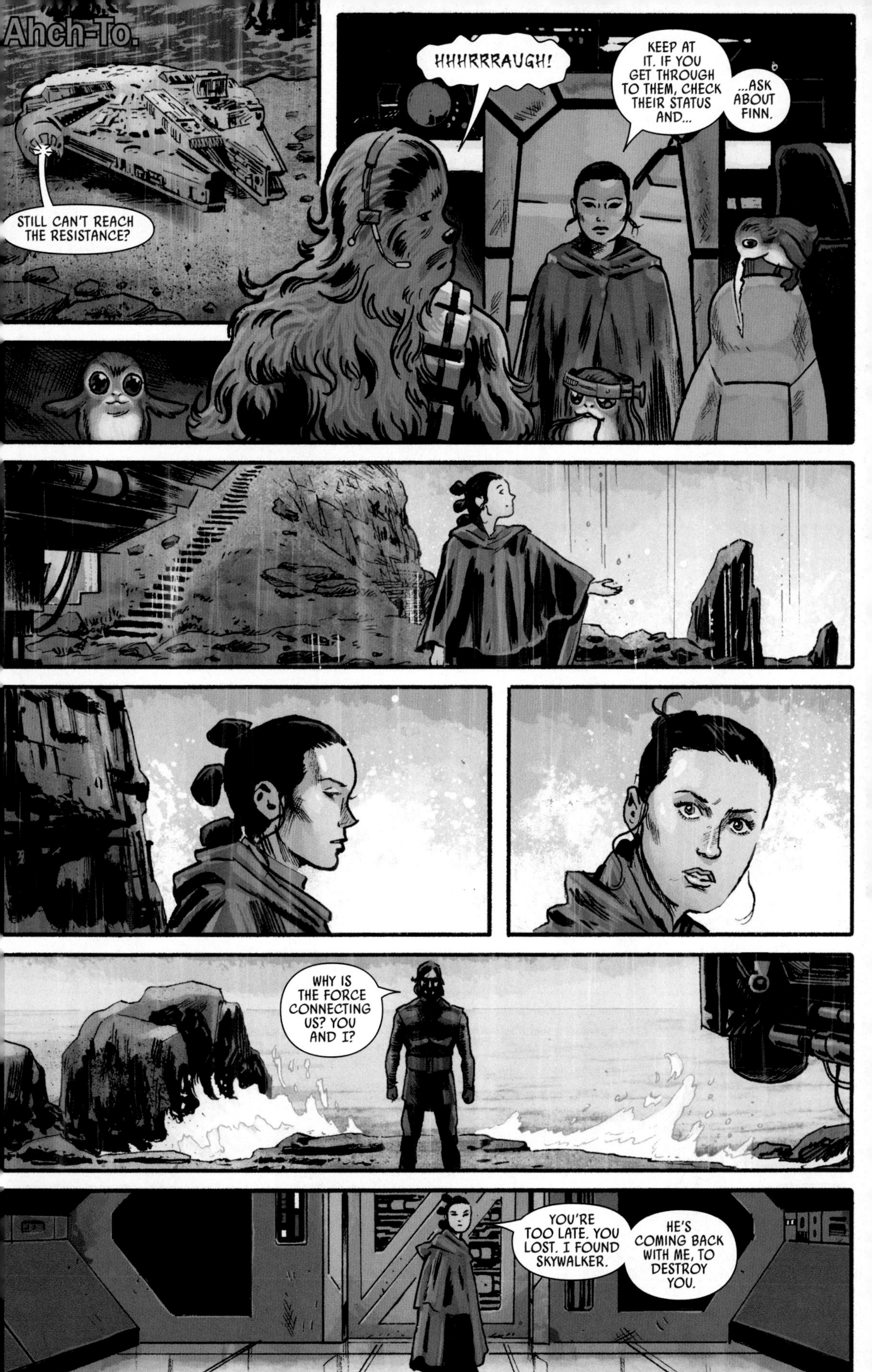

Ahch-To.
STILL CAN'T REACH THE RESISTANCE?
HHHRRRAUGH!
KEEP AT IT. IF YOU GET THROUGH TO THEM, CHECK THEIR STATUS AND...
...ASK ABOUT FINN.
WHY IS THE FORCE CONNECTING US? YOU AND I?
YOU'RE TOO LATE. YOU LOST. I FOUND SKYWALKER.
HE'S COMING BACK WITH ME, TO DESTROY YOU.

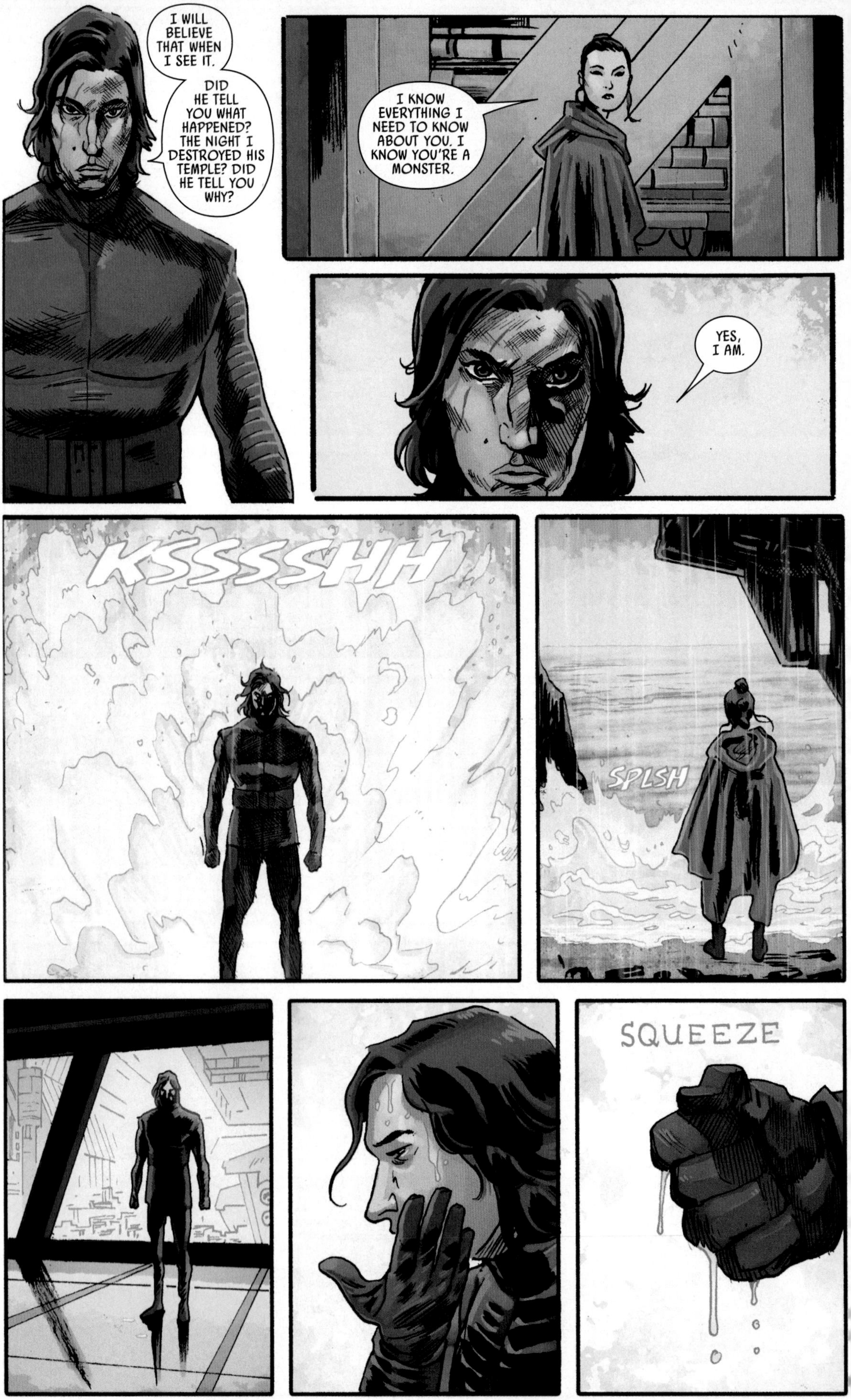

I WILL BELIEVE THAT WHEN I SEE IT.
DID HE TELL YOU WHAT HAPPENED? THE NIGHT I DESTROYED HIS TEMPLE? DID HE TELL YOU WHY?
I KNOW EVERYTHING I NEED TO KNOW ABOUT YOU. I KNOW YOU'RE A MONSTER.
YES, I AM.
KSSSSHH
SPLSH
SQUEEZE

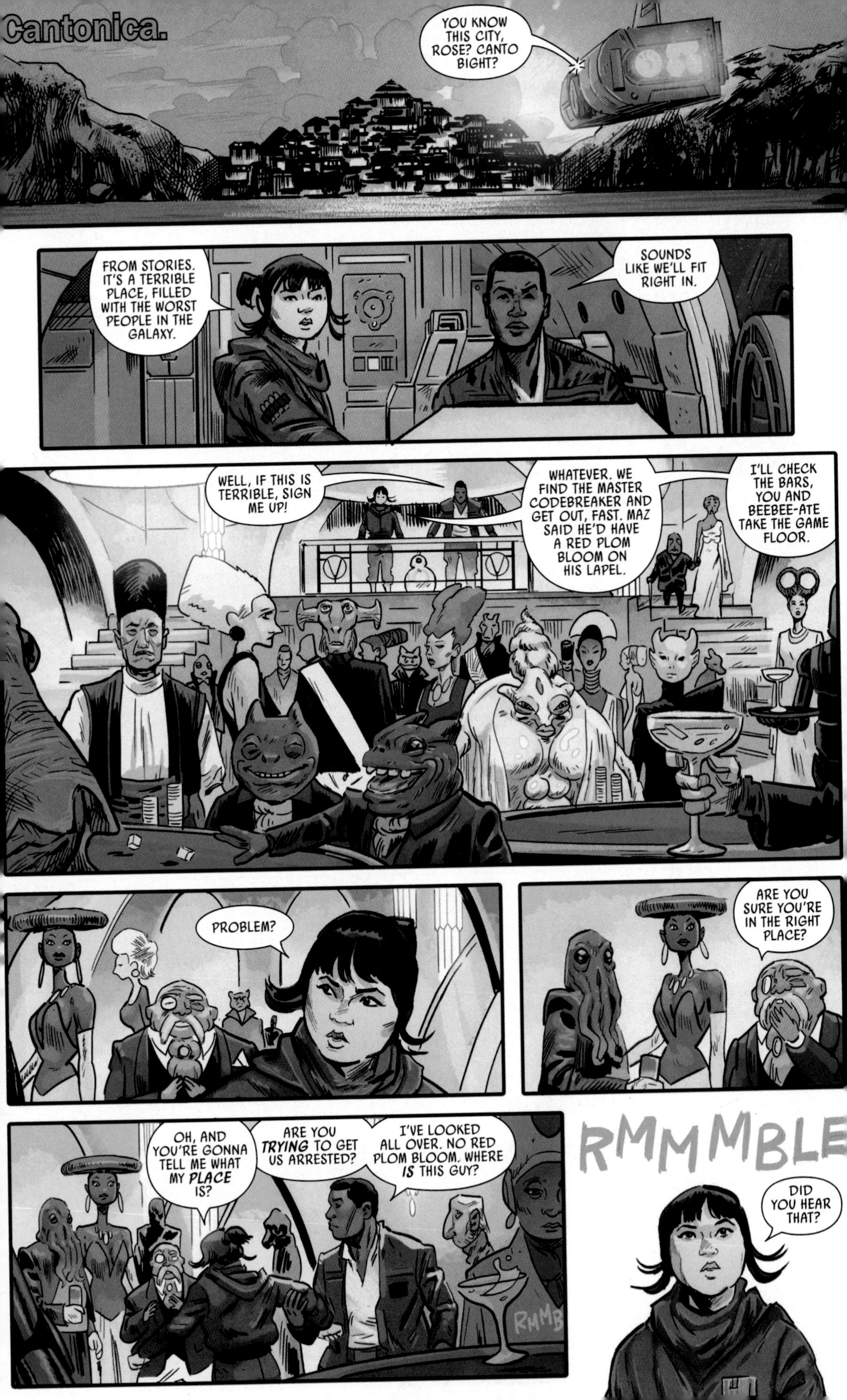
Cantonica.
YOU KNOW THIS CITY, ROSE? CANTO BIGHT?
FROM STORIES. IT'S A TERRIBLE PLACE, FILLED WITH THE WORST PEOPLE IN THE GALAXY.
SOUNDS LIKE WE'LL FIT RIGHT IN.
WELL, IF THIS IS TERRIBLE, SIGN ME UP!
WHATEVER. WE FIND THE MASTER CODEBREAKER AND GET OUT, FAST. MAZ SAID HE'D HAVE A RED PLOM BLOOM ON HIS LAPEL.
I'LL CHECK THE BARS, YOU AND BEEBEE-ATE TAKE THE GAME FLOOR.
PROBLEM?
ARE YOU SURE YOU'RE IN THE RIGHT PLACE?
OH, AND YOU'RE GONNA TELL ME WHAT MY *PLACE* IS?
ARE YOU *TRYING* TO GET US ARRESTED?
I'VE LOOKED ALL OVER. NO RED PLOM BLOOM. WHERE *IS* THIS GUY?
RMMB
RMMMBLE
DID YOU HEAR THAT?

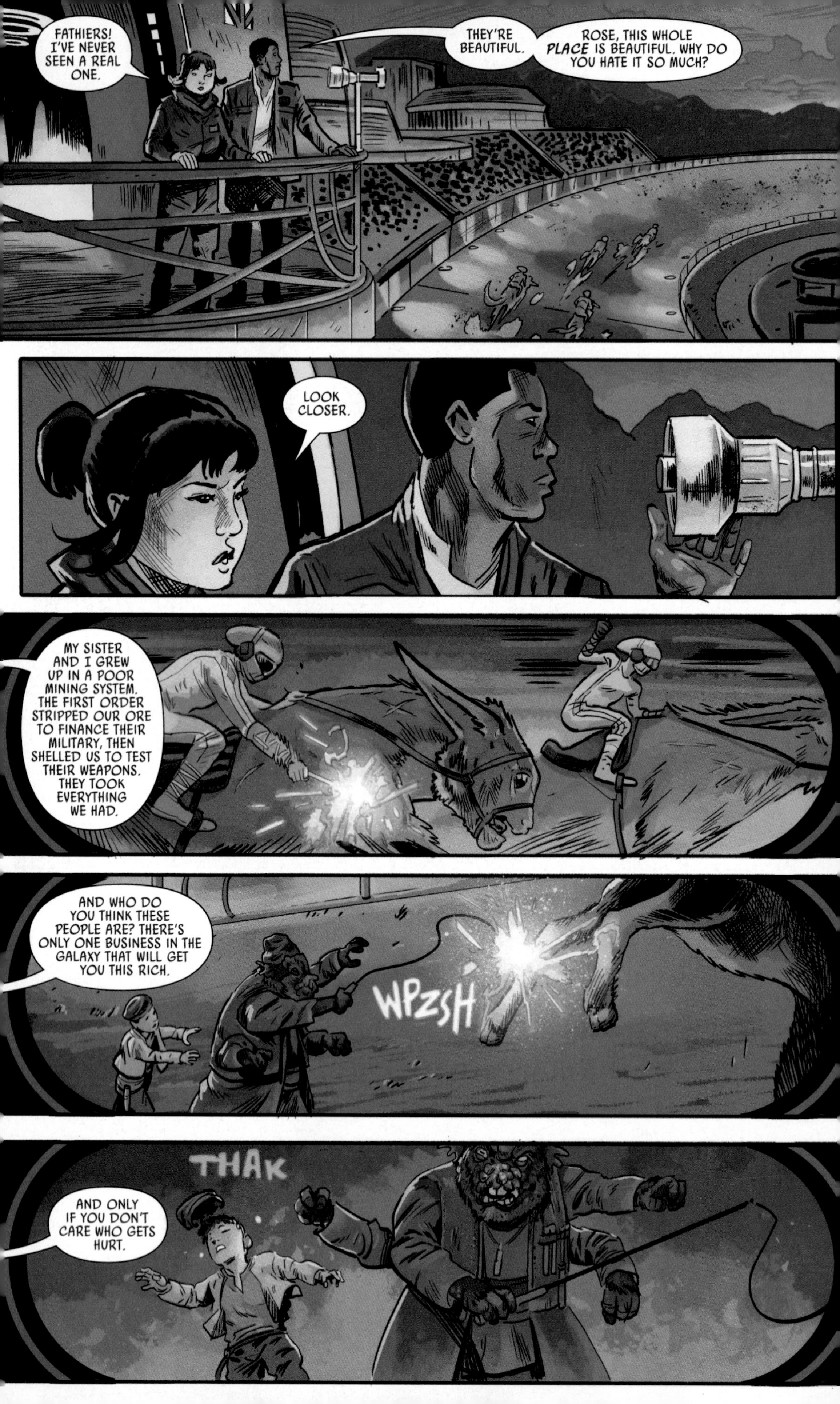

FATHIERS! I'VE NEVER SEEN A REAL ONE.
THEY'RE BEAUTIFUL.
ROSE, THIS WHOLE PLACE IS BEAUTIFUL. WHY DO YOU HATE IT SO MUCH?
LOOK CLOSER.
MY SISTER AND I GREW UP IN A POOR MINING SYSTEM. THE FIRST ORDER STRIPPED OUR ORE TO FINANCE THEIR MILITARY, THEN SHELLED US TO TEST THEIR WEAPONS. THEY TOOK EVERYTHING WE HAD.
AND WHO DO YOU THINK THESE PEOPLE ARE? THERE'S ONLY ONE BUSINESS IN THE GALAXY THAT WILL GET YOU THIS RICH.
WPZSH
THAK
AND ONLY IF YOU DON'T CARE WHO GETS HURT.

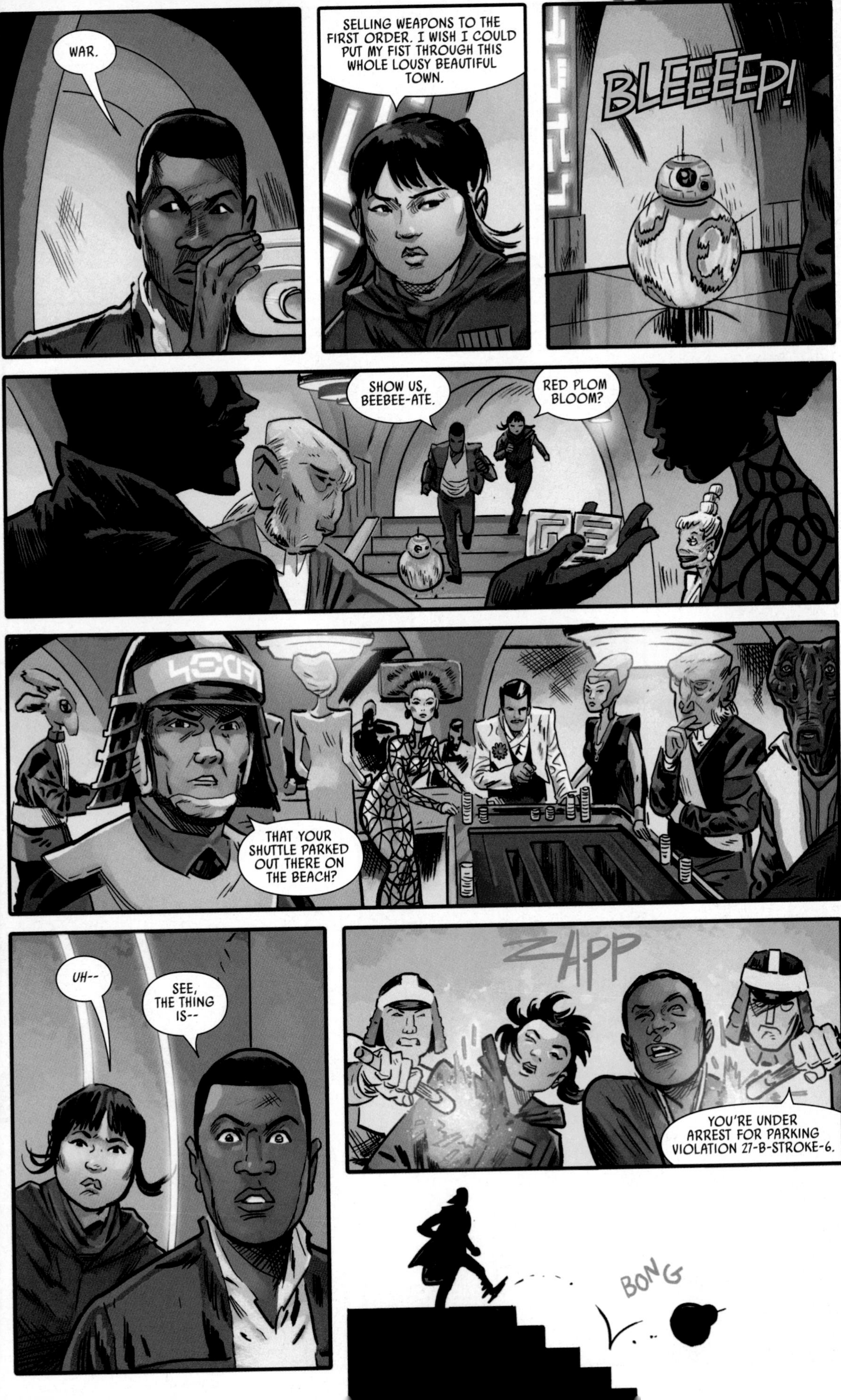
WAR.
SELLING WEAPONS TO THE FIRST ORDER. I WISH I COULD PUT MY FIST THROUGH THIS WHOLE LOUSY BEAUTIFUL TOWN.
BLEEEEP!
SHOW US, BEEBEE-ATE.
RED PLOM BLOOM?
THAT YOUR SHUTTLE PARKED OUT THERE ON THE BEACH?
UH--
SEE, THE THING IS--
ZAPP
YOU'RE UNDER ARREST FOR PARKING VIOLATION 27-B-STROKE-6.
BONG

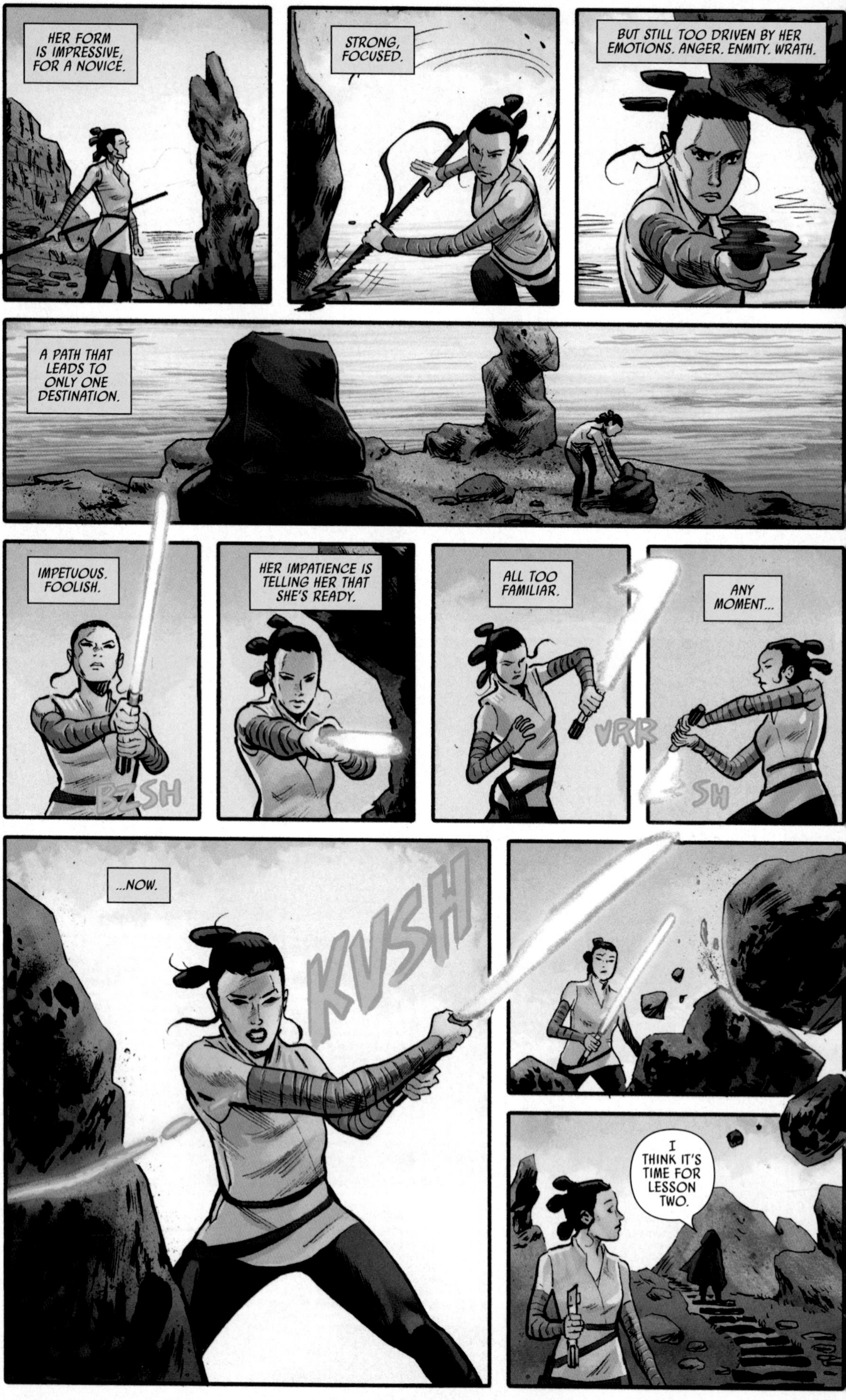
HER FORM IS IMPRESSIVE, FOR A NOVICE.
STRONG, FOCUSED.
BUT STILL TOO DRIVEN BY HER EMOTIONS. ANGER. ENMITY. WRATH.
A PATH THAT LEADS TO ONLY ONE DESTINATION.
IMPETUOUS. FOOLISH.
BZSH
HER IMPATIENCE IS TELLING HER THAT SHE'S READY.
ALL TOO FAMILIAR.
VRR
ANY MOMENT...
SH
...NOW.
KVSH
I THINK IT'S TIME FOR LESSON TWO.

NOW THAT THEY'RE EXTINCT, THE JEDI ARE ROMANTICIZED. DEIFIED. BUT IF YOU STRIP AWAY THE MYTH AND LOOK AT THEIR DEEDS, THE LEGACY OF THE JEDI IS FAILURE, HYPOCRISY, HUBRIS.

THAT'S NOT TRUE.

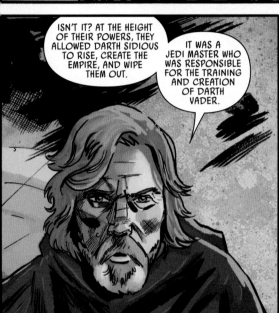

ISN'T IT? AT THE HEIGHT OF THEIR POWERS, THEY ALLOWED DARTH SIDIOUS TO RISE, CREATE THE EMPIRE, AND WIPE THEM OUT.

IT WAS A JEDI MASTER WHO WAS RESPONSIBLE FOR THE TRAINING AND CREATION OF DARTH VADER.

AND A JEDI WHO SAVED HIM. THE MOST HATED MAN IN THE GALAXY, BUT YOU SAW THAT THERE WAS CONFLICT INSIDE HIM. YOU BELIEVED THAT HE WASN'T LOST, THAT HE COULD BE SAVED.

OH, HOW I WISH I HAD NEVER TOLD ANYONE THAT STORY. I SHOULD HAVE JUST LET WHAT HAPPENED DIE WITH MY FATHER, WITH SIDIOUS.

BUT I LEARNED HOW QUICKLY A GOOD TALE SPREADS LIKE FIRE THROUGHOUT THE GALAXY AND BECOMES LEGEND.

FOR MANY YEARS THERE WAS BALANCE, AND THEN I SAW BEN, MY NEPHEW, WITH THAT MIGHTY SKYWALKER BLOOD.

IN MY HUBRIS, I THOUGHT I COULD TRAIN HIM, PASS ON WHAT I HAD LEARNED AS MY OWN MASTER HAD INSTRUCTED. AND LEIA TRUSTED ME. WITH HER ONLY SON.

I TOOK HIM, AND A DOZEN STUDENTS, AND BEGAN A TRAINING TEMPLE. AND BY THE TIME I REALIZED I WAS NO MATCH FOR THE DARKNESS RISING IN HIM, IT WAS TOO LATE.

WHAT HAPPENED?

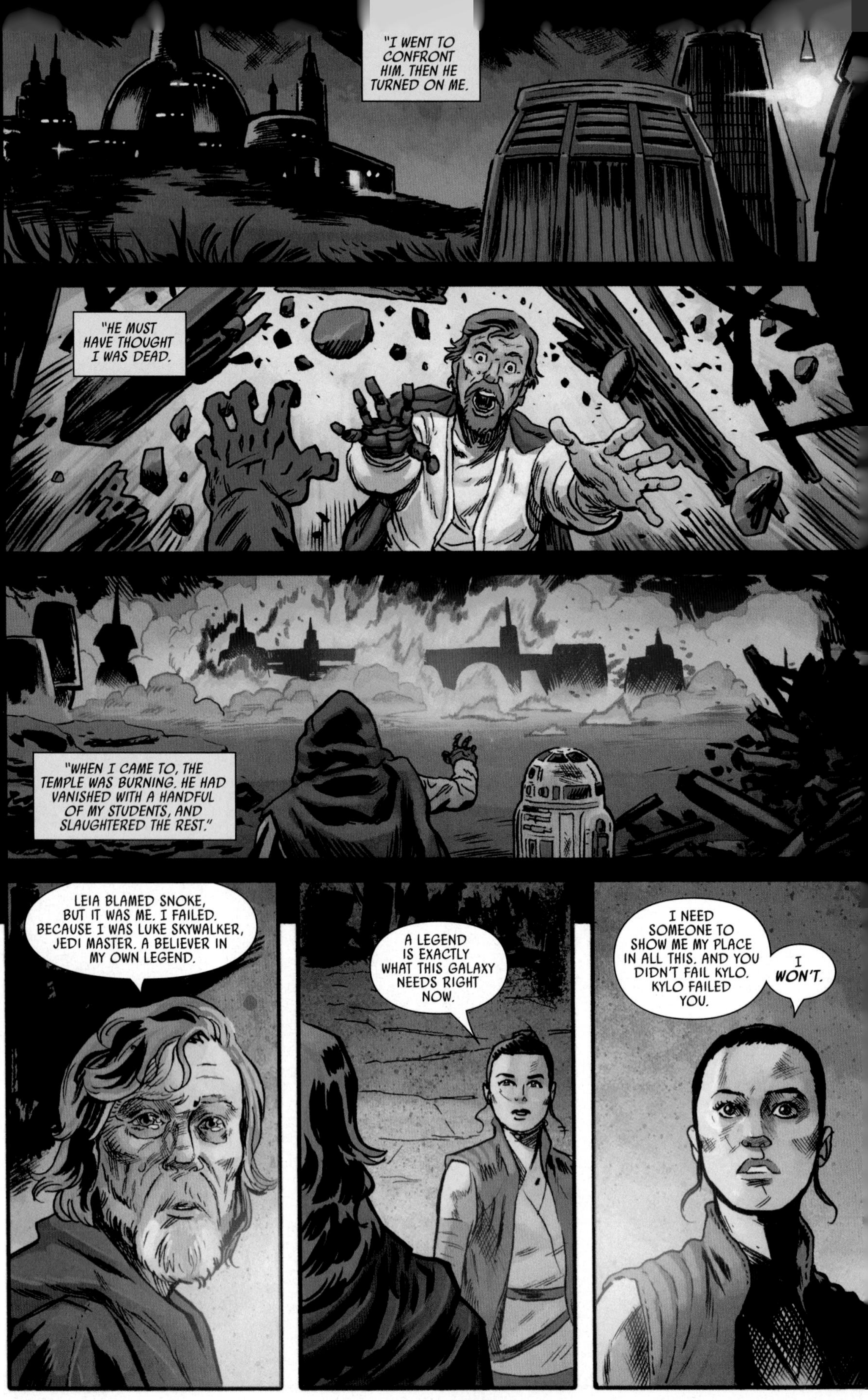

"I WENT TO CONFRONT HIM. THEN HE TURNED ON ME.
"HE MUST HAVE THOUGHT I WAS DEAD.
"WHEN I CAME TO, THE TEMPLE WAS BURNING. HE HAD VANISHED WITH A HANDFUL OF MY STUDENTS, AND SLAUGHTERED THE REST."
LEIA BLAMED SNOKE, BUT IT WAS ME. I FAILED. BECAUSE I WAS LUKE SKYWALKER, JEDI MASTER. A BELIEVER IN MY OWN LEGEND.
A LEGEND IS EXACTLY WHAT THIS GALAXY NEEDS RIGHT NOW.
I NEED SOMEONE TO SHOW ME MY PLACE IN ALL THIS. AND YOU DIDN'T FAIL KYLO. KYLO FAILED YOU.
I WON'T.

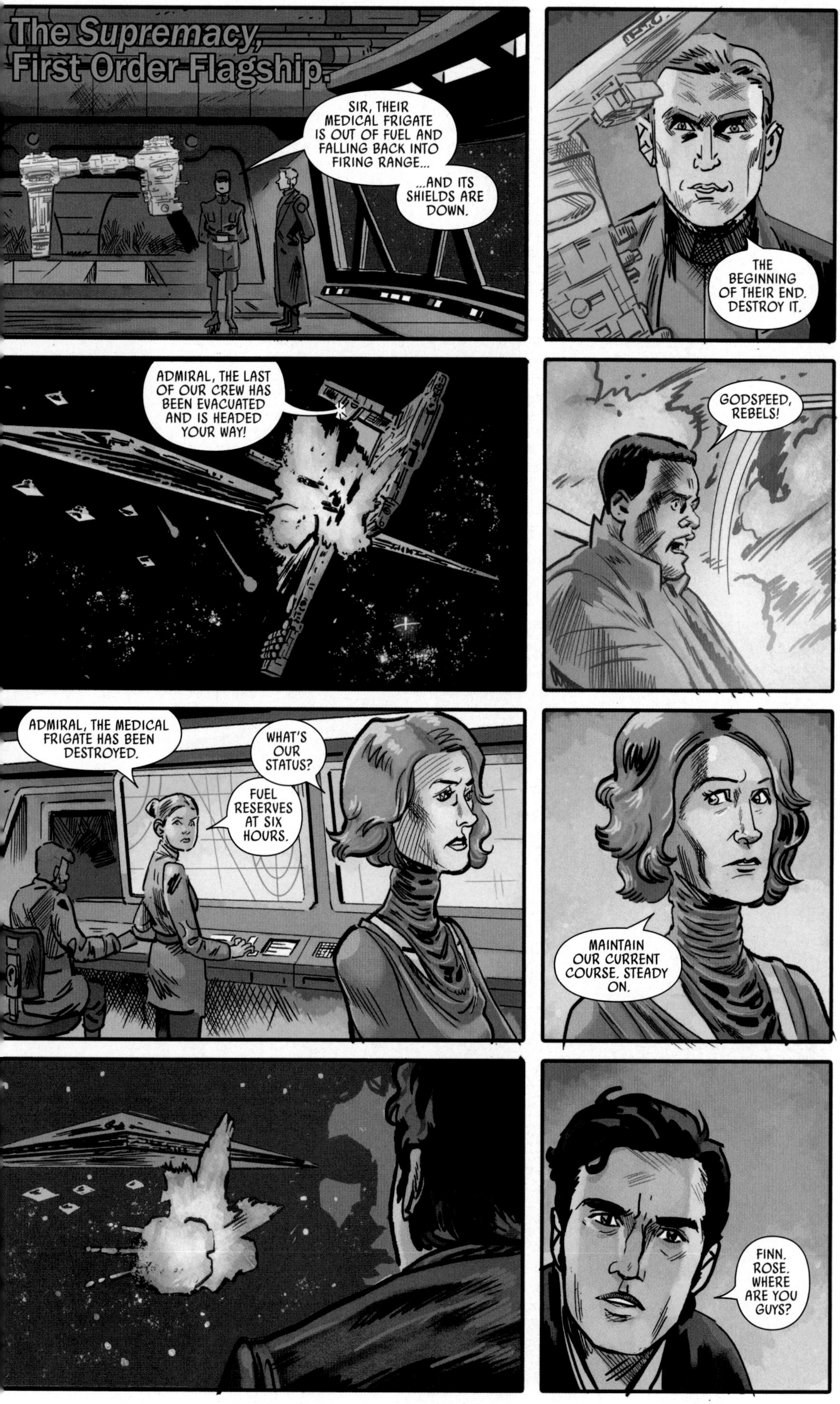
The Supremacy, First Order Flagship.
SIR, THEIR MEDICAL FRIGATE IS OUT OF FUEL AND FALLING BACK INTO FIRING RANGE...
...AND ITS SHIELDS ARE DOWN.
THE BEGINNING OF THEIR END. DESTROY IT.
ADMIRAL, THE LAST OF OUR CREW HAS BEEN EVACUATED AND IS HEADED YOUR WAY!
GODSPEED, REBELS!
ADMIRAL, THE MEDICAL FRIGATE HAS BEEN DESTROYED.
WHAT'S OUR STATUS?
FUEL RESERVES AT SIX HOURS.
MAINTAIN OUR CURRENT COURSE. STEADY ON.
FINN. ROSE. WHERE ARE YOU GUYS?

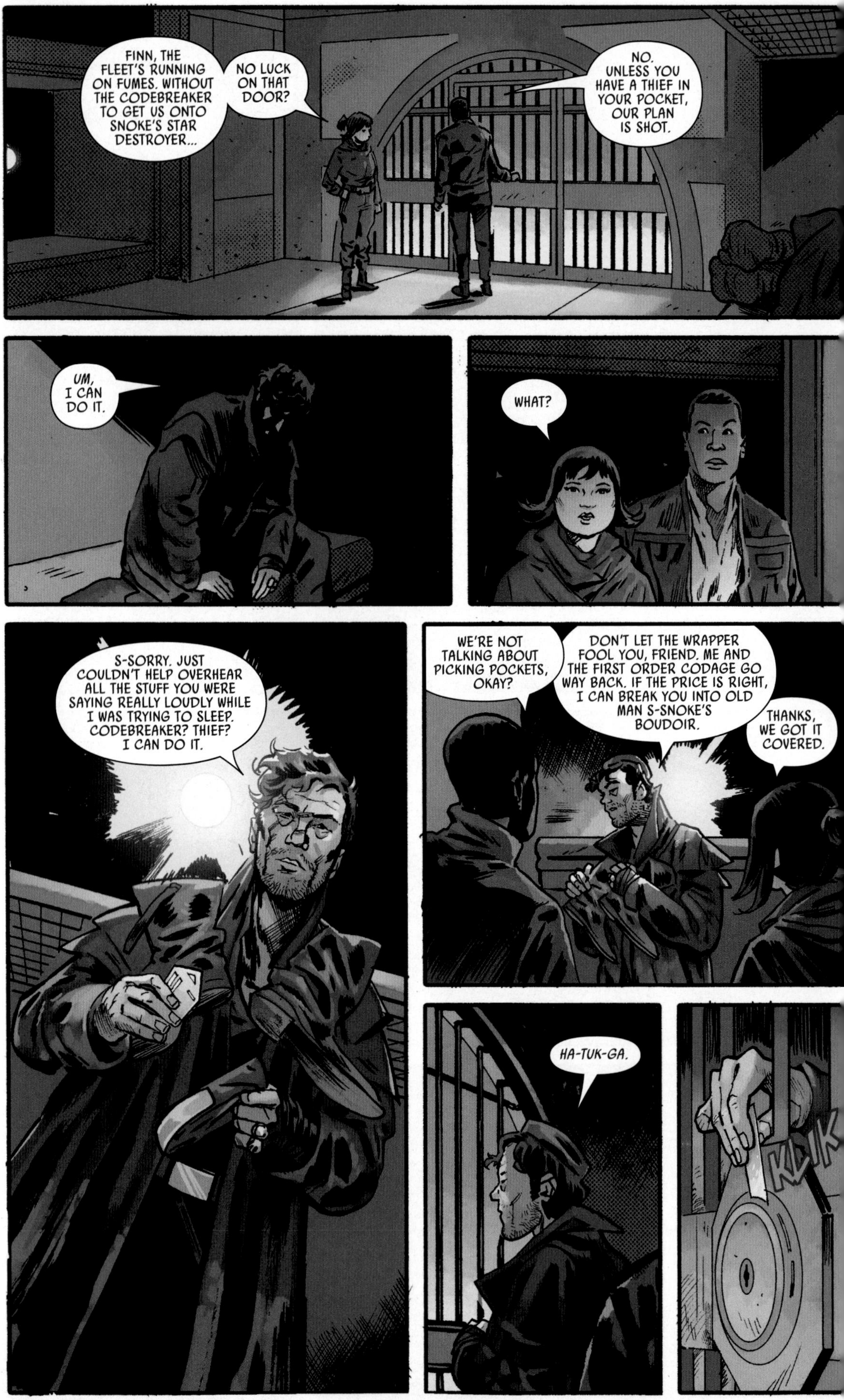
FINN, THE FLEET'S RUNNING ON FUMES. WITHOUT THE CODEBREAKER TO GET US ONTO SNOKE'S STAR DESTROYER...
NO LUCK ON THAT DOOR?
NO. UNLESS YOU HAVE A THIEF IN YOUR POCKET, OUR PLAN IS SHOT.
UM, I CAN DO IT.
WHAT?
S-SORRY. JUST COULDN'T HELP OVERHEAR ALL THE STUFF YOU WERE SAYING REALLY LOUDLY WHILE I WAS TRYING TO SLEEP. CODEBREAKER? THIEF? I CAN DO IT.
WE'RE NOT TALKING ABOUT PICKING POCKETS, OKAY?
DON'T LET THE WRAPPER FOOL YOU, FRIEND. ME AND THE FIRST ORDER CODAGE GO WAY BACK. IF THE PRICE IS RIGHT, I CAN BREAK YOU INTO OLD MAN S-SNOKE'S BOUDOIR.
THANKS, WE GOT IT COVERED.
HA-TUK-GA.
KLIK

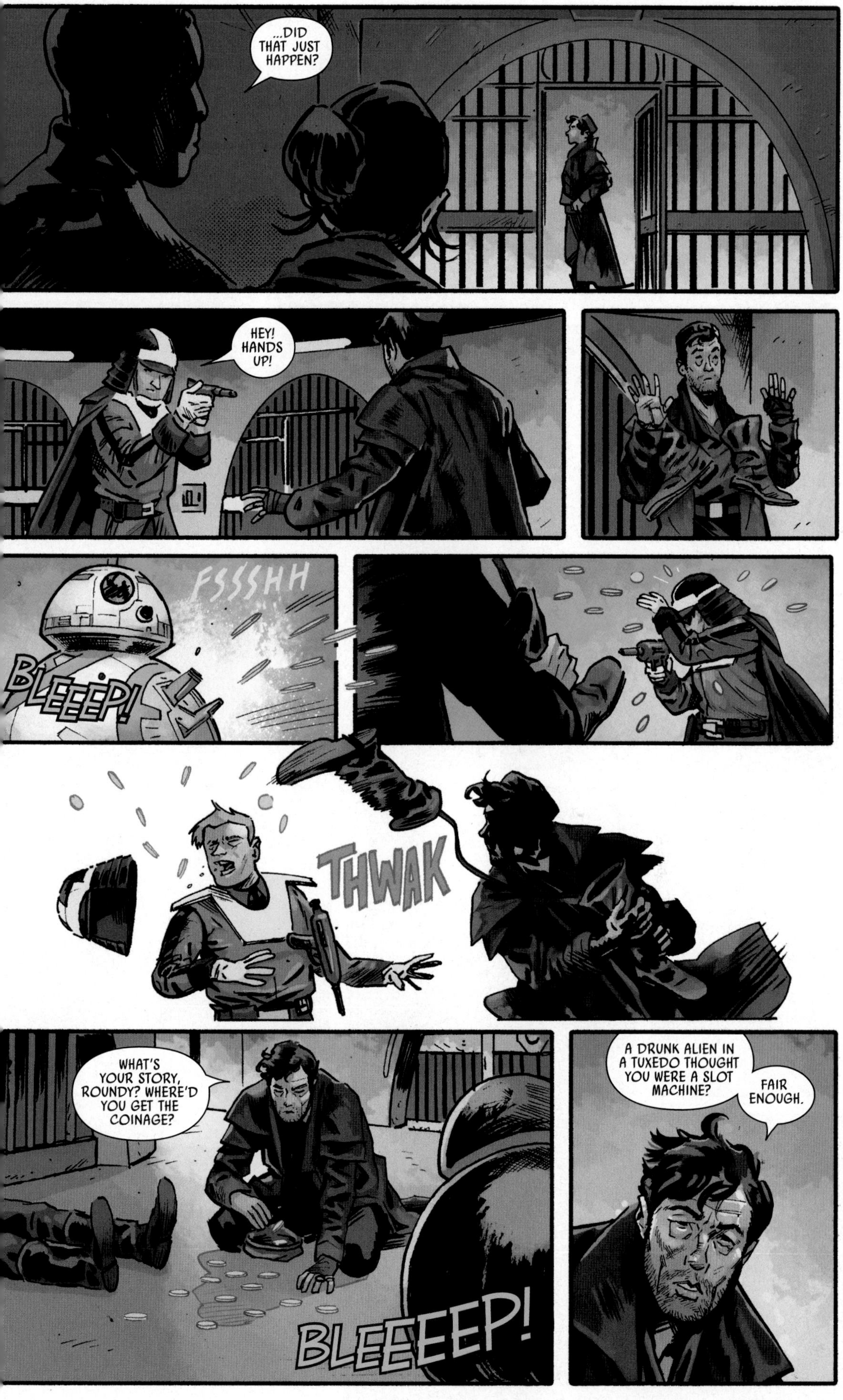

...DID THAT JUST HAPPEN?
HEY! HANDS UP!
FSSSHH
BLEEEP!
THWAK
WHAT'S YOUR STORY, ROUNDY? WHERE'D YOU GET THE COINAGE?
BLEEEEP!
A DRUNK ALIEN IN A TUXEDO THOUGHT YOU WERE A SLOT MACHINE?
FAIR ENOUGH.

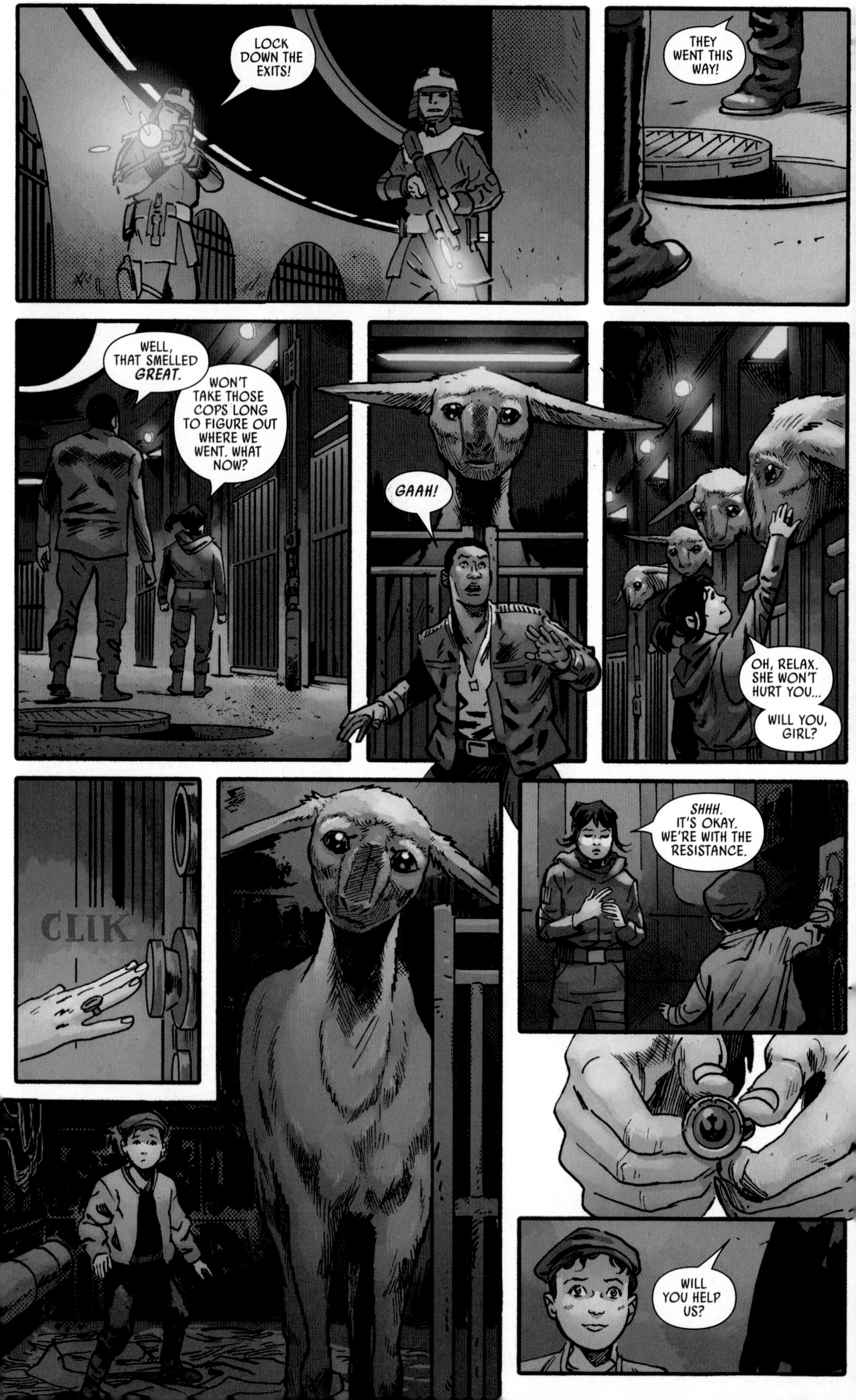
LOCK DOWN THE EXITS!
THEY WENT THIS WAY!
WELL, THAT SMELLED GREAT.
WON'T TAKE THOSE COPS LONG TO FIGURE OUT WHERE WE WENT. WHAT NOW?
GAAH!
OH, RELAX. SHE WON'T HURT YOU...
WILL YOU, GIRL?
CLIK
SHHH. IT'S OKAY. WE'RE WITH THE RESISTANCE.
WILL YOU HELP US?

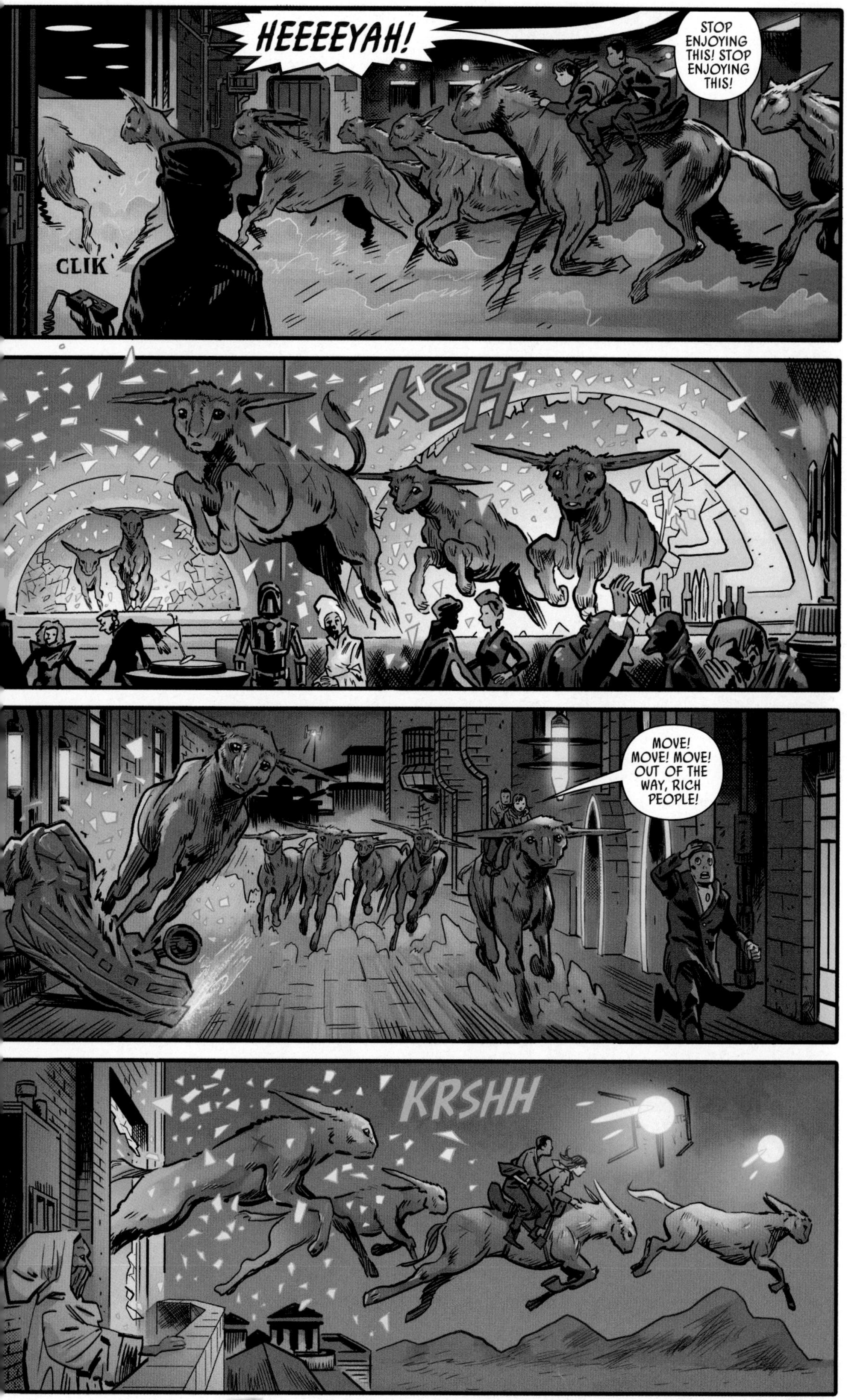
HEEEEYAH!
STOP ENJOYING THIS! STOP ENJOYING THIS!
CLIK
KSH
MOVE! MOVE! MOVE! OUT OF THE WAY, RICH PEOPLE!
KRSHH

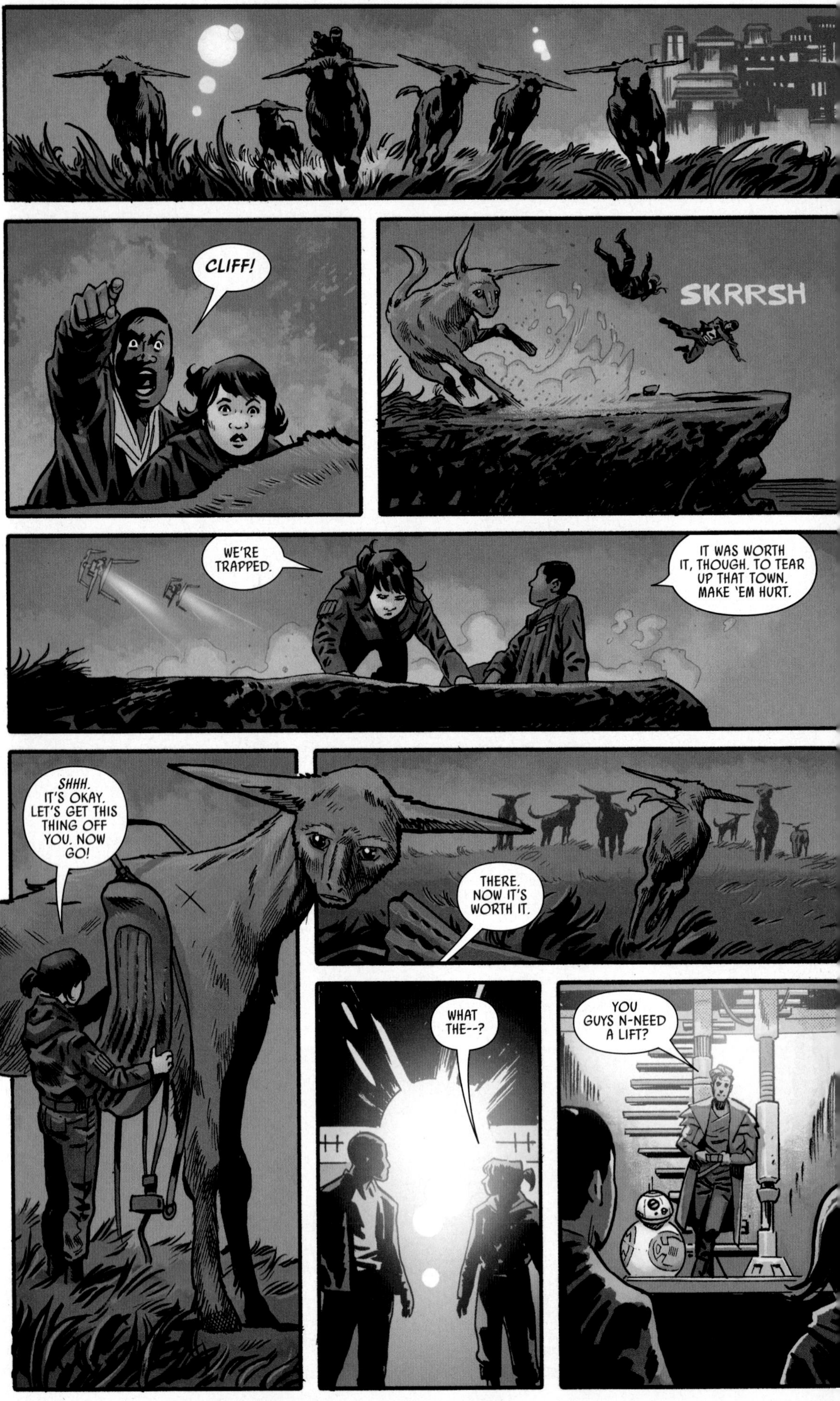

CLIFF!
SKRRSH
WE'RE TRAPPED.
IT WAS WORTH IT, THOUGH. TO TEAR UP THAT TOWN. MAKE 'EM HURT.
SHHH. IT'S OKAY. LET'S GET THIS THING OFF YOU. NOW GO!
THERE. NOW IT'S WORTH IT.
WHAT THE--?
YOU GUYS N-NEED A LIFT?

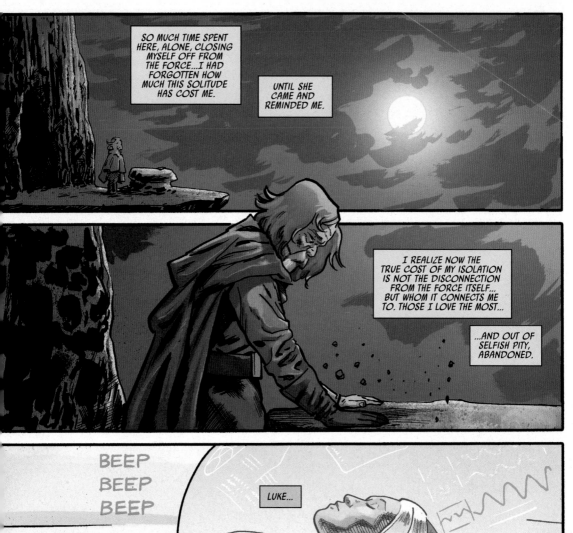

SO MUCH TIME SPENT HERE, ALONE, CLOSING MYSELF OFF FROM THE FORCE...I HAD FORGOTTEN HOW MUCH THIS SOLITUDE HAS COST ME.

UNTIL SHE CAME AND REMINDED ME.

I REALIZE NOW THE TRUE COST OF MY ISOLATION IS NOT THE DISCONNECTION FROM THE FORCE ITSELF... BUT WHOM IT CONNECTS ME TO. THOSE I LOVE THE MOST...

...AND OUT OF SELFISH PITY, ABANDONED.

BEEP BEEP BEEP

LUKE...

LEIA...

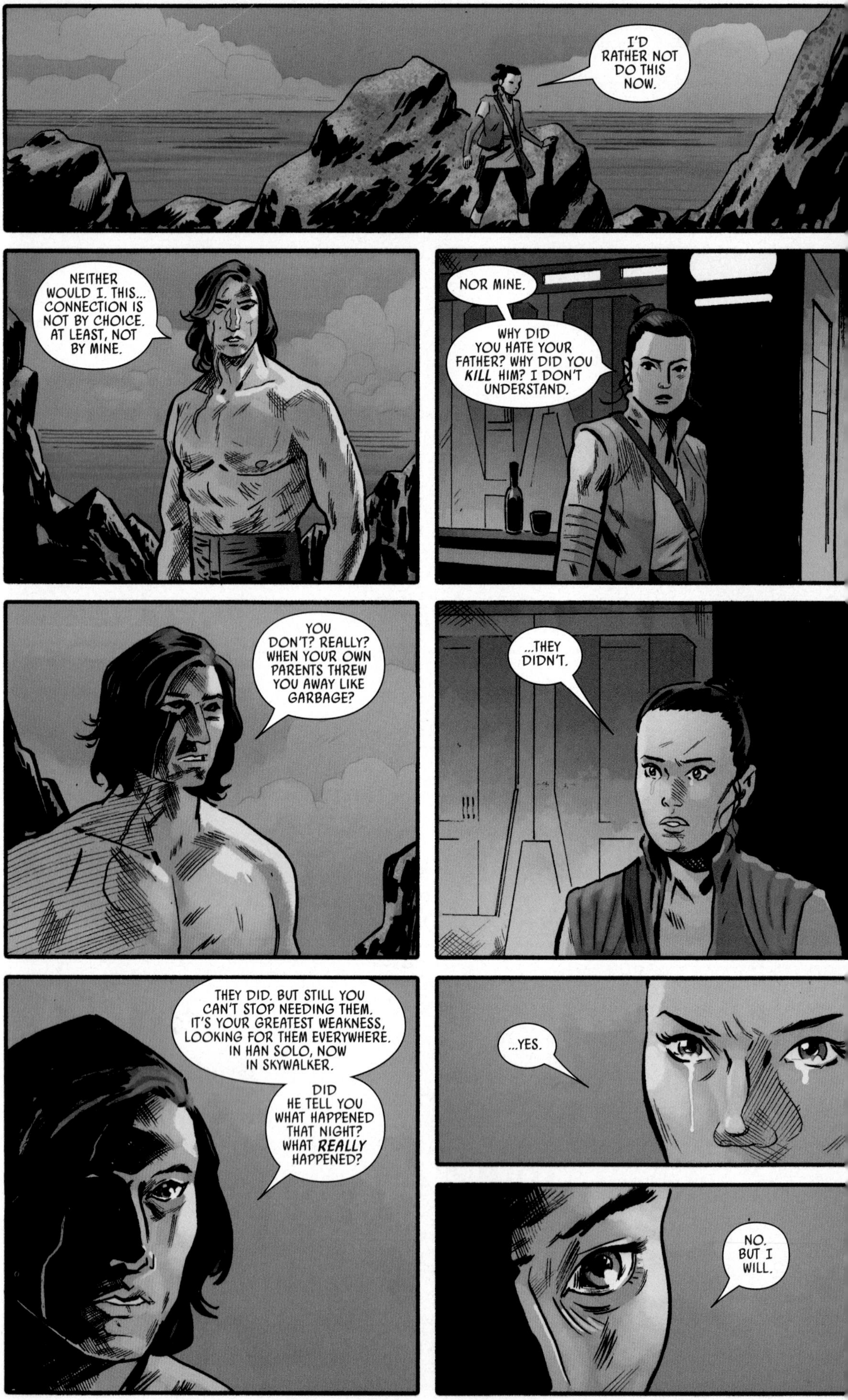
I'D RATHER NOT DO THIS NOW.
NEITHER WOULD I. THIS... CONNECTION IS NOT BY CHOICE. AT LEAST, NOT BY MINE.
NOR MINE.
WHY DID YOU HATE YOUR FATHER? WHY DID YOU KILL HIM? I DON'T UNDERSTAND.
YOU DON'T? REALLY? WHEN YOUR OWN PARENTS THREW YOU AWAY LIKE GARBAGE?
...THEY DIDN'T.
THEY DID. BUT STILL YOU CAN'T STOP NEEDING THEM. IT'S YOUR GREATEST WEAKNESS, LOOKING FOR THEM EVERYWHERE. IN HAN SOLO, NOW IN SKYWALKER.
DID HE TELL YOU WHAT HAPPENED THAT NIGHT? WHAT REALLY HAPPENED?
...YES.
NO. BUT I WILL.

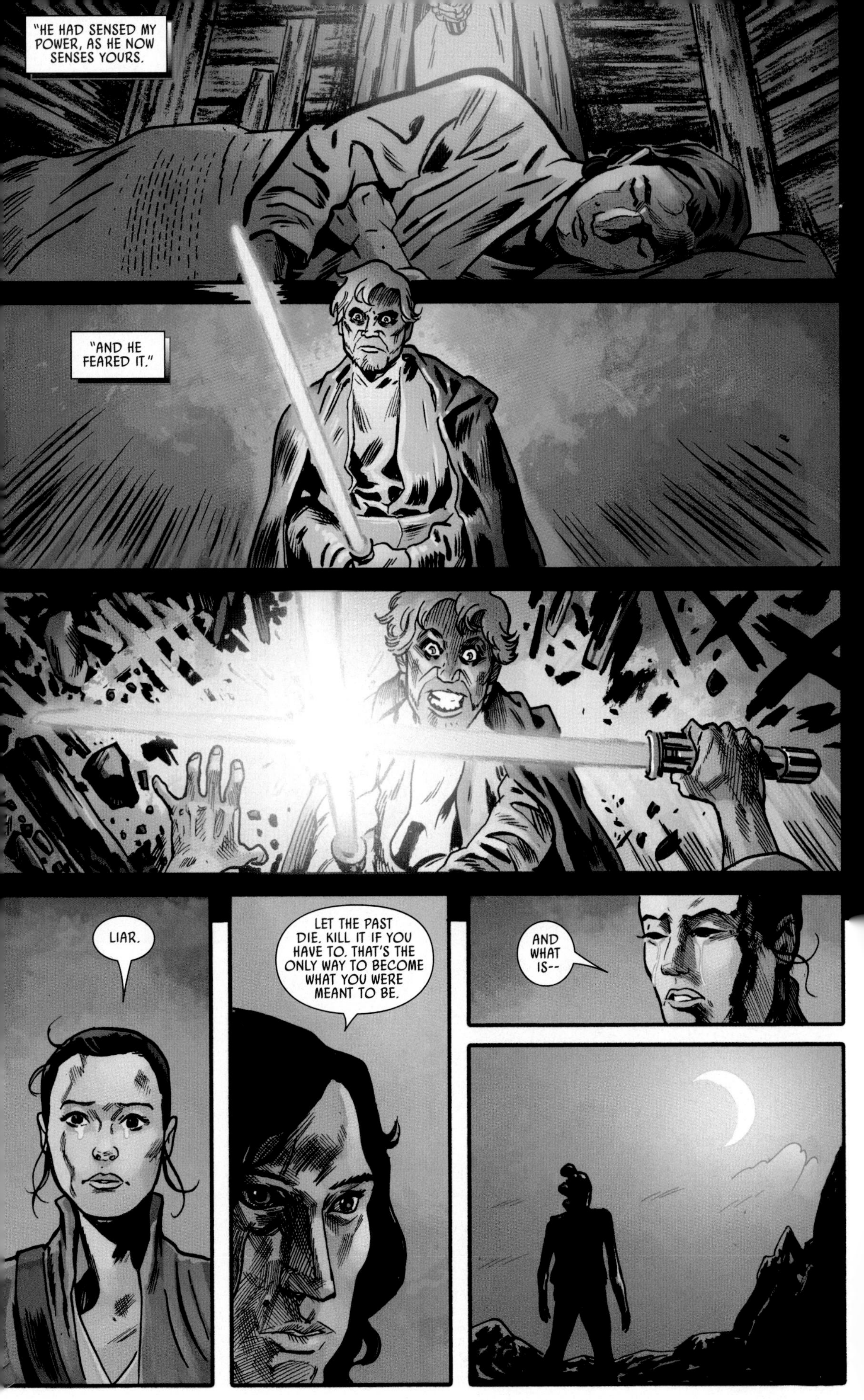
"HE HAD SENSED MY POWER, AS HE NOW SENSES YOURS.
"AND HE FEARED IT."
LIAR.
LET THE PAST DIE. KILL IT IF YOU HAVE TO. THAT'S THE ONLY WAY TO BECOME WHAT YOU WERE MEANT TO BE.
AND WHAT IS--

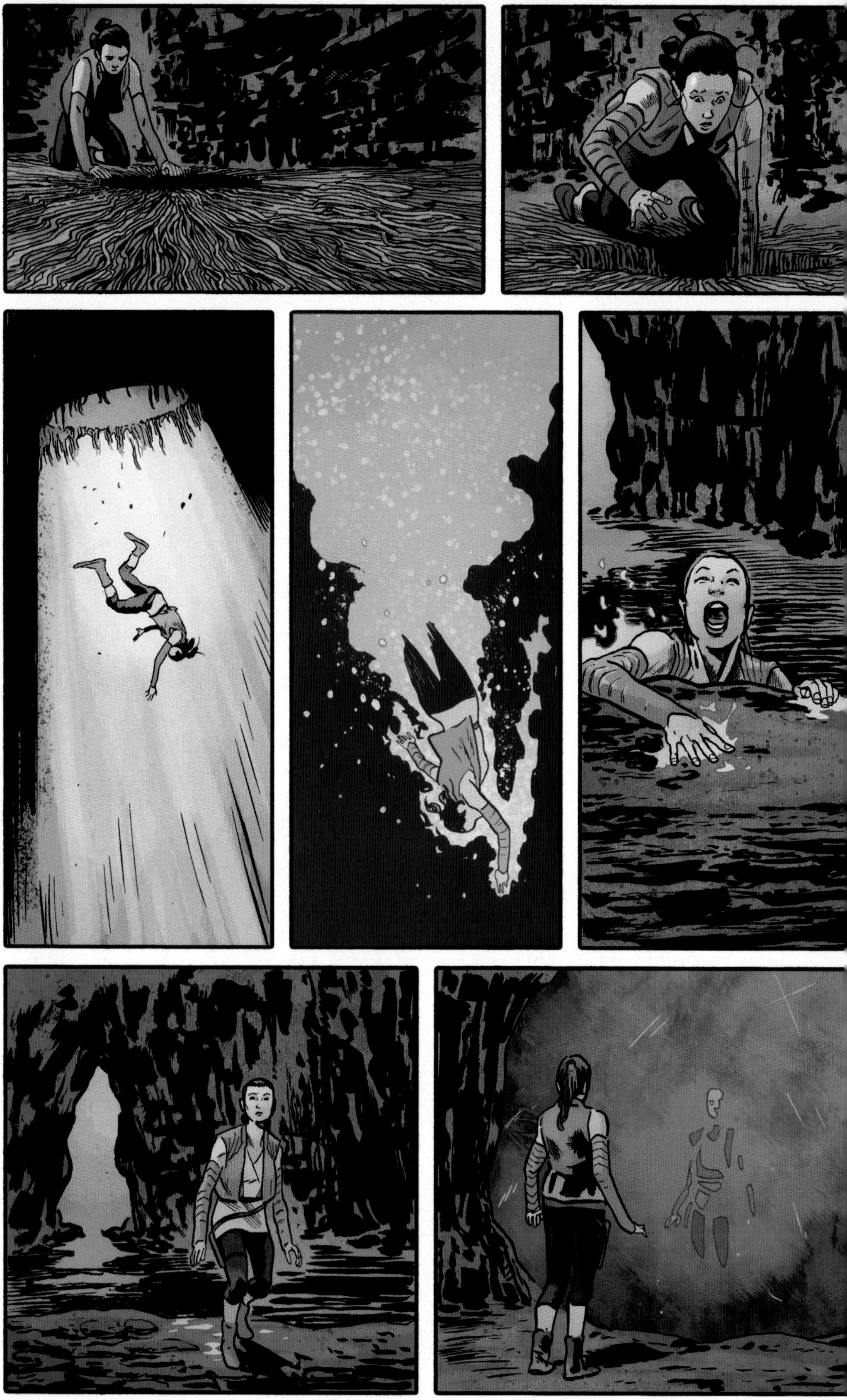

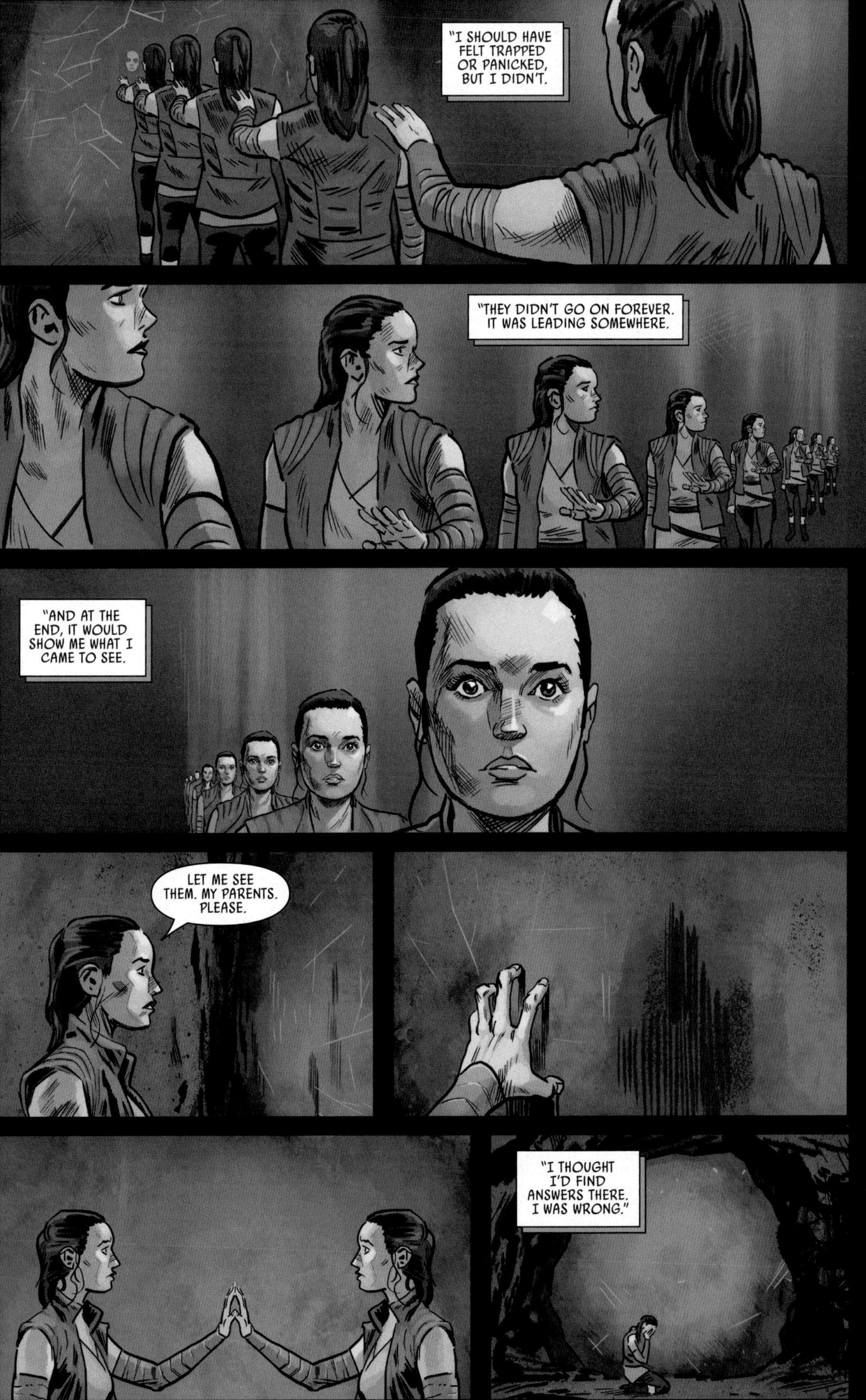
"I SHOULD HAVE FELT TRAPPED OR PANICKED, BUT I DIDN'T.
"THEY DIDN'T GO ON FOREVER. IT WAS LEADING SOMEWHERE.
"AND AT THE END, IT WOULD SHOW ME WHAT I CAME TO SEE.
LET ME SEE THEM. MY PARENTS. PLEASE.
"I THOUGHT I'D FIND ANSWERS THERE. I WAS WRONG."

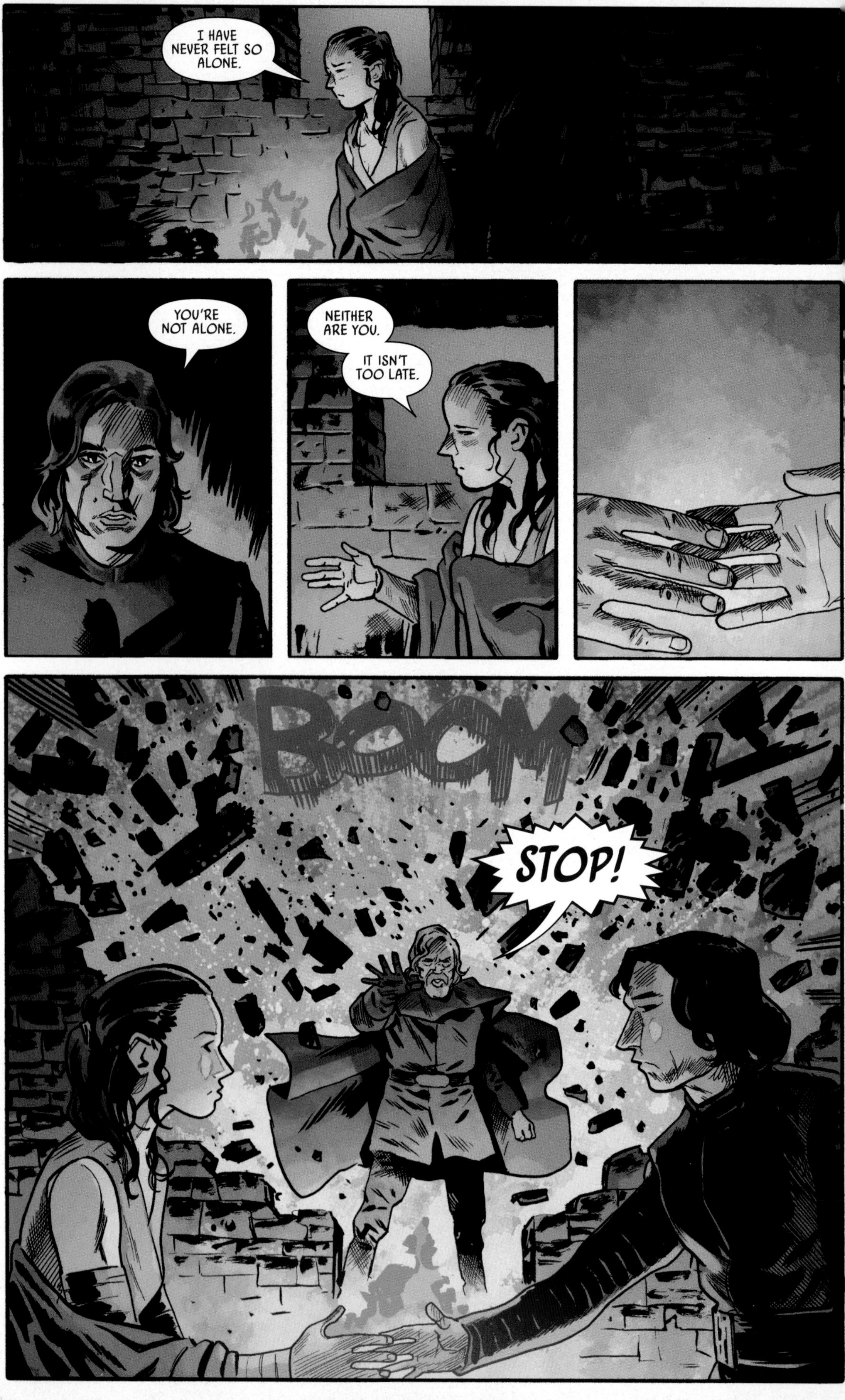
I HAVE NEVER FELT SO ALONE.
YOU'RE NOT ALONE.
NEITHER ARE YOU.
IT ISN'T TOO LATE.
BOOM
STOP!

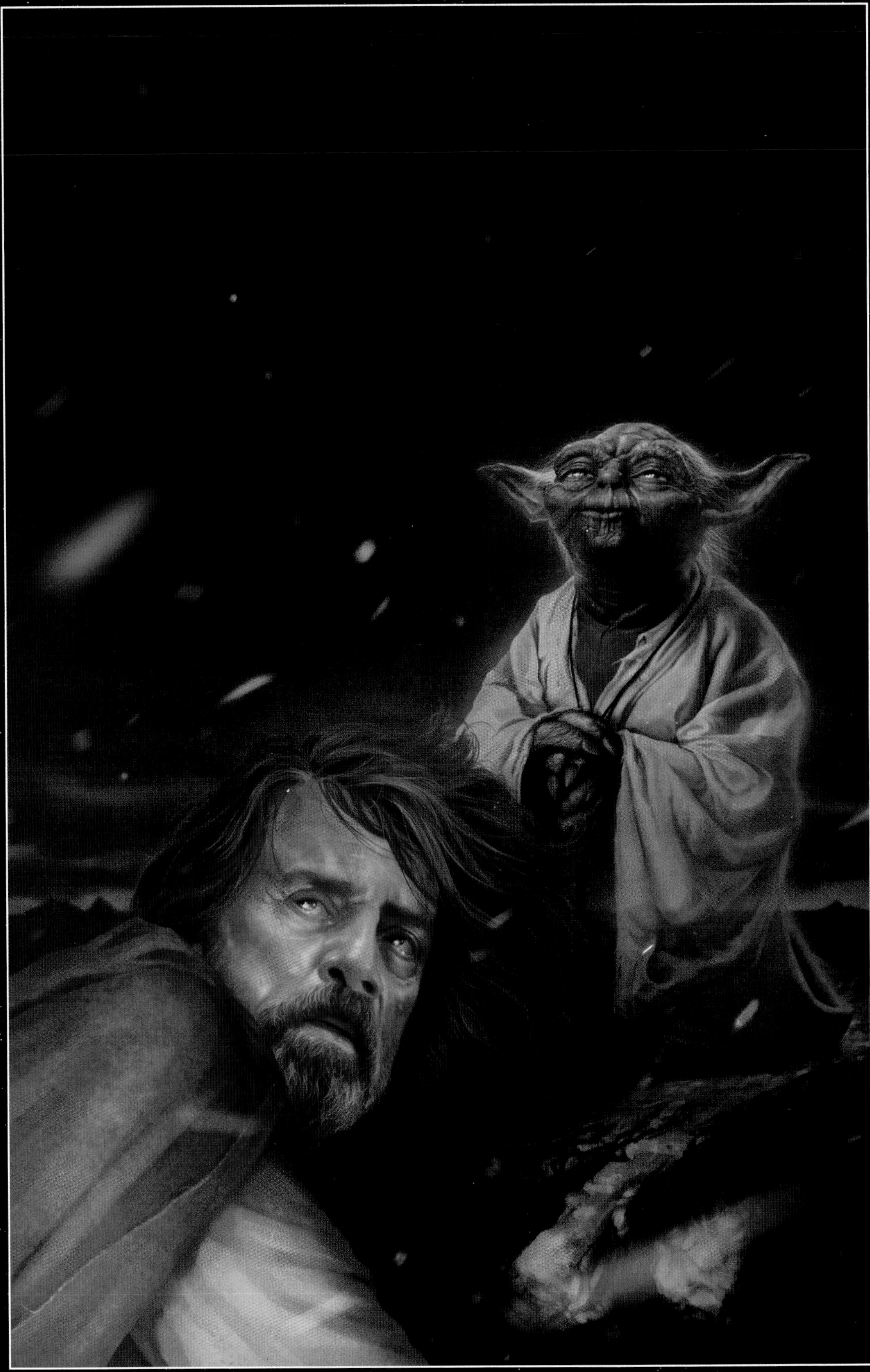

THE LAST JEDI #4

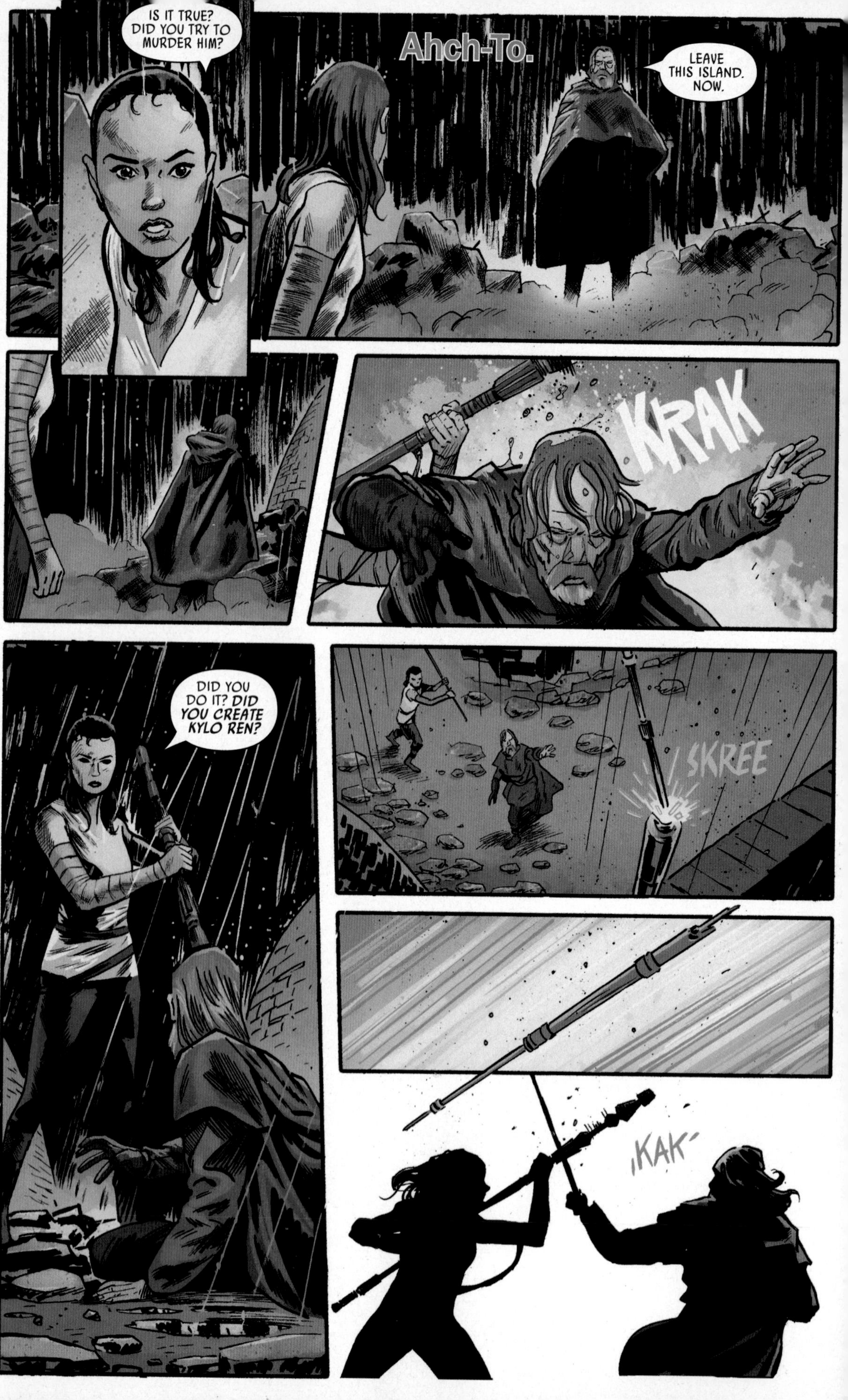
Ahch-To.
IS IT TRUE? DID YOU TRY TO MURDER HIM?
LEAVE THIS ISLAND. NOW.
KRAK
DID YOU DO IT? DID YOU CREATE KYLO REN?
SKREE
KAK

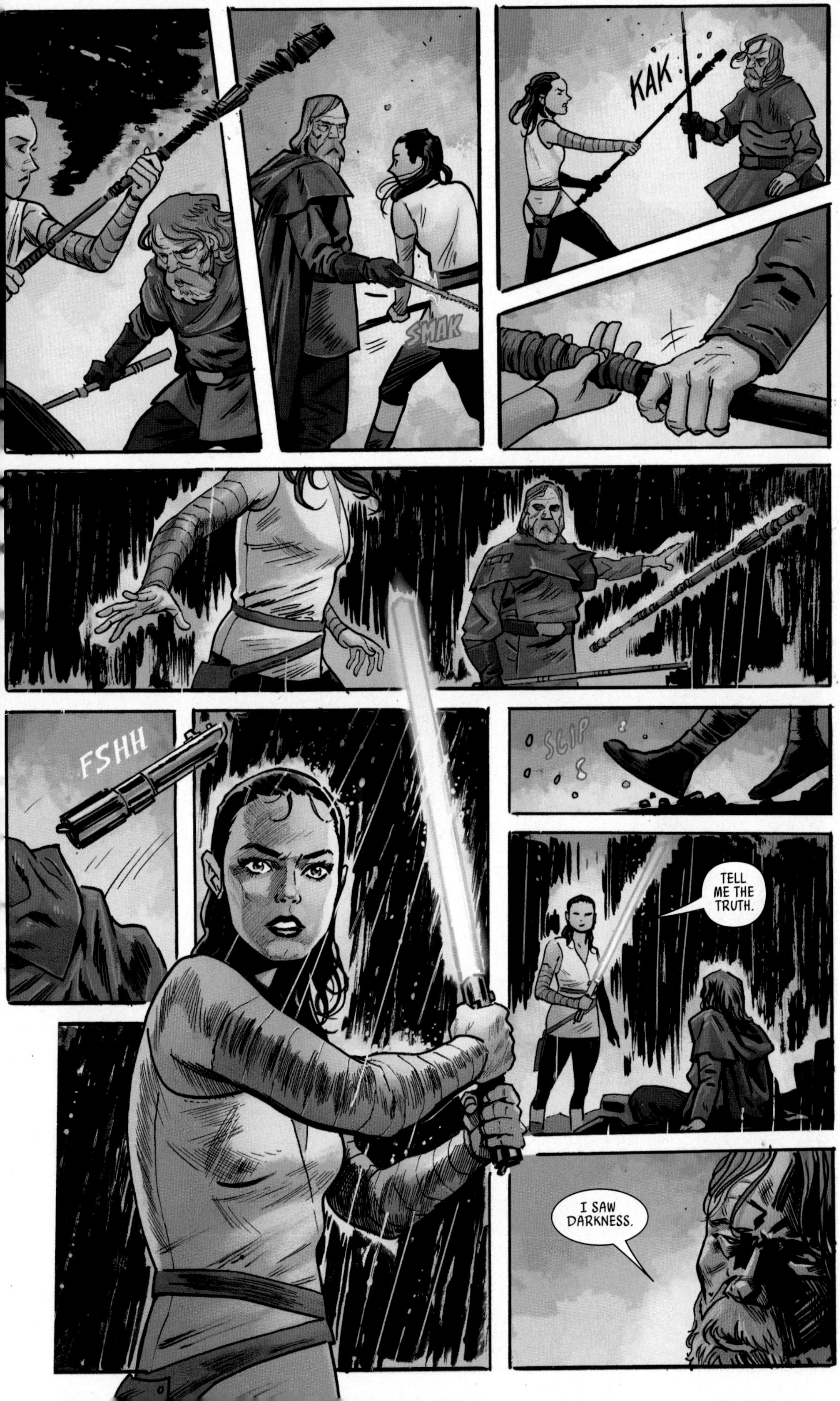
SMAK
KAK
FSHH
SLIP
TELL ME THE TRUTH.
I SAW DARKNESS.

"I HAD SENSED IT BUILDING IN HIM. SEEN IT IN MOMENTS DURING HIS TRAINING.

"BUT THEN I LOOKED INSIDE HIM, AND IT WAS BEYOND ANYTHING I COULD HAVE IMAGINED.

"SNOKE HAD ALREADY TURNED HIS HEART. HE WOULD BRING DESTRUCTION AND PAIN AND DEATH AND THE END OF EVERYTHING I LOVED BECAUSE OF WHAT HE WOULD BECOME.

"AND FOR THE BRIEFEST MOMENT OF PURE INSTINCT, I THOUGHT I COULD STOP IT.

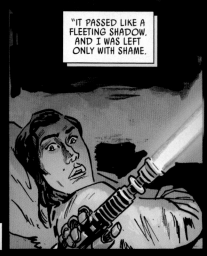

"IT PASSED LIKE A FLEETING SHADOW. AND I WAS LEFT ONLY WITH SHAME.

"AND WITH CONSEQUENCE."

THE LAST THING I SAW WERE THE EYES OF A FRIGHTENED BOY... WHOSE MASTER HAD FAILED HIM.

YOU ONLY FAILED HIM BY THINKING HIS CHOICE WAS MADE. IT WASN'T. THERE'S STILL CONFLICT WITHIN HIM. I'VE SENSED IT. IF HE TURNED FROM THE DARK SIDE, THAT COULD SHIFT THE TIDE OF THE ENTIRE WAR. THIS COULD BE HOW WE *WIN!*

IF I GO TO HIM, I BELIEVE BEN SOLO WILL TURN. IF *WE* GO TO HIM, I *KNOW* HE WILL.

THIS IS NOT GOING TO GO THE WAY YOU THINK.

AND I CAN'T HELP YOU.

THEN HE IS OUR ONLY HOPE.

RUSHING OFF BEFORE SHE IS READY, TO CONFRONT AN ADVERSARY FAR MORE POWERFUL, WITH THE FOOLISH HOPE OF TURNING HIM FROM THE DARK SIDE, DESPITE THE WARNINGS OF HER MASTER.

NOW WHERE HAVE I HEARD *THAT* BEFORE?

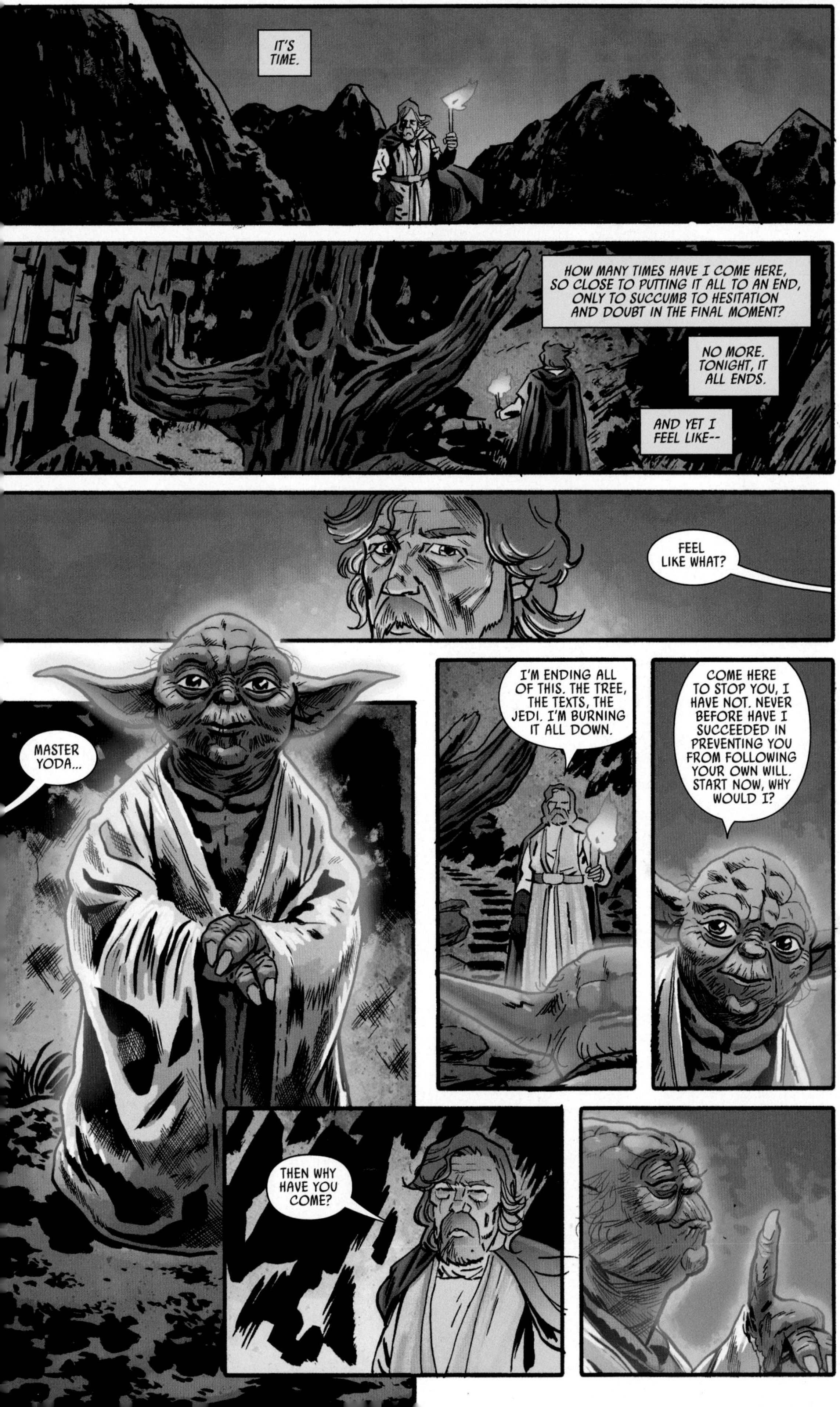

IT'S TIME.
HOW MANY TIMES HAVE I COME HERE, SO CLOSE TO PUTTING IT ALL TO AN END, ONLY TO SUCCUMB TO HESITATION AND DOUBT IN THE FINAL MOMENT?
NO MORE. TONIGHT, IT ALL ENDS.
AND YET I FEEL LIKE--
FEEL LIKE WHAT?
MASTER YODA...
I'M ENDING ALL OF THIS. THE TREE, THE TEXTS, THE JEDI. I'M BURNING IT ALL DOWN.
COME HERE TO STOP YOU, I HAVE NOT. NEVER BEFORE HAVE I SUCCEEDED IN PREVENTING YOU FROM FOLLOWING YOUR OWN WILL. START NOW, WHY WOULD I?
THEN WHY HAVE YOU COME?

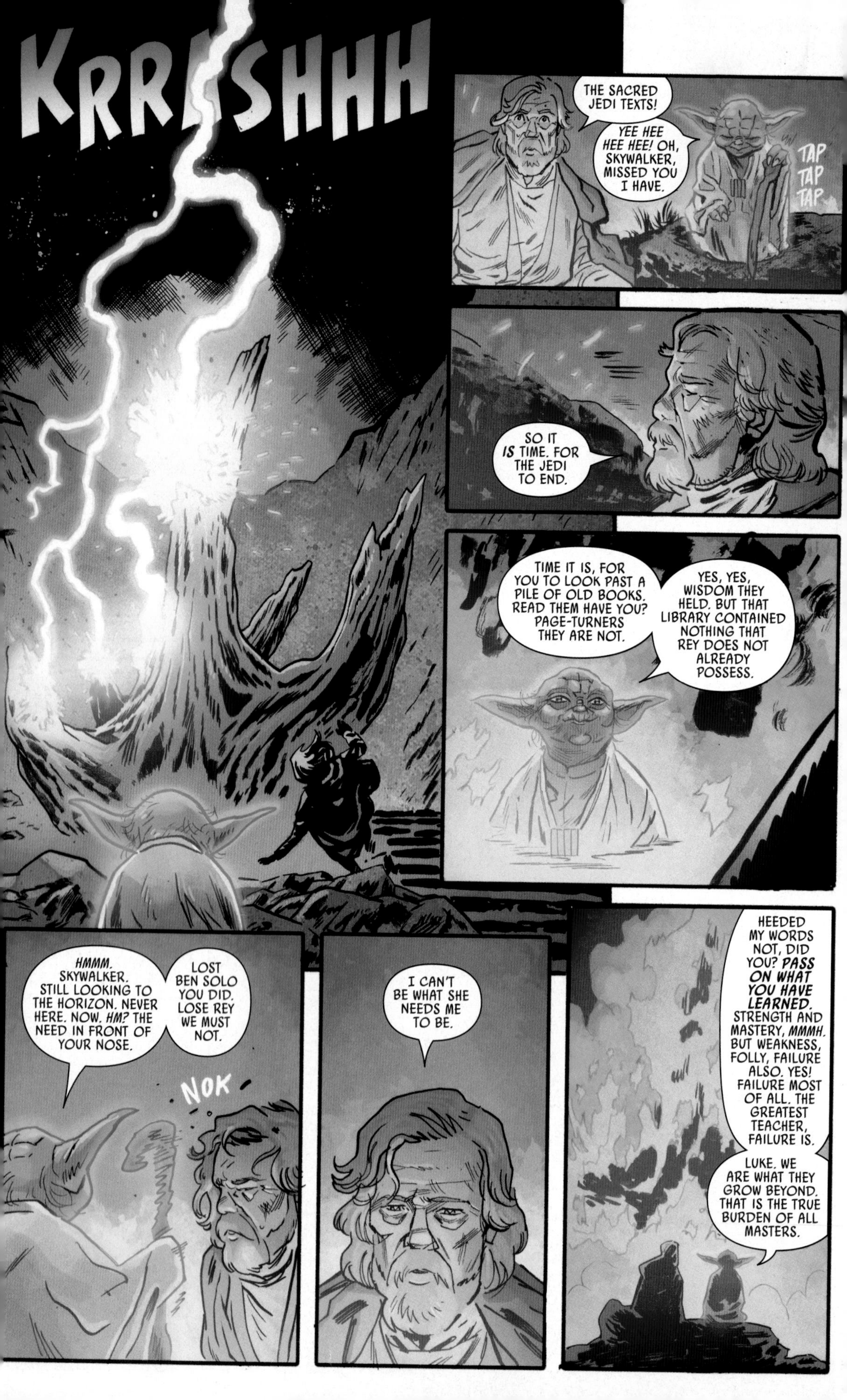
KRRISHHH
THE SACRED JEDI TEXTS!
YEE HEE HEE HEE! OH, SKYWALKER, MISSED YOU I HAVE.
TAP TAP TAP
SO IT IS TIME. FOR THE JEDI TO END.
TIME IT IS, FOR YOU TO LOOK PAST A PILE OF OLD BOOKS. READ THEM HAVE YOU? PAGE-TURNERS THEY ARE NOT.
YES, YES, WISDOM THEY HELD. BUT THAT LIBRARY CONTAINED NOTHING THAT REY DOES NOT ALREADY POSSESS.
HMMM. SKYWALKER. STILL LOOKING TO THE HORIZON. NEVER HERE. NOW. HM? THE NEED IN FRONT OF YOUR NOSE.
LOST BEN SOLO YOU DID. LOSE REY WE MUST NOT.
NOK
I CAN'T BE WHAT SHE NEEDS ME TO BE.
HEEDED MY WORDS NOT, DID YOU? PASS ON WHAT YOU HAVE LEARNED. STRENGTH AND MASTERY, MMMH. BUT WEAKNESS, FOLLY, FAILURE ALSO. YES! FAILURE MOST OF ALL. THE GREATEST TEACHER, FAILURE IS.
LUKE. WE ARE WHAT THEY GROW BEYOND. THAT IS THE TRUE BURDEN OF ALL MASTERS.

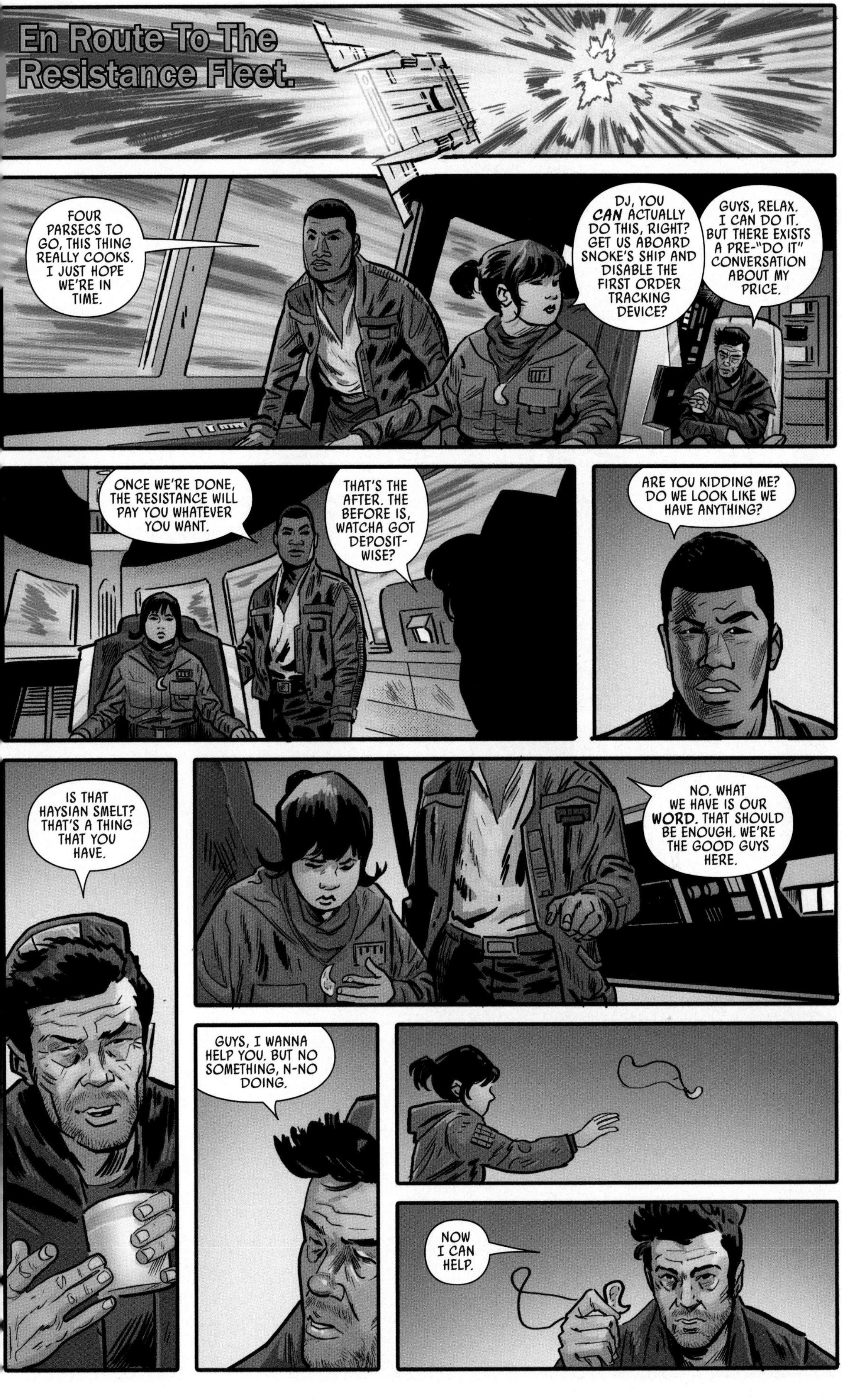
En Route To The Resistance Fleet.
FOUR PARSECS TO GO, THIS THING REALLY COOKS. I JUST HOPE WE'RE IN TIME.
DJ, YOU CAN ACTUALLY DO THIS, RIGHT? GET US ABOARD SNOKE'S SHIP AND DISABLE THE FIRST ORDER TRACKING DEVICE?
GUYS, RELAX. I CAN DO IT. BUT THERE EXISTS A PRE-"DO IT" CONVERSATION ABOUT MY PRICE.
ONCE WE'RE DONE, THE RESISTANCE WILL PAY YOU WHATEVER YOU WANT.
THAT'S THE AFTER. THE BEFORE IS, WATCHA GOT DEPOSIT-WISE?
ARE YOU KIDDING ME? DO WE LOOK LIKE WE HAVE ANYTHING?
IS THAT HAYSIAN SMELT? THAT'S A THING THAT YOU HAVE.
NO. WHAT WE HAVE IS OUR WORD. THAT SHOULD BE ENOUGH. WE'RE THE GOOD GUYS HERE.
GUYS, I WANNA HELP YOU. BUT NO SOMETHING, N-NO DOING.
NOW I CAN HELP.

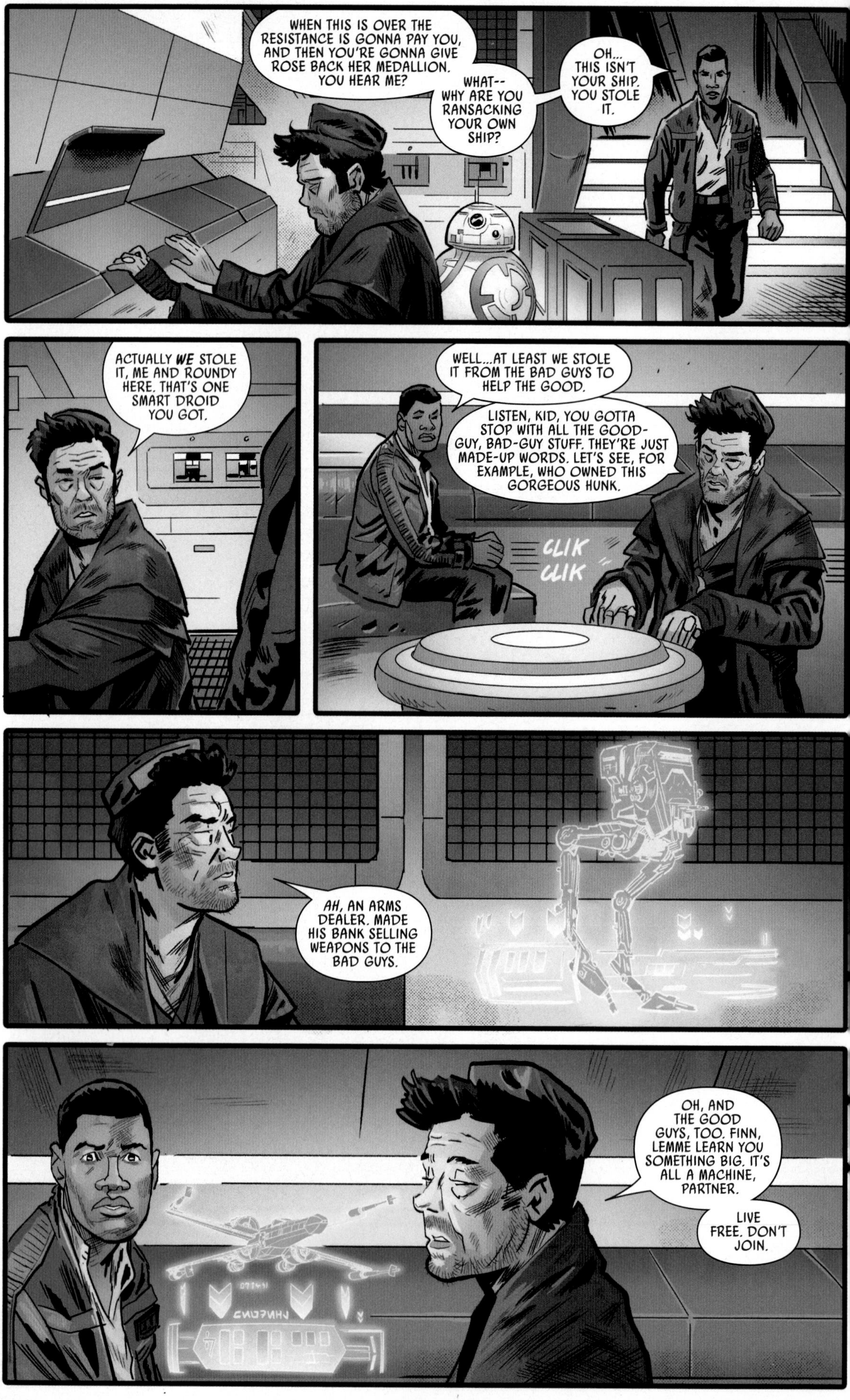
WHEN THIS IS OVER THE RESISTANCE IS GONNA PAY YOU, AND THEN YOU'RE GONNA GIVE ROSE BACK HER MEDALLION. YOU HEAR ME?
WHAT-- WHY ARE YOU RANSACKING YOUR OWN SHIP?
OH... THIS ISN'T YOUR SHIP. YOU STOLE IT.
ACTUALLY WE STOLE IT, ME AND ROUNDY HERE. THAT'S ONE SMART DROID YOU GOT.
WELL...AT LEAST WE STOLE IT FROM THE BAD GUYS TO HELP THE GOOD.
LISTEN, KID, YOU GOTTA STOP WITH ALL THE GOOD-GUY, BAD-GUY STUFF. THEY'RE JUST MADE-UP WORDS. LET'S SEE, FOR EXAMPLE, WHO OWNED THIS GORGEOUS HUNK.
CLIK CLIK
AH, AN ARMS DEALER. MADE HIS BANK SELLING WEAPONS TO THE BAD GUYS.
OH, AND THE GOOD GUYS, TOO. FINN, LEMME LEARN YOU SOMETHING BIG. IT'S ALL A MACHINE, PARTNER.
LIVE FREE. DON'T JOIN.

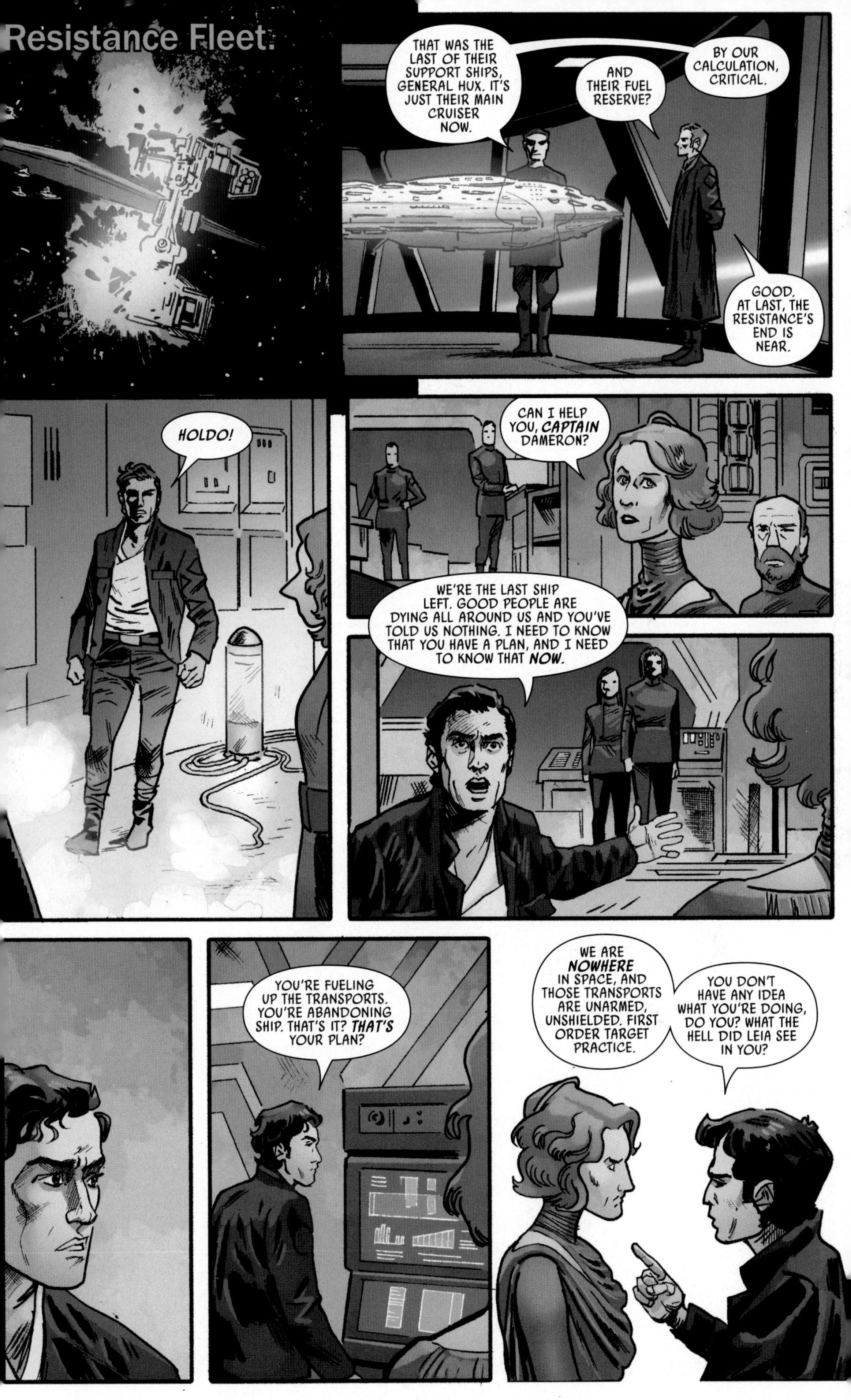
Resistance Fleet.
THAT WAS THE LAST OF THEIR SUPPORT SHIPS, GENERAL HUX. IT'S JUST THEIR MAIN CRUISER NOW.
AND THEIR FUEL RESERVE?
BY OUR CALCULATION, CRITICAL.
GOOD. AT LAST, THE RESISTANCE'S END IS NEAR.
HOLDO!
CAN I HELP YOU, CAPTAIN DAMERON?
WE'RE THE LAST SHIP LEFT. GOOD PEOPLE ARE DYING ALL AROUND US AND YOU'VE TOLD US NOTHING. I NEED TO KNOW THAT YOU HAVE A PLAN, AND I NEED TO KNOW THAT NOW.
YOU'RE FUELING UP THE TRANSPORTS. YOU'RE ABANDONING SHIP. THAT'S IT? THAT'S YOUR PLAN?
WE ARE NOWHERE IN SPACE, AND THOSE TRANSPORTS ARE UNARMED, UNSHIELDED. FIRST ORDER TARGET PRACTICE.
YOU DON'T HAVE ANY IDEA WHAT YOU'RE DOING, DO YOU? WHAT THE HELL DID LEIA SEE IN YOU?

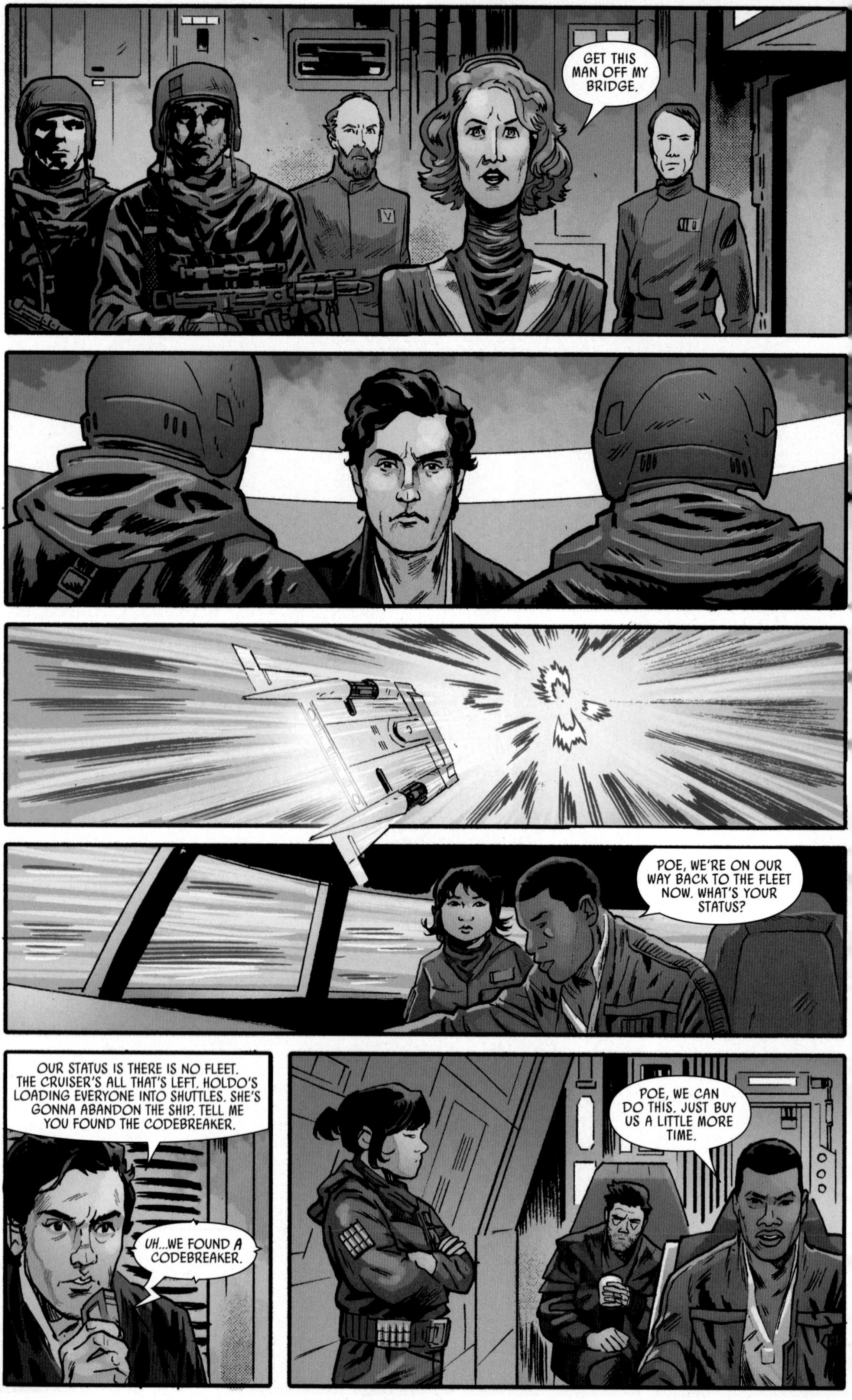
GET THIS MAN OFF MY BRIDGE.
POE, WE'RE ON OUR WAY BACK TO THE FLEET NOW. WHAT'S YOUR STATUS?
OUR STATUS IS THERE IS NO FLEET. THE CRUISER'S ALL THAT'S LEFT. HOLDO'S LOADING EVERYONE INTO SHUTTLES. SHE'S GONNA ABANDON THE SHIP. TELL ME YOU FOUND THE CODEBREAKER.
UH...WE FOUND A CODEBREAKER.
POE, WE CAN DO THIS. JUST BUY US A LITTLE MORE TIME.

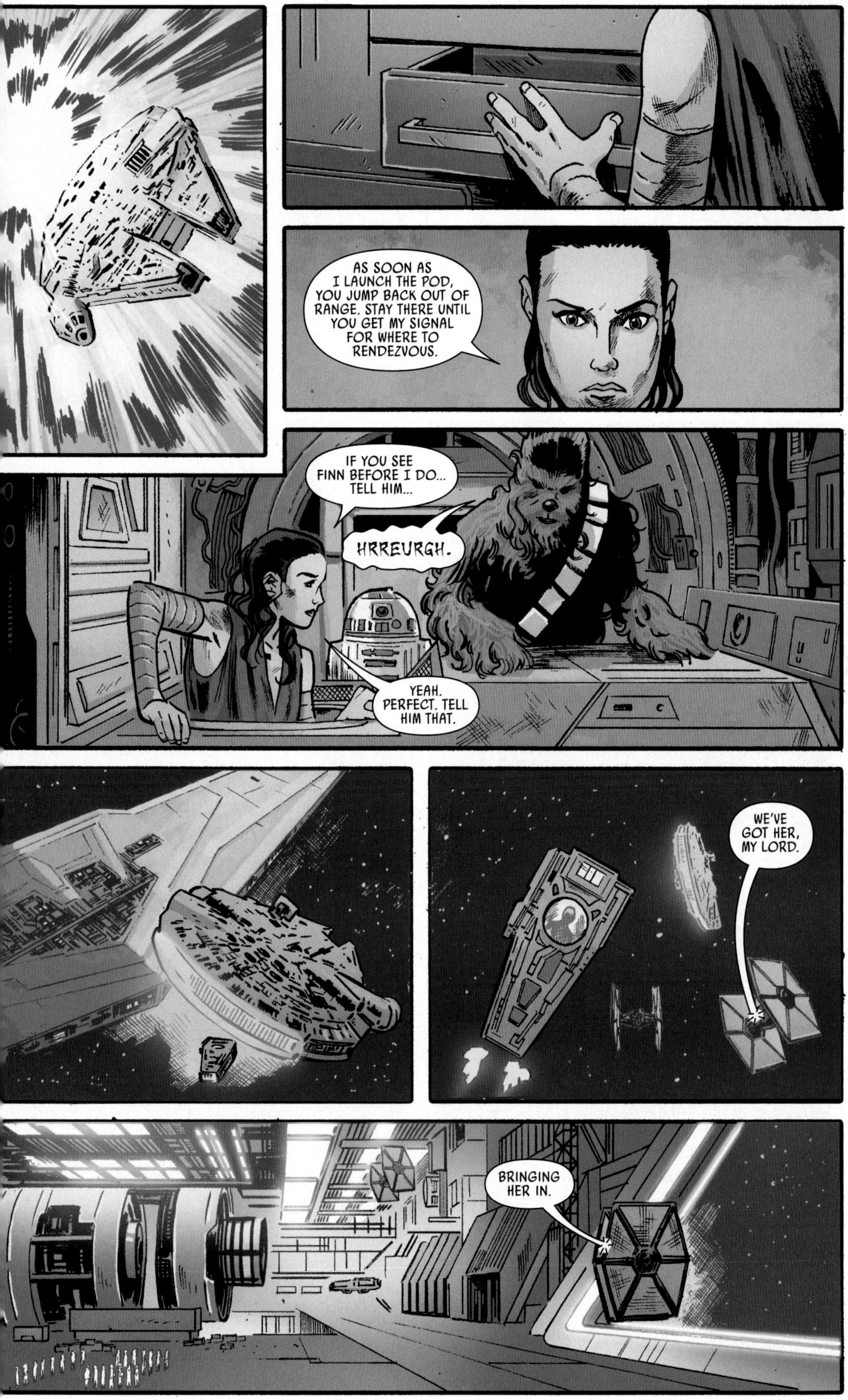
AS SOON AS I LAUNCH THE POD, YOU JUMP BACK OUT OF RANGE. STAY THERE UNTIL YOU GET MY SIGNAL FOR WHERE TO RENDEZVOUS.
IF YOU SEE FINN BEFORE I DO... TELL HIM...
HRREURGH.
YEAH. PERFECT. TELL HIM THAT.
WE'VE GOT HER, MY LORD.
BRINGING HER IN.

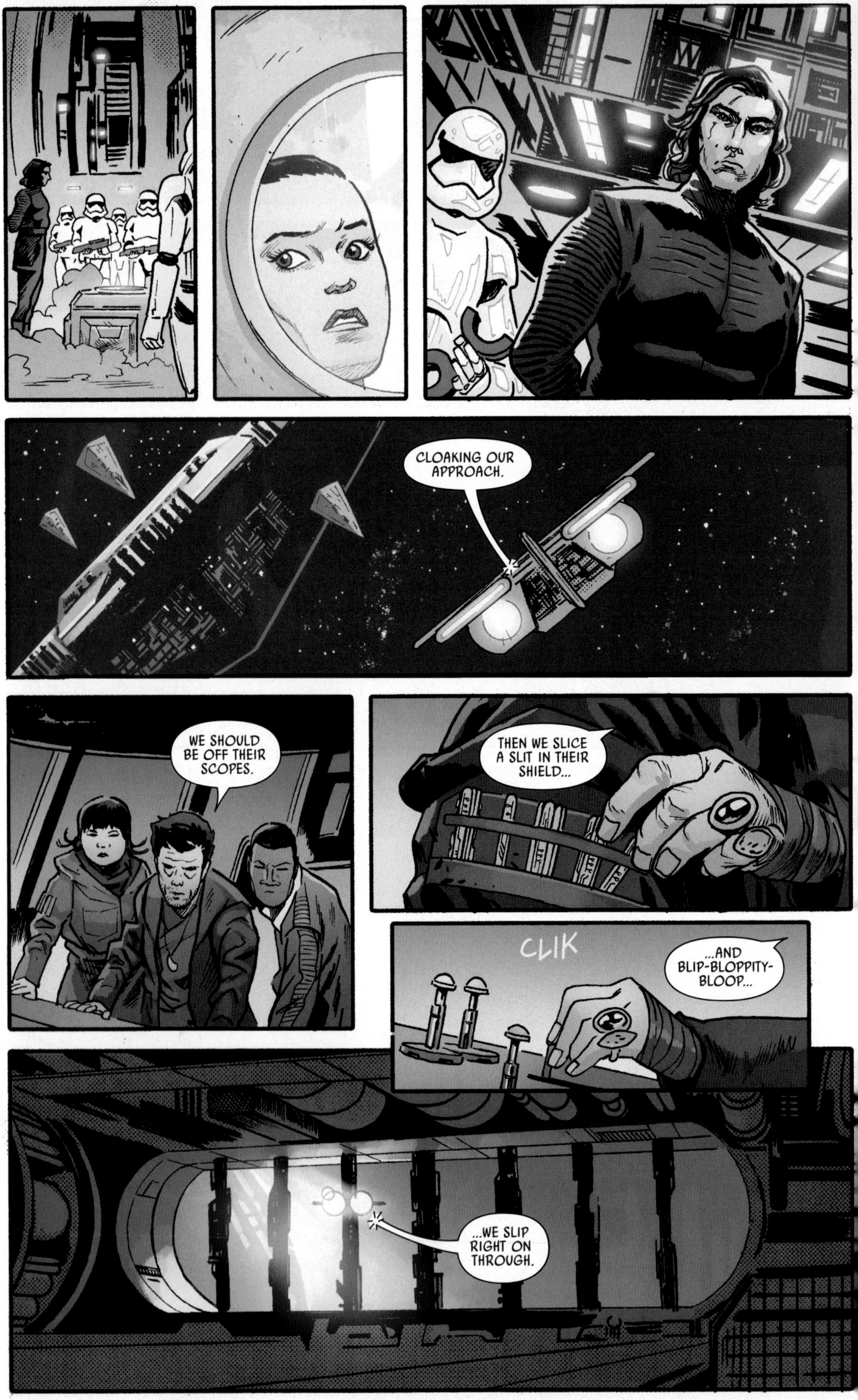
CLOAKING OUR APPROACH.
WE SHOULD BE OFF THEIR SCOPES.
THEN WE SLICE A SLIT IN THEIR SHIELD...
CLIK
...AND BLIP-BLOPPITY-BLOOP...
...WE SLIP RIGHT ON THROUGH.

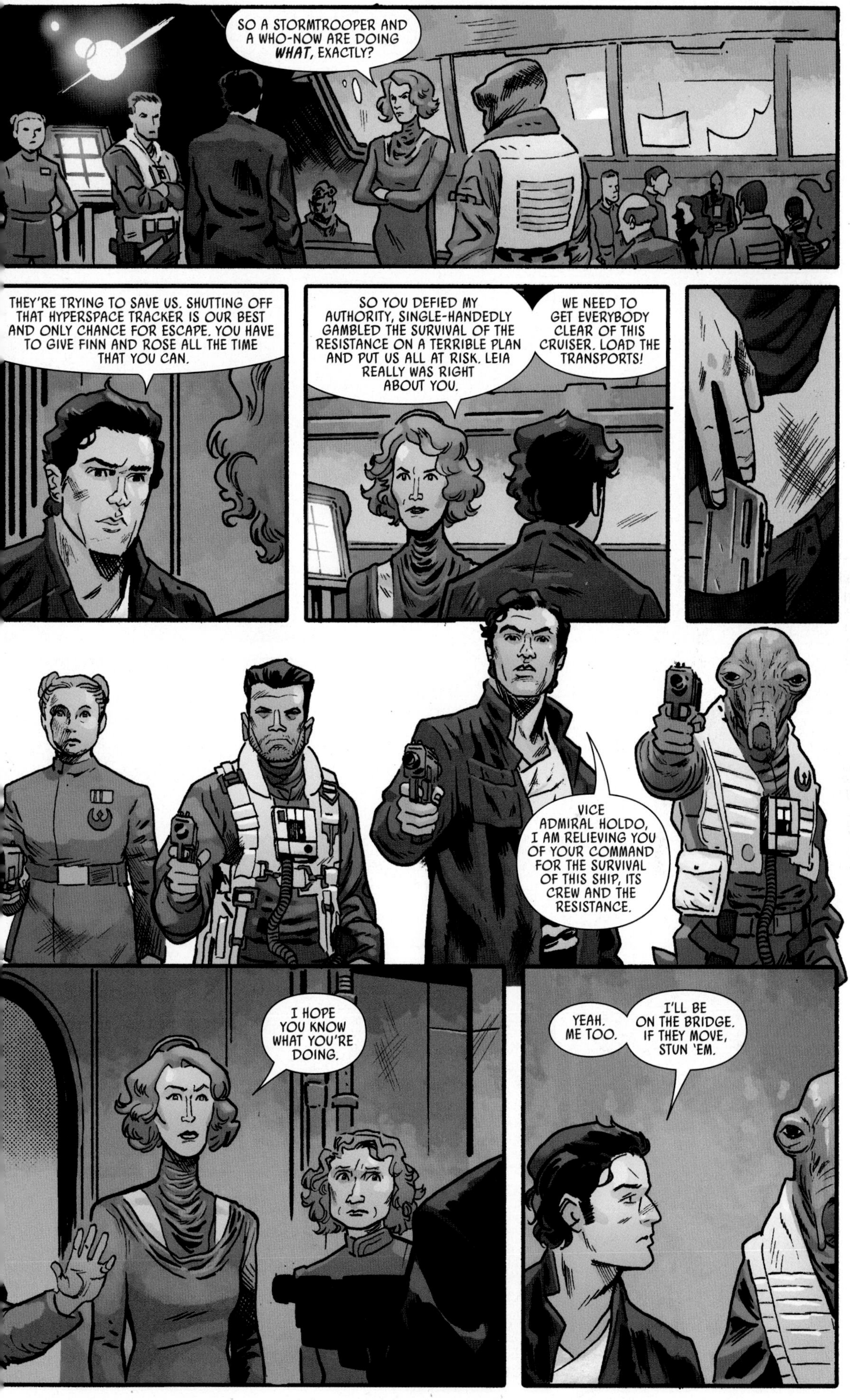
SO A STORMTROOPER AND A WHO-NOW ARE DOING *WHAT*, EXACTLY?
THEY'RE TRYING TO SAVE US. SHUTTING OFF THAT HYPERSPACE TRACKER IS OUR BEST AND ONLY CHANCE FOR ESCAPE. YOU HAVE TO GIVE FINN AND ROSE ALL THE TIME THAT YOU CAN.
SO YOU DEFIED MY AUTHORITY, SINGLE-HANDEDLY GAMBLED THE SURVIVAL OF THE RESISTANCE ON A TERRIBLE PLAN AND PUT US ALL AT RISK. LEIA REALLY WAS RIGHT ABOUT YOU.
WE NEED TO GET EVERYBODY CLEAR OF THIS CRUISER. LOAD THE TRANSPORTS!
VICE ADMIRAL HOLDO, I AM RELIEVING YOU OF YOUR COMMAND FOR THE SURVIVAL OF THIS SHIP, ITS CREW AND THE RESISTANCE.
I HOPE YOU KNOW WHAT YOU'RE DOING.
YEAH. ME TOO.
I'LL BE ON THE BRIDGE. IF THEY MOVE, STUN 'EM.

SORRY, PAL, GOTTA WORK WITH WHAT WE HAVE HERE.

OKAY, LET'S DO THIS.

BLOO BLEEP!

IT'S RIGHT UP AHEAD. ALMOST THERE. JUST STAY COOL...

BLEEO BEEP

BRUP BROOP?!

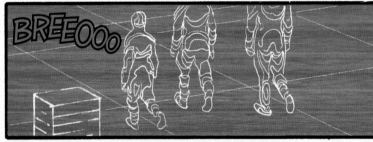

BREEOOO

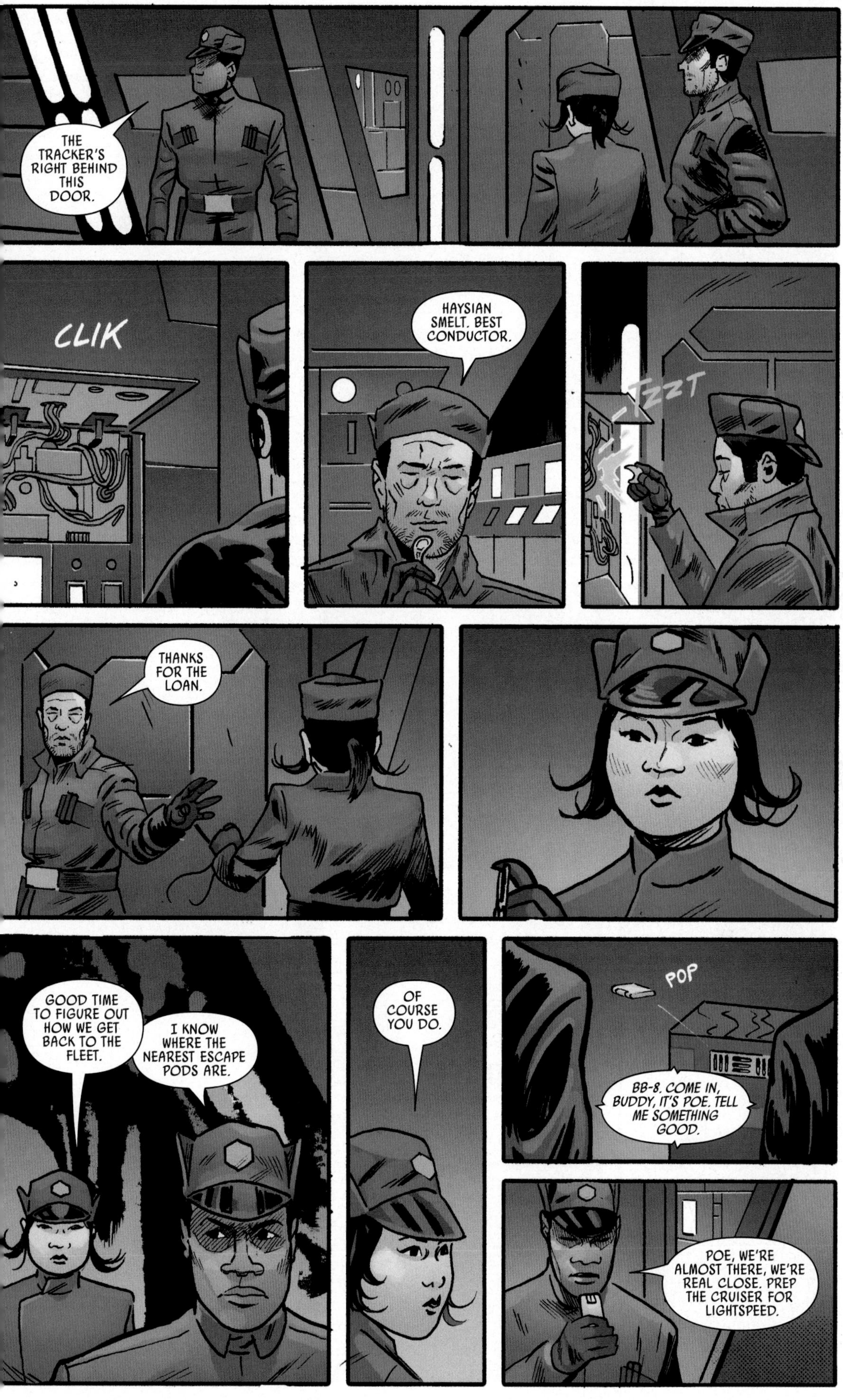
THE TRACKER'S RIGHT BEHIND THIS DOOR.
CLIK
HAYSIAN SMELT. BEST CONDUCTOR.
TZZT
THANKS FOR THE LOAN.
GOOD TIME TO FIGURE OUT HOW WE GET BACK TO THE FLEET.
I KNOW WHERE THE NEAREST ESCAPE PODS ARE.
OF COURSE YOU DO.
POP
BB-8. COME IN, BUDDY, IT'S POE. TELL ME SOMETHING GOOD.
POE, WE'RE ALMOST THERE, WE'RE REAL CLOSE. PREP THE CRUISER FOR LIGHTSPEED.

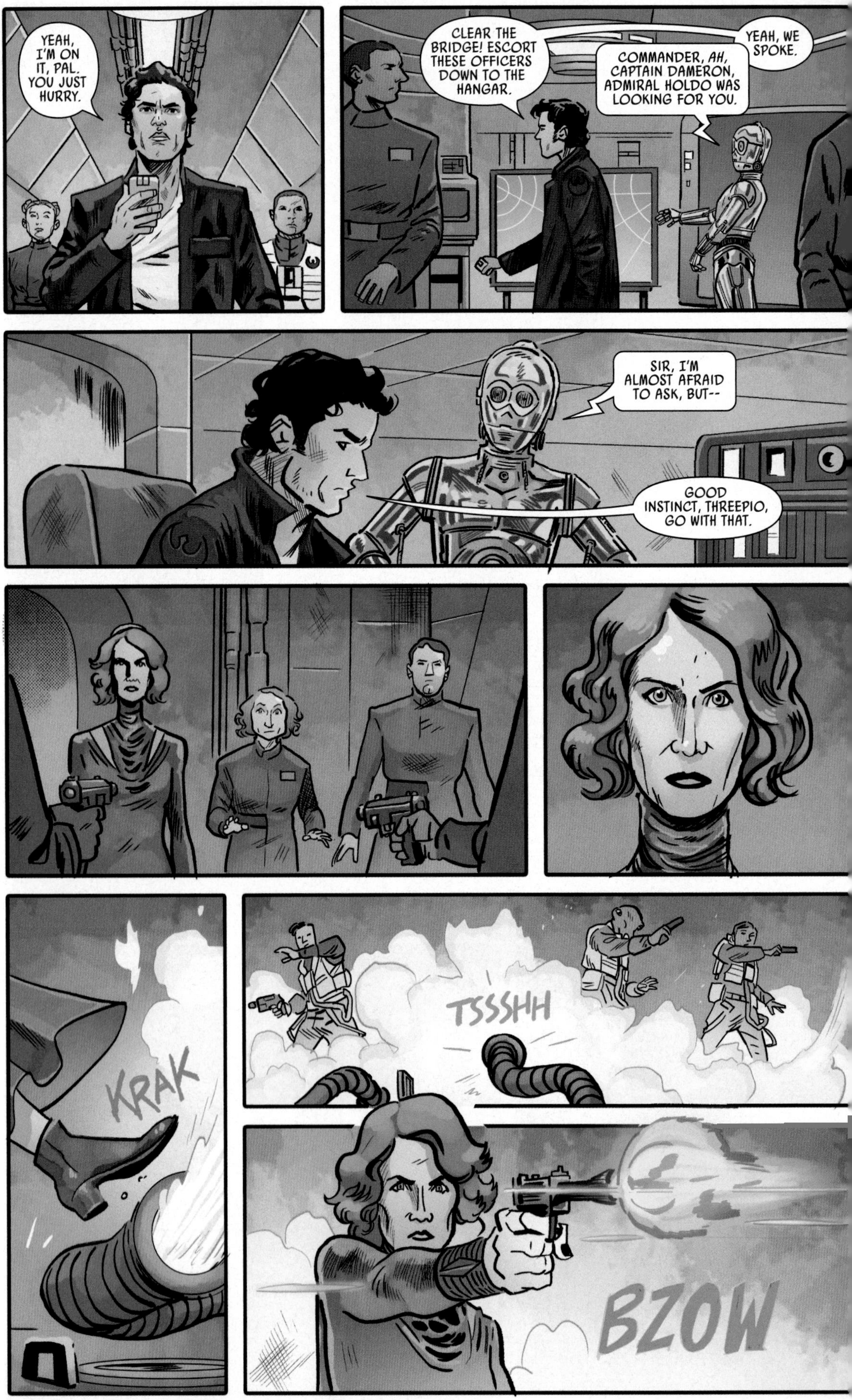

YEAH, I'M ON IT, PAL. YOU JUST HURRY.
CLEAR THE BRIDGE! ESCORT THESE OFFICERS DOWN TO THE HANGAR.
COMMANDER, AH, CAPTAIN DAMERON, ADMIRAL HOLDO WAS LOOKING FOR YOU.
YEAH, WE SPOKE.
SIR, I'M ALMOST AFRAID TO ASK, BUT--
GOOD INSTINCT, THREEPIO, GO WITH THAT.
KRAK
TSSSHH
BZOW

FINN, I'M ON THE BRIDGE AND READY TO MAKE THE JUMP. WHAT'S GOING ON?

ALMOST THERE...

WE DON'T HAVE TIME, IT'S NOW OR NEVER!

NOW.

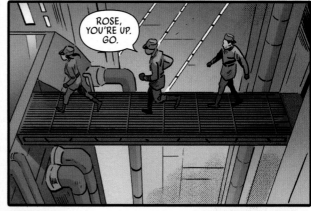

ROSE, YOU'RE UP. GO.

BREE BEEP!

DROP YOUR WEAPONS, HANDS IN THE AIR, NOW!

I HAD A BAD FEELING ABOUT THIS...

FN-2187.

SO GOOD TO HAVE YOU BACK.

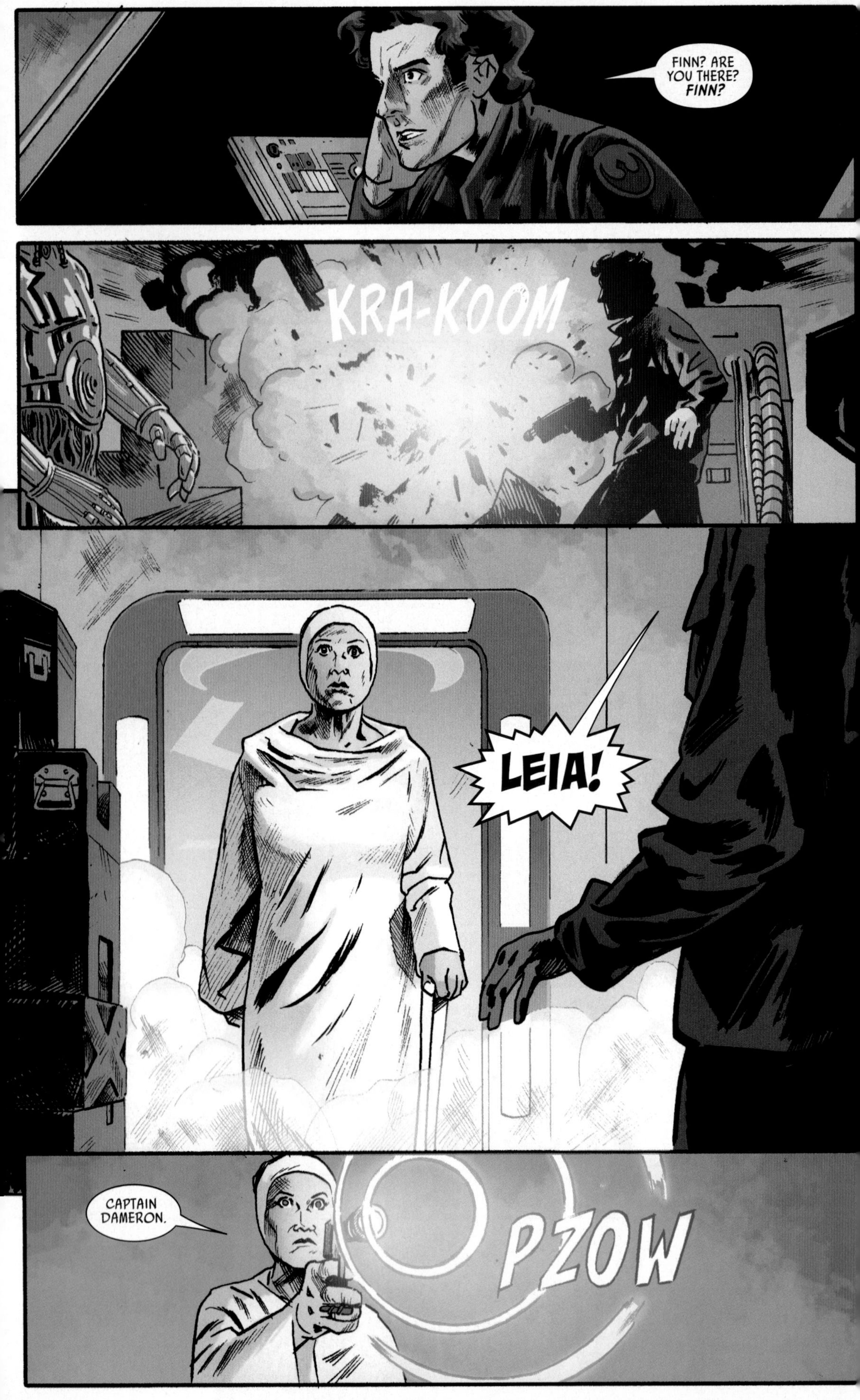
FINN? ARE YOU THERE? FINN?
KRA-KOOM
LEIA!
CAPTAIN DAMERON.
PZOW

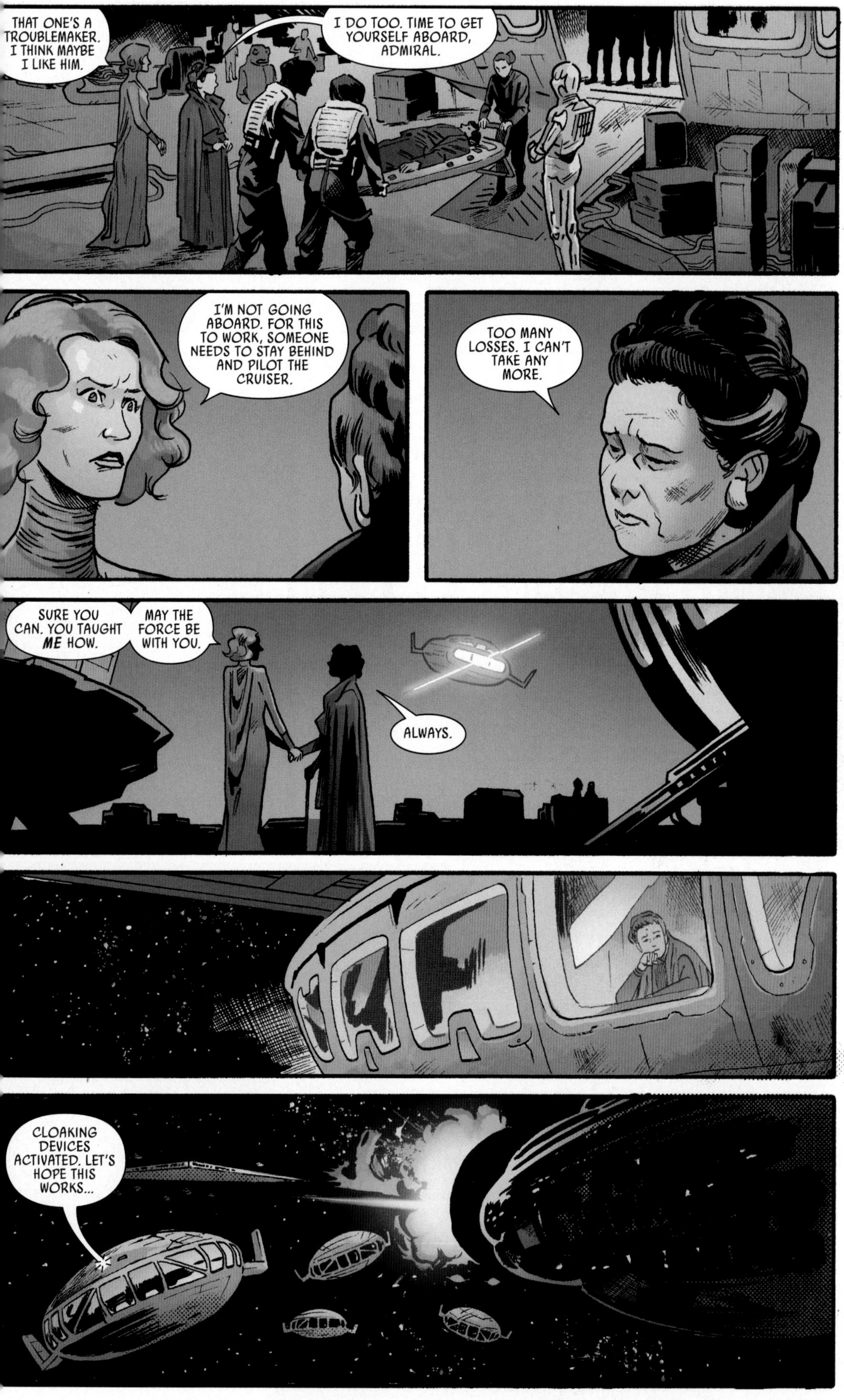
THAT ONE'S A TROUBLEMAKER. I THINK MAYBE I LIKE HIM.
I DO TOO. TIME TO GET YOURSELF ABOARD, ADMIRAL.
I'M NOT GOING ABOARD. FOR THIS TO WORK, SOMEONE NEEDS TO STAY BEHIND AND PILOT THE CRUISER.
TOO MANY LOSSES. I CAN'T TAKE ANY MORE.
SURE YOU CAN. YOU TAUGHT ME HOW.
MAY THE FORCE BE WITH YOU.
ALWAYS.
CLOAKING DEVICES ACTIVATED. LET'S HOPE THIS WORKS...

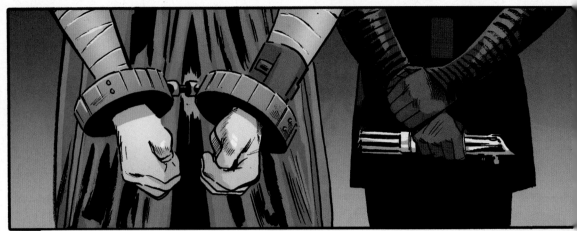

YOU DON'T HAVE TO DO THIS. I FEEL THE CONFLICT IN YOU. IT'S TEARING YOU APART.

BEN, WHEN WE TOUCHED HANDS I SAW YOUR FUTURE. JUST THE SHAPE OF IT, BUT SOLID AND CLEAR. YOU WILL NOT BOW BEFORE SNOKE. YOU'LL TURN. I'LL HELP YOU. I SAW IT.

I SAW SOMETHING, TOO. I KNOW THAT WHEN THE MOMENT COMES, YOU'LL BE THE ONE TO TURN. YOU'LL STAND WITH ME.

REY.

I SAW WHO YOUR PARENTS ARE.

TSSSSSS

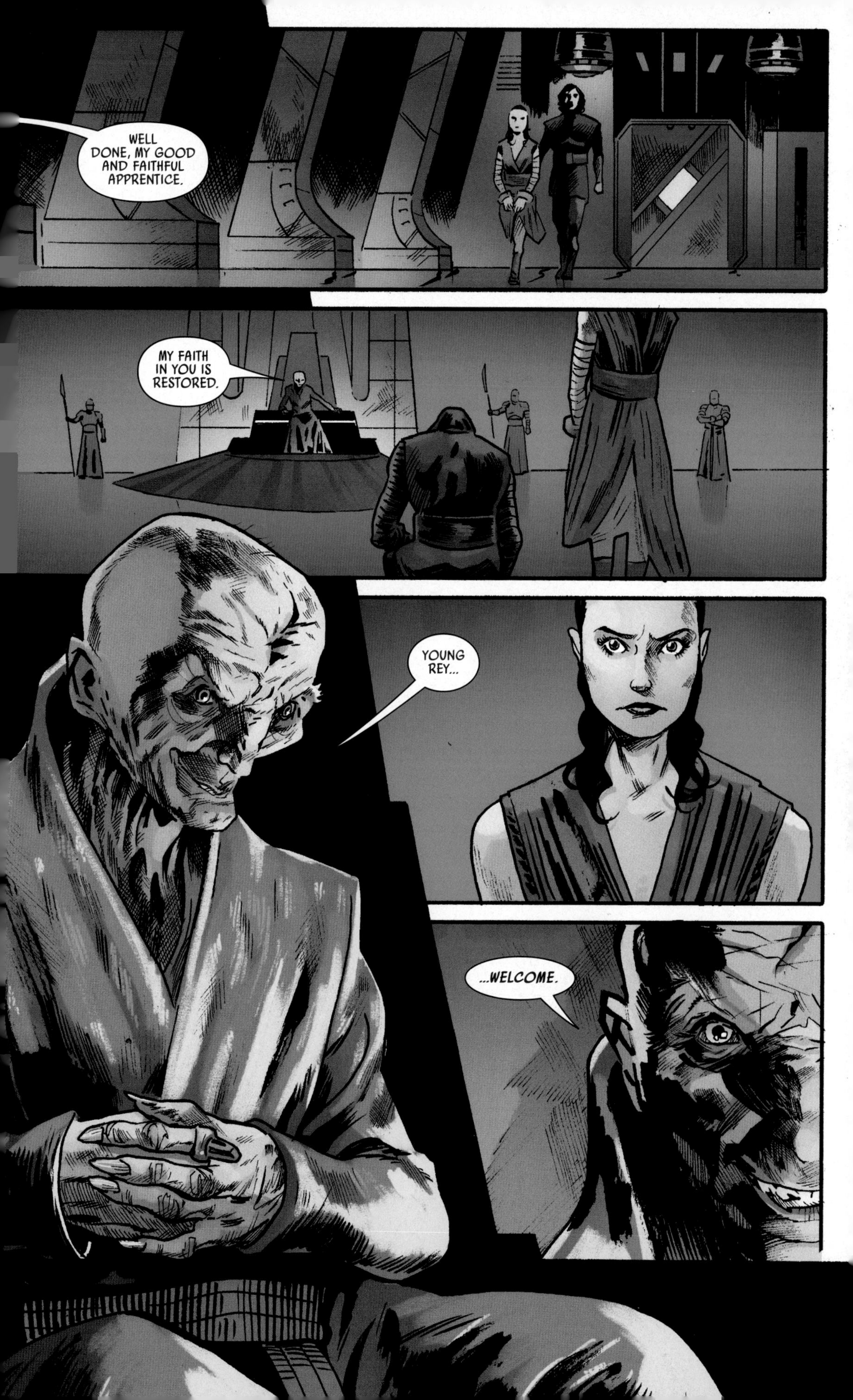
WELL DONE, MY GOOD AND FAITHFUL APPRENTICE.
MY FAITH IN YOU IS RESTORED.
YOUNG REY...
...WELCOME.

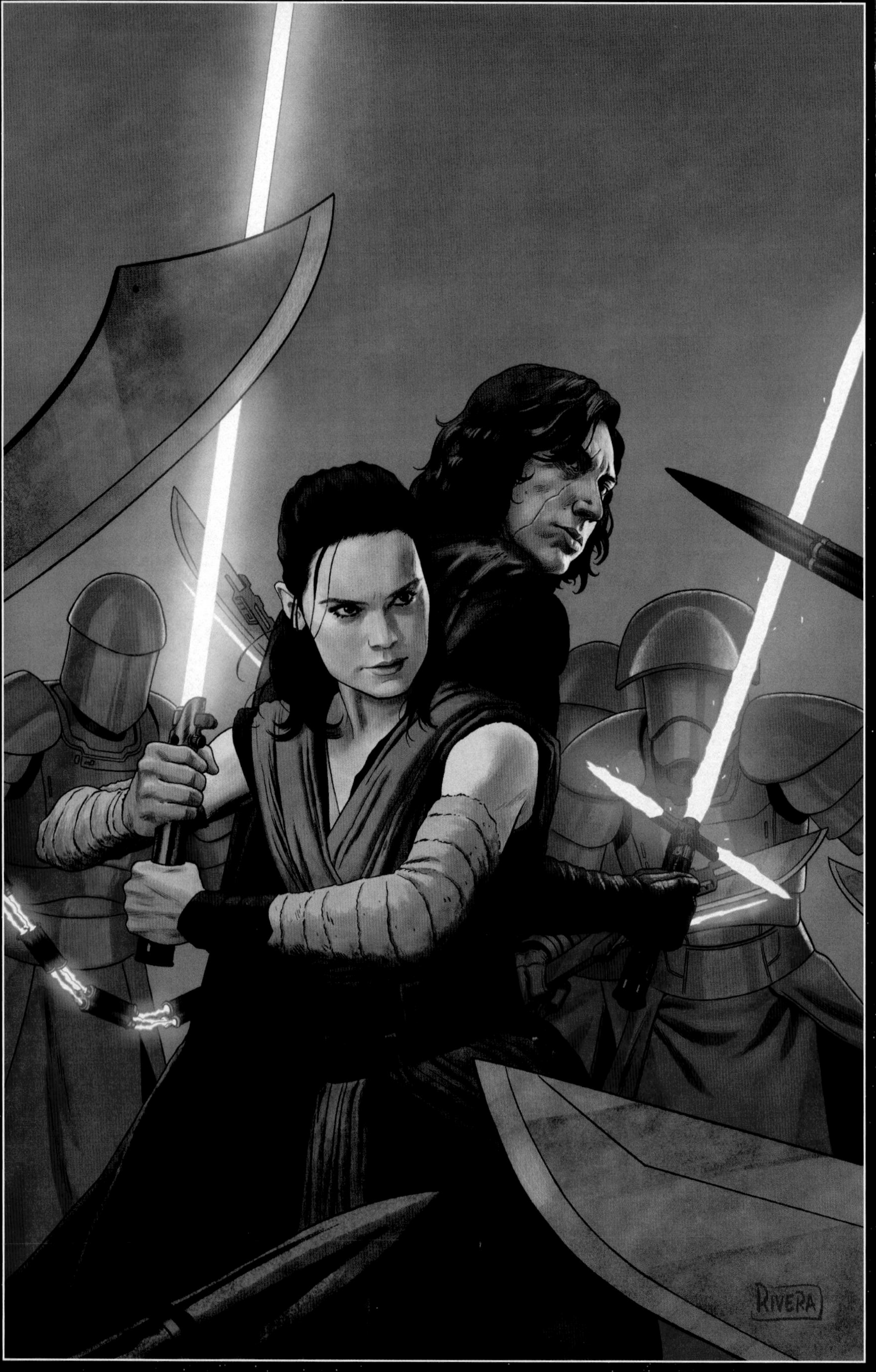
RIVERA

THE LAST JEDI #5

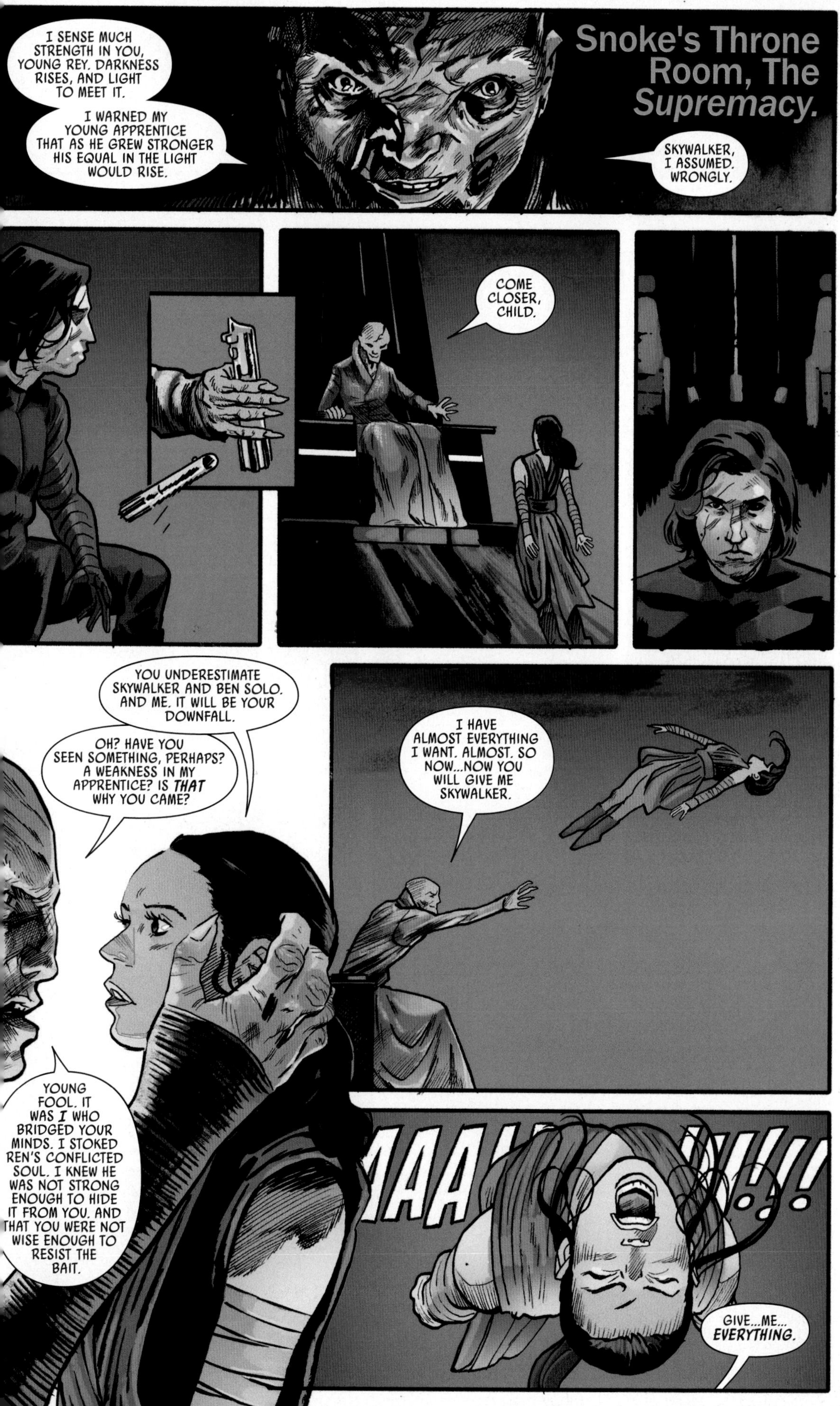
Snoke's Throne Room, The *Supremacy.*
I SENSE MUCH STRENGTH IN YOU, YOUNG REY. DARKNESS RISES, AND LIGHT TO MEET IT.
I WARNED MY YOUNG APPRENTICE THAT AS HE GREW STRONGER HIS EQUAL IN THE LIGHT WOULD RISE.
SKYWALKER, I ASSUMED. WRONGLY.
COME CLOSER, CHILD.
YOU UNDERESTIMATE SKYWALKER AND BEN SOLO. AND ME. IT WILL BE YOUR DOWNFALL.
OH? HAVE YOU SEEN SOMETHING, PERHAPS? A WEAKNESS IN MY APPRENTICE? IS *THAT* WHY YOU CAME?
YOUNG FOOL. IT WAS *I* WHO BRIDGED YOUR MINDS. I STOKED REN'S CONFLICTED SOUL. I KNEW HE WAS NOT STRONG ENOUGH TO HIDE IT FROM YOU. AND THAT YOU WERE NOT WISE ENOUGH TO RESIST THE BAIT.
I HAVE ALMOST EVERYTHING I WANT. ALMOST. SO NOW...NOW YOU WILL GIVE ME SKYWALKER.
GIVE...ME... *EVERYTHING.*

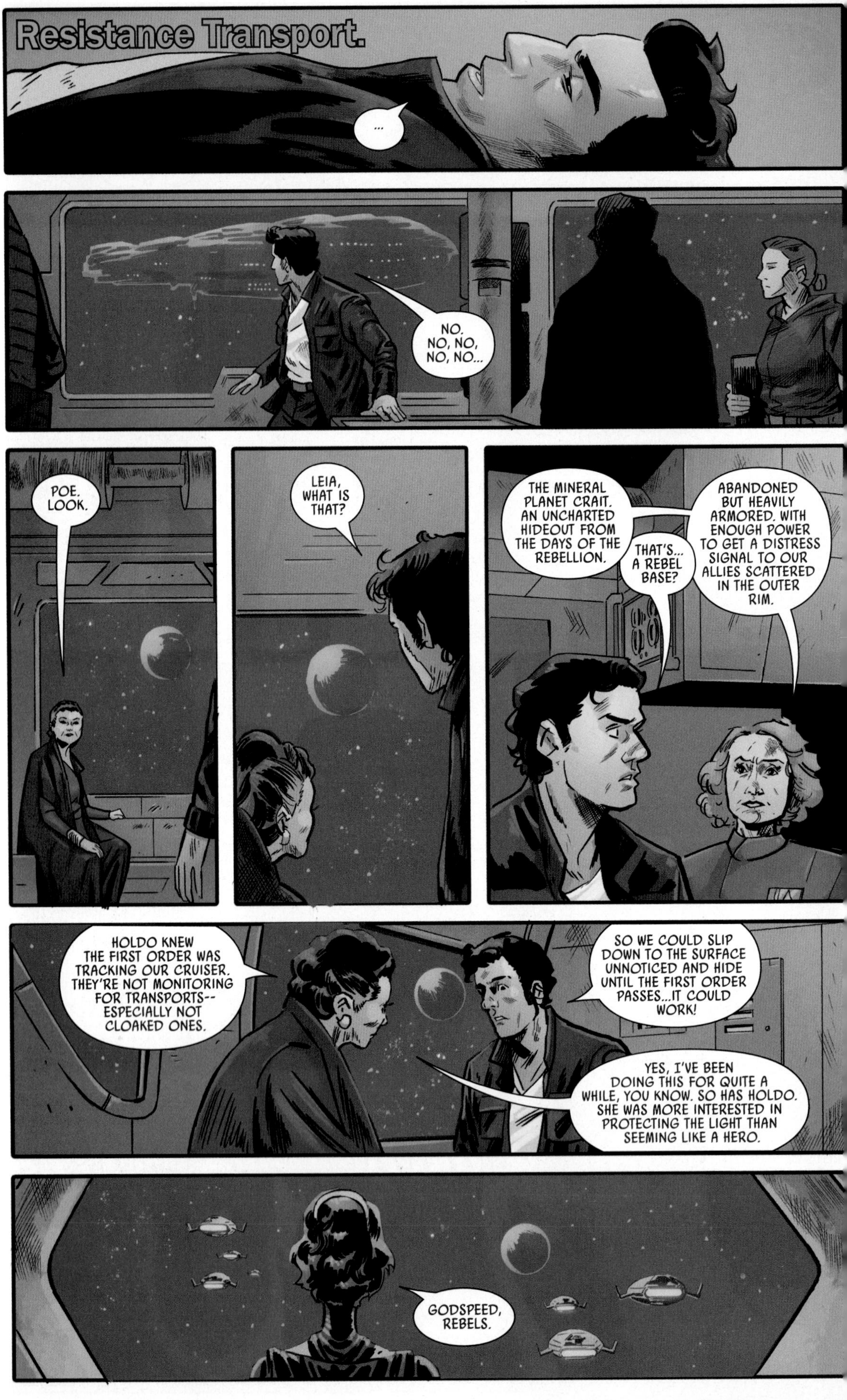
Resistance Transport.
...
NO. NO, NO, NO, NO...
POE. LOOK.
LEIA, WHAT IS THAT?
THE MINERAL PLANET CRAIT. AN UNCHARTED HIDEOUT FROM THE DAYS OF THE REBELLION.
THAT'S... A REBEL BASE?
ABANDONED BUT HEAVILY ARMORED. WITH ENOUGH POWER TO GET A DISTRESS SIGNAL TO OUR ALLIES SCATTERED IN THE OUTER RIM.
HOLDO KNEW THE FIRST ORDER WAS TRACKING OUR CRUISER. THEY'RE NOT MONITORING FOR TRANSPORTS-- ESPECIALLY NOT CLOAKED ONES.
SO WE COULD SLIP DOWN TO THE SURFACE UNNOTICED AND HIDE UNTIL THE FIRST ORDER PASSES...IT COULD WORK!
YES, I'VE BEEN DOING THIS FOR QUITE A WHILE, YOU KNOW. SO HAS HOLDO. SHE WAS MORE INTERESTED IN PROTECTING THE LIGHT THAN SEEMING LIKE A HERO.
GODSPEED, REBELS.

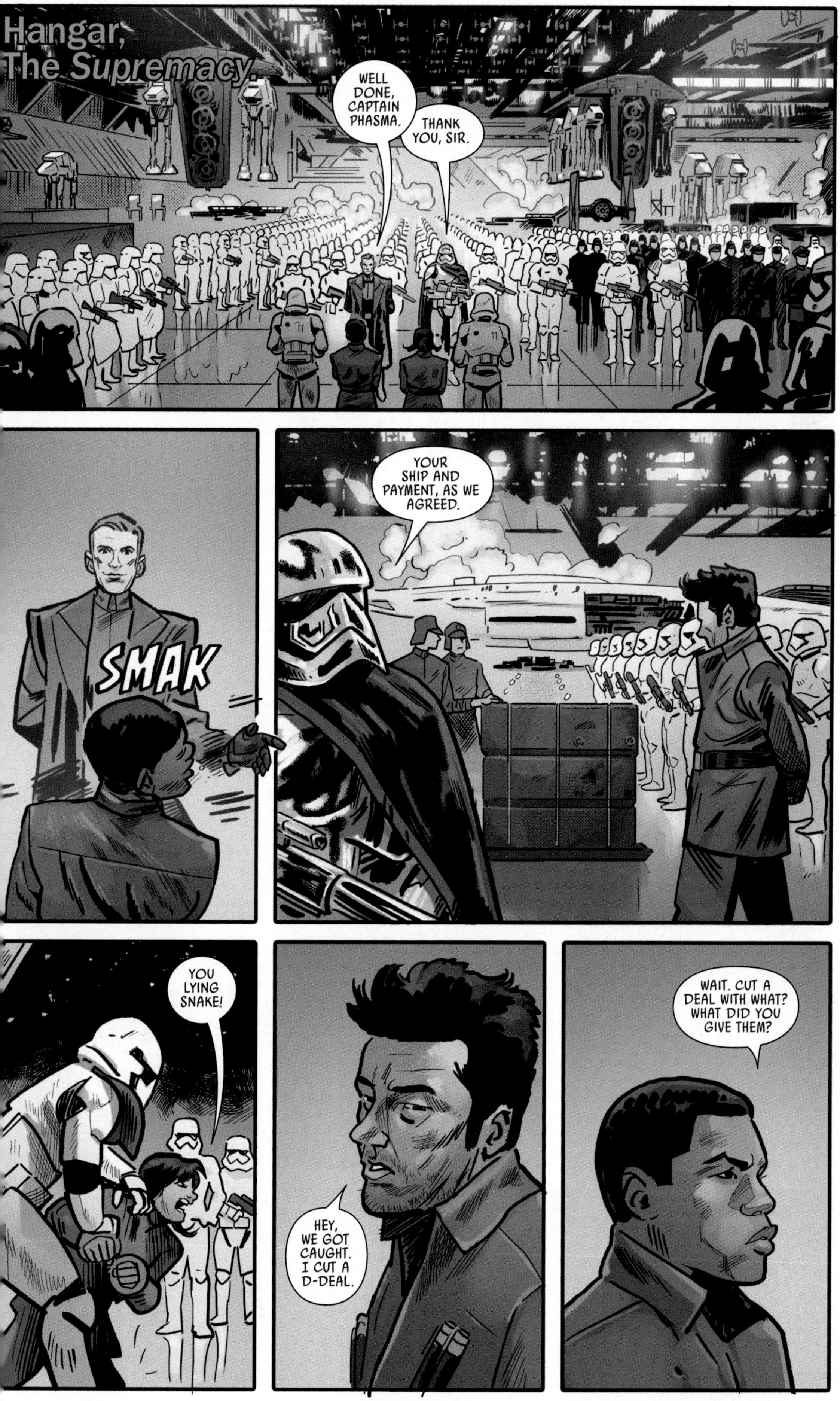
Hangar, The Supremacy.
WELL DONE, CAPTAIN PHASMA.
THANK YOU, SIR.
SMAK
YOUR SHIP AND PAYMENT, AS WE AGREED.
YOU LYING SNAKE!
HEY, WE GOT CAUGHT. I CUT A D-DEAL.
WAIT. CUT A DEAL WITH WHAT? WHAT DID YOU GIVE THEM?

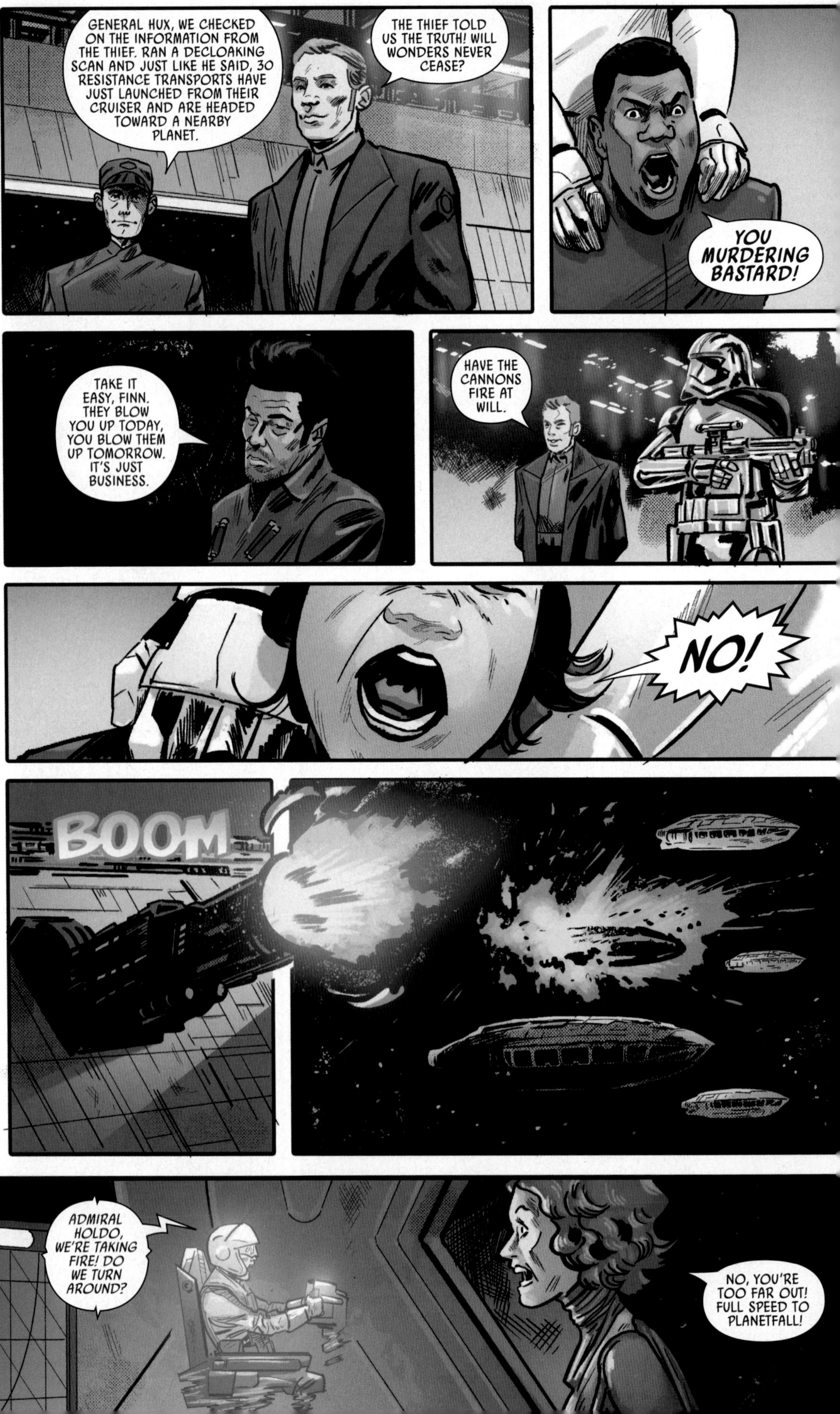

GENERAL HUX, WE CHECKED ON THE INFORMATION FROM THE THIEF. RAN A DECLOAKING SCAN AND JUST LIKE HE SAID, 30 RESISTANCE TRANSPORTS HAVE JUST LAUNCHED FROM THEIR CRUISER AND ARE HEADED TOWARD A NEARBY PLANET.
THE THIEF TOLD US THE TRUTH! WILL WONDERS NEVER CEASE?
YOU MURDERING BASTARD!
TAKE IT EASY, FINN. THEY BLOW YOU UP TODAY, YOU BLOW THEM UP TOMORROW. IT'S JUST BUSINESS.
HAVE THE CANNONS FIRE AT WILL.
NO!
BOOM
ADMIRAL HOLDO, WE'RE TAKING FIRE! DO WE TURN AROUND?
NO, YOU'RE TOO FAR OUT! FULL SPEED TO PLANETFALL!

LOOK HERE NOW.

WELL, WELL. I DID NOT EXPECT SKYWALKER TO BE SO WISE. WE WILL GIVE HIM AND THE JEDI ORDER THE DEATH HE SO DESIRES.

WE WILL GO TO HIS PLANET AND OBLITERATE THE ENTIRE ISLAND. AS SOON AS WE HAVE FINISHED WIPING OUT YOUR REBEL FRIENDS.

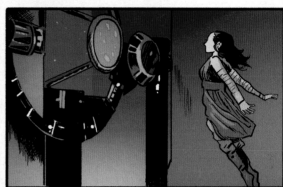

ALL THAT REMAINS OF THE RESISTANCE IS ON THOSE TRANSPORTS, BEING PICKED OFF LIKE FLIES, ONE BY ONE. SOON THEY WILL ALL BE GONE. FOR YOU, ALL IS LOST.

AND STILL HOPE PERSISTS? YOU HAVE THE SPIRIT OF A TRUE JEDI.

KLAK

MY WORTHY APPRENTICE, SON OF DARKNESS. HEIR APPARENT TO LORD VADER. WHERE THERE WAS CONFLICT I NOW SENSE RESOLVE. WHERE THERE WAS WEAKNESS, STRENGTH. COMPLETE YOUR TRAINING AND FULFILL YOUR DESTINY.

I KNOW WHAT I HAVE TO DO.

BEN...

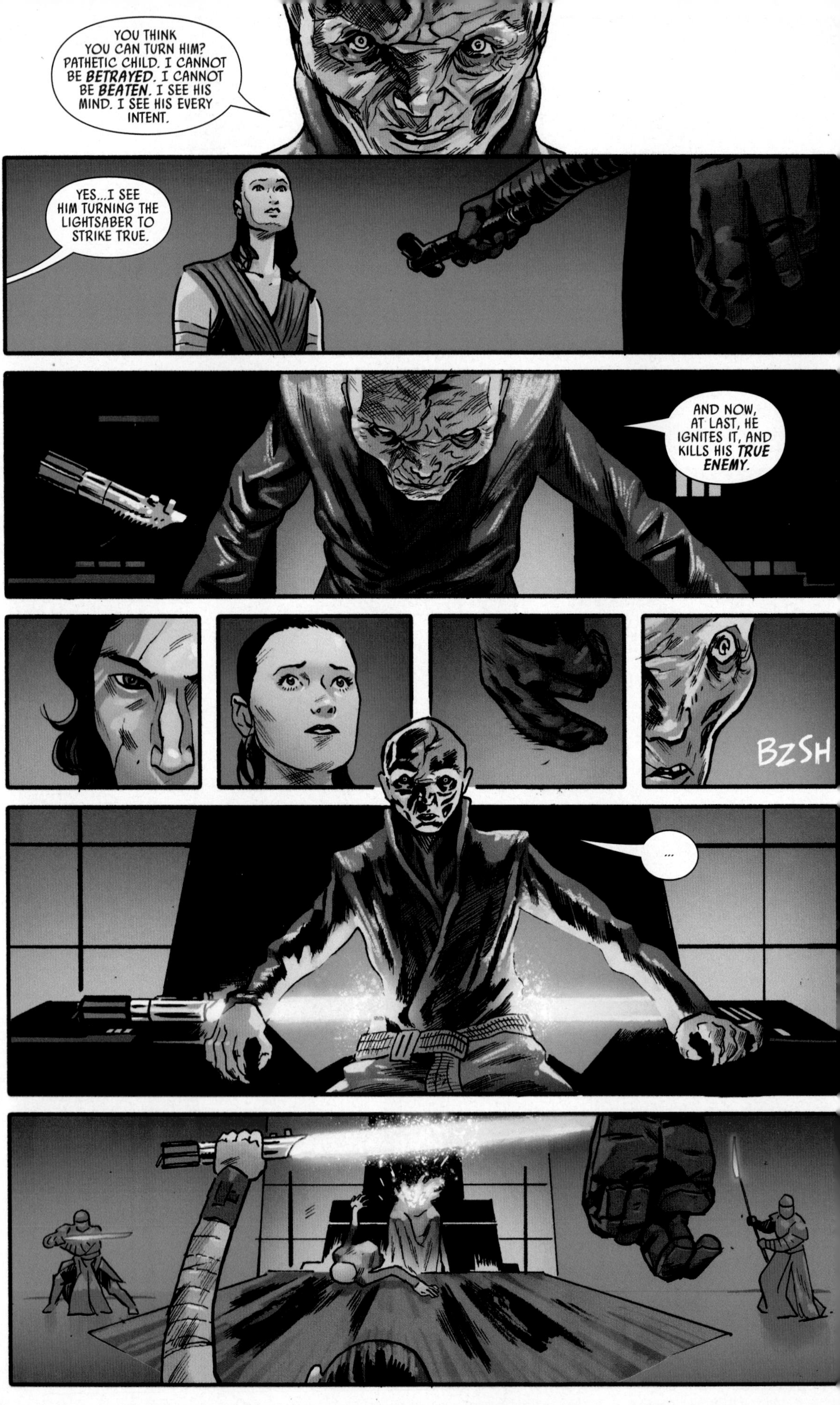

YOU THINK YOU CAN TURN HIM? PATHETIC CHILD. I CANNOT BE *BETRAYED*. I CANNOT BE *BEATEN*. I SEE HIS MIND. I SEE HIS EVERY INTENT.
YES...I SEE HIM TURNING THE LIGHTSABER TO STRIKE TRUE.
AND NOW, AT LAST, HE IGNITES IT, AND KILLS HIS *TRUE ENEMY*.
BZSH
...

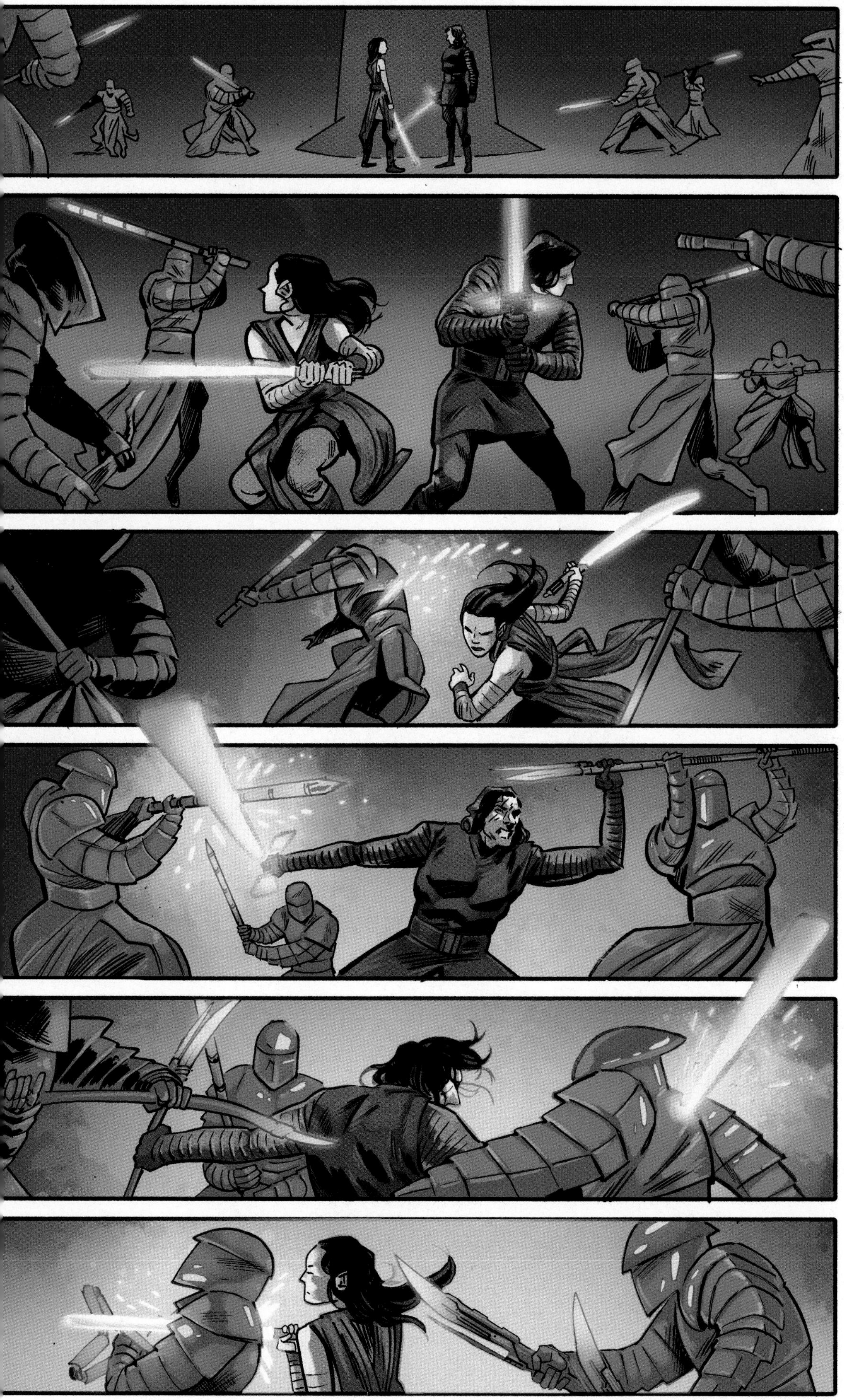

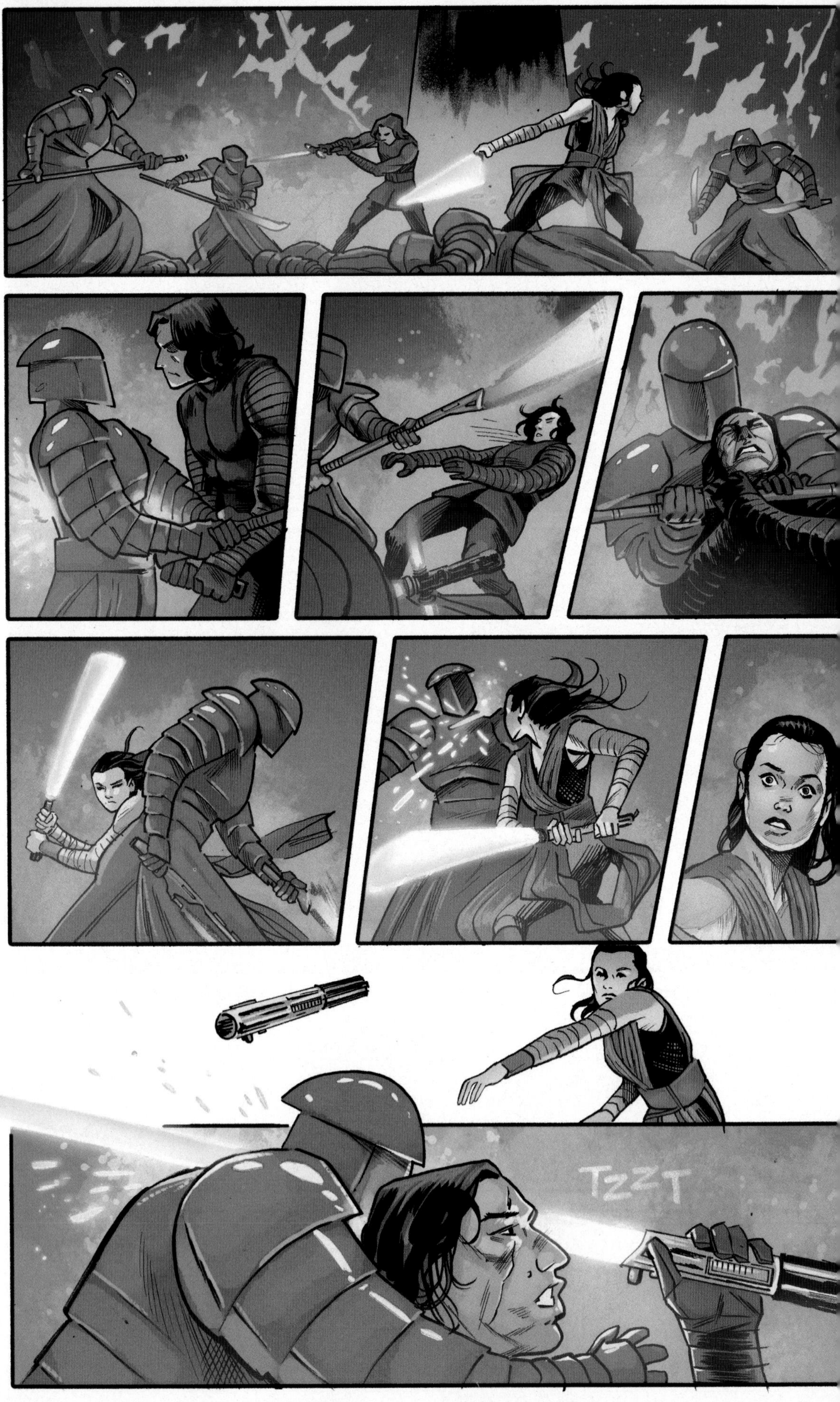
TZZT

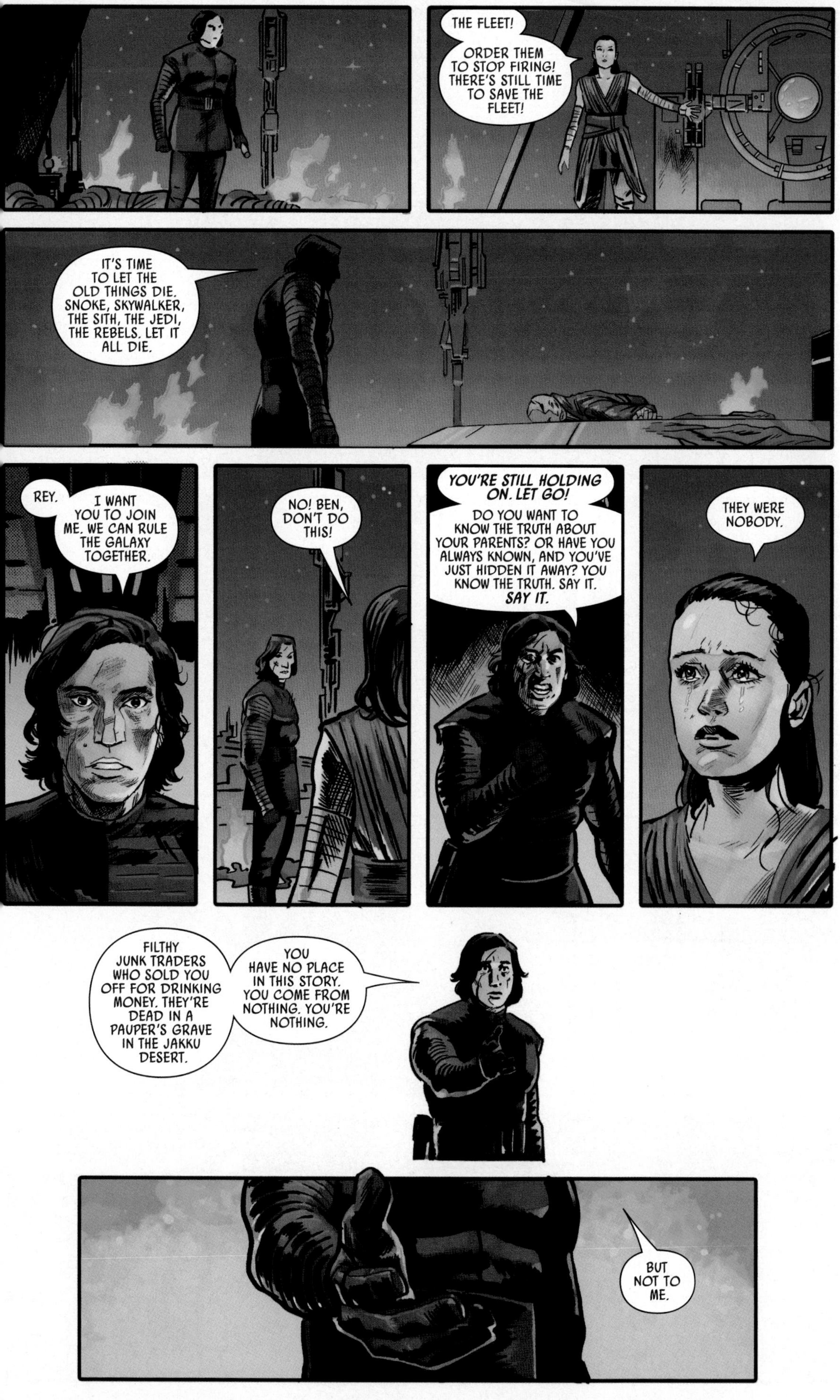
THE FLEET!
ORDER THEM TO STOP FIRING! THERE'S STILL TIME TO SAVE THE FLEET!
IT'S TIME TO LET THE OLD THINGS DIE. SNOKE, SKYWALKER, THE SITH, THE JEDI, THE REBELS. LET IT ALL DIE.
REY.
I WANT YOU TO JOIN ME. WE CAN RULE THE GALAXY TOGETHER.
NO! BEN, DON'T DO THIS!
YOU'RE STILL HOLDING ON. LET GO!
DO YOU WANT TO KNOW THE TRUTH ABOUT YOUR PARENTS? OR HAVE YOU ALWAYS KNOWN, AND YOU'VE JUST HIDDEN IT AWAY? YOU KNOW THE TRUTH. SAY IT. SAY IT.
THEY WERE NOBODY.
FILTHY JUNK TRADERS WHO SOLD YOU OFF FOR DRINKING MONEY. THEY'RE DEAD IN A PAUPER'S GRAVE IN THE JAKKU DESERT.
YOU HAVE NO PLACE IN THIS STORY. YOU COME FROM NOTHING. YOU'RE NOTHING.
BUT NOT TO ME.

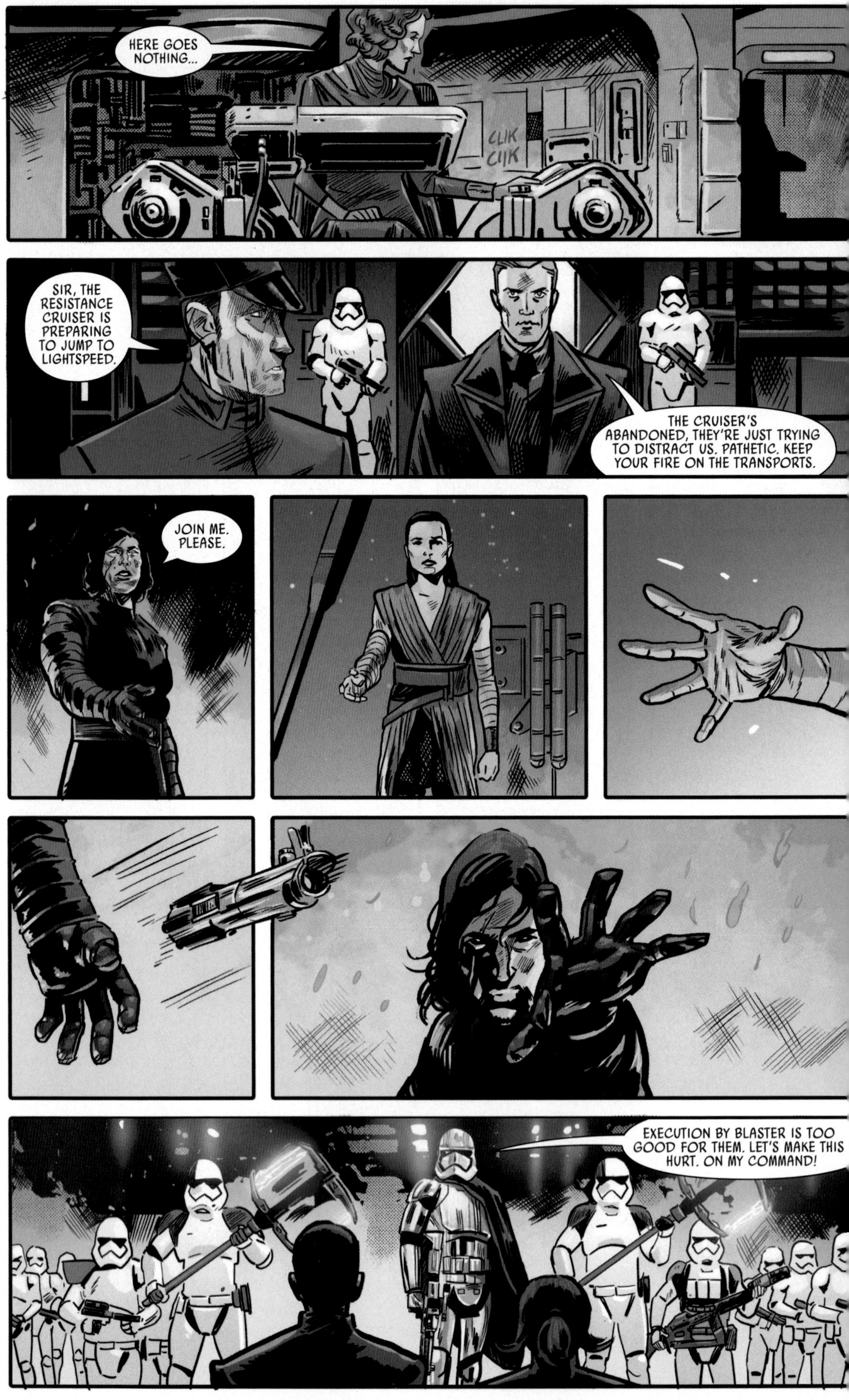
HERE GOES NOTHING...
CLIK CLIK
SIR, THE RESISTANCE CRUISER IS PREPARING TO JUMP TO LIGHTSPEED.
THE CRUISER'S ABANDONED, THEY'RE JUST TRYING TO DISTRACT US. PATHETIC. KEEP YOUR FIRE ON THE TRANSPORTS.
JOIN ME. PLEASE.
EXECUTION BY BLASTER IS TOO GOOD FOR THEM. LET'S MAKE THIS HURT. ON MY COMMAND!

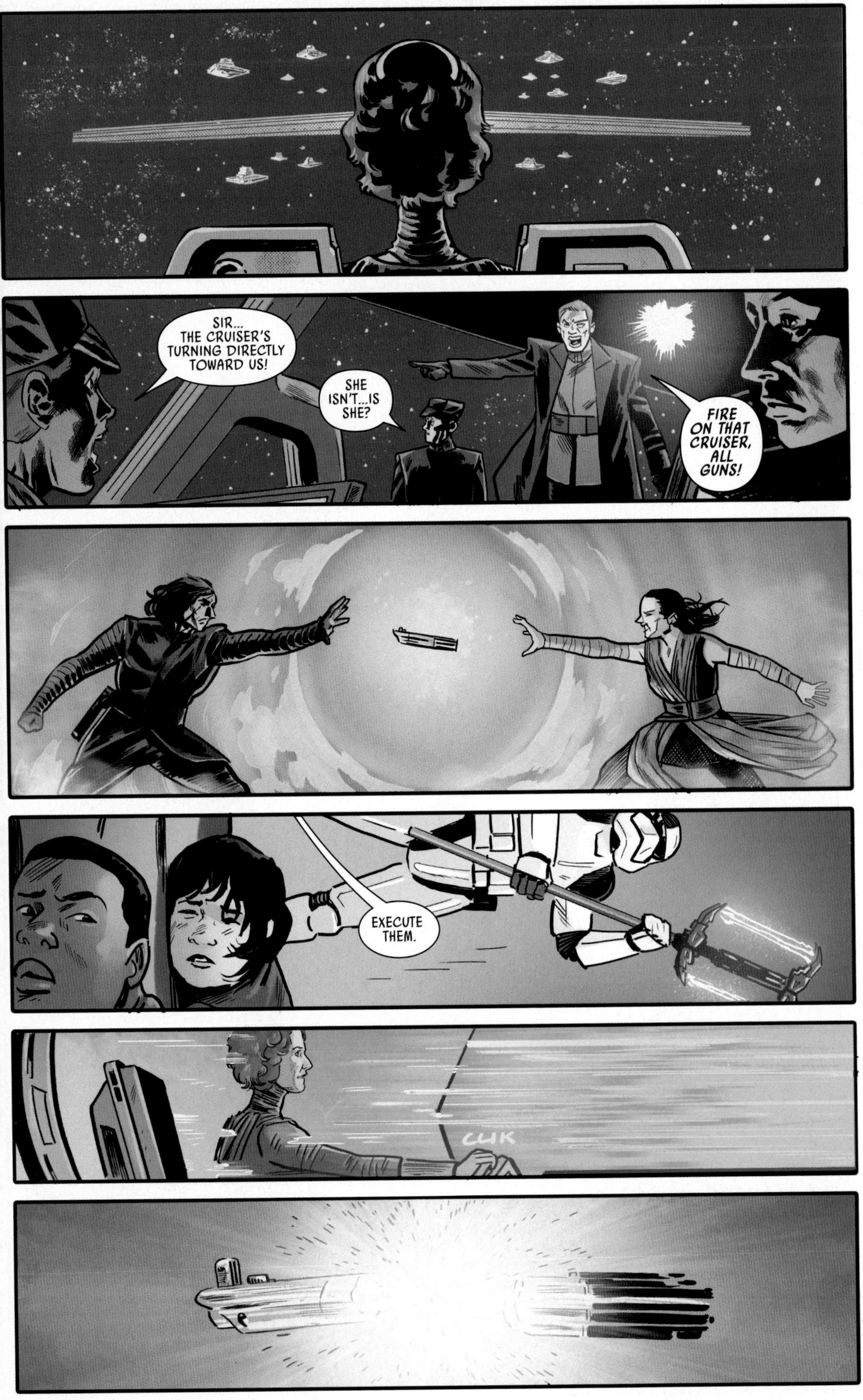
SIR... THE CRUISER'S TURNING DIRECTLY TOWARD US!
SHE ISN'T...IS SHE?
FIRE ON THAT CRUISER, ALL GUNS!
EXECUTE THEM.
CLIK

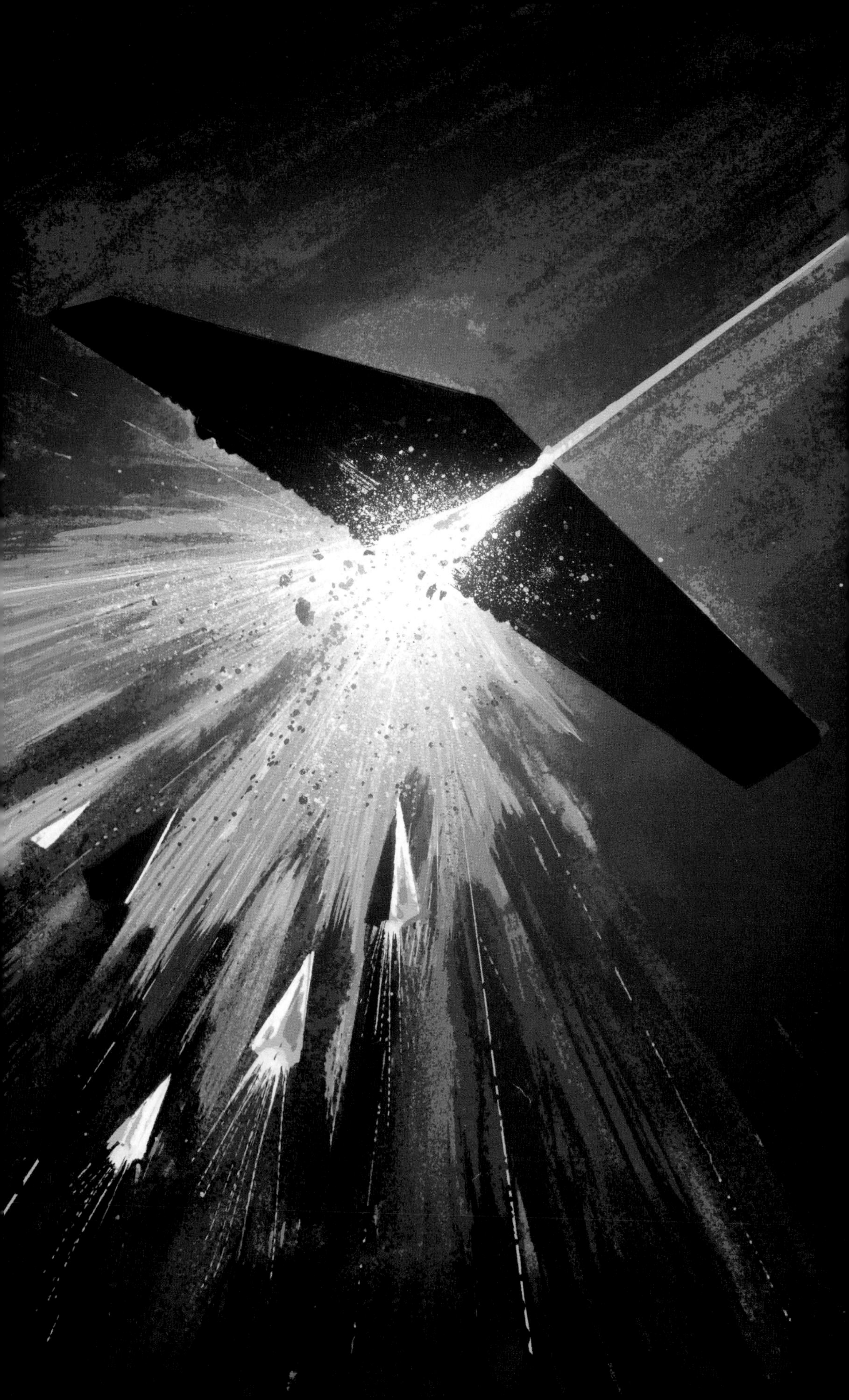

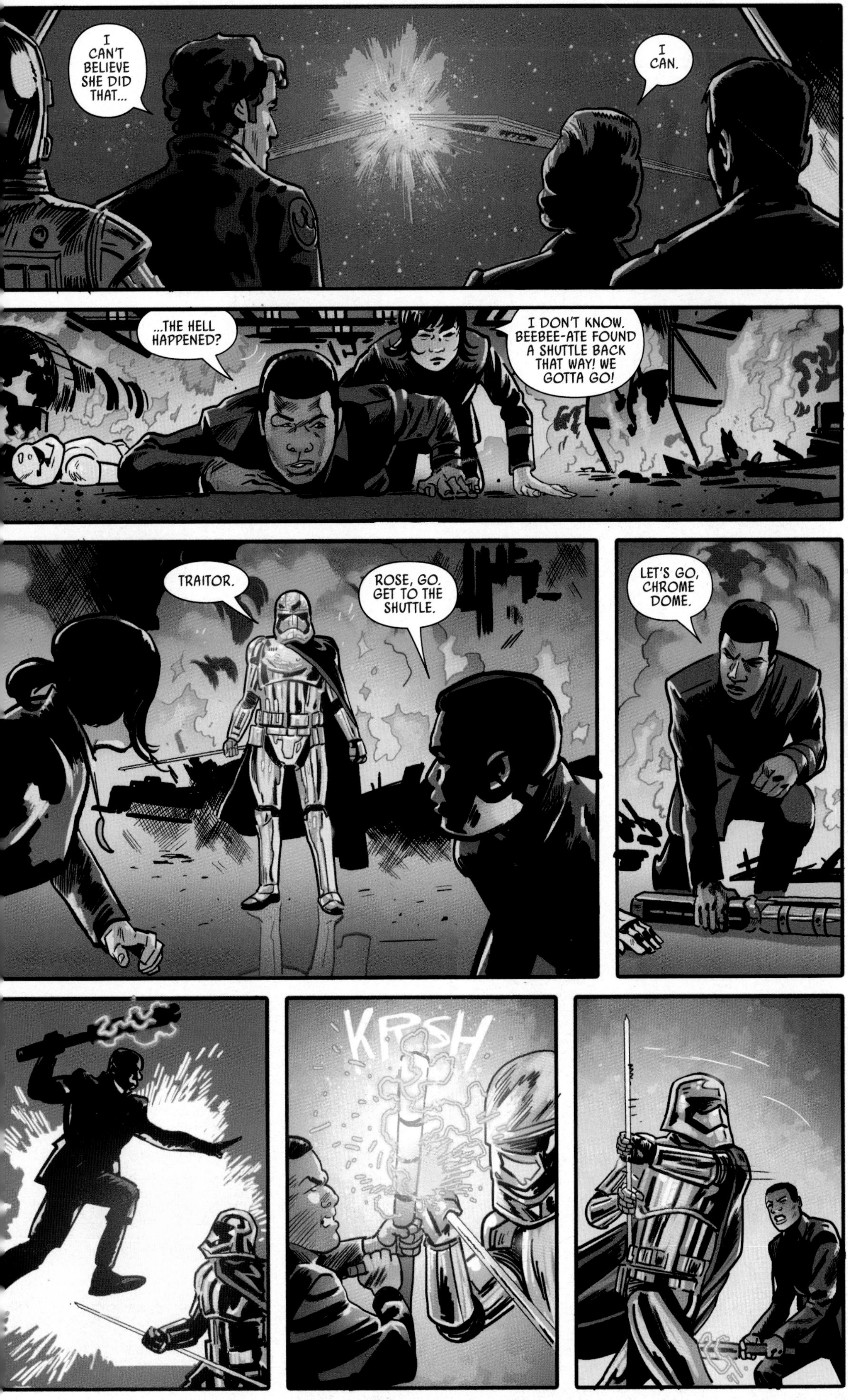
I CAN'T BELIEVE SHE DID THAT...
I CAN.
...THE HELL HAPPENED?
I DON'T KNOW. BEEBEE-ATE FOUND A SHUTTLE BACK THAT WAY! WE GOTTA GO!
TRAITOR.
ROSE, GO. GET TO THE SHUTTLE.
LET'S GO, CHROME DOME.
KRSH

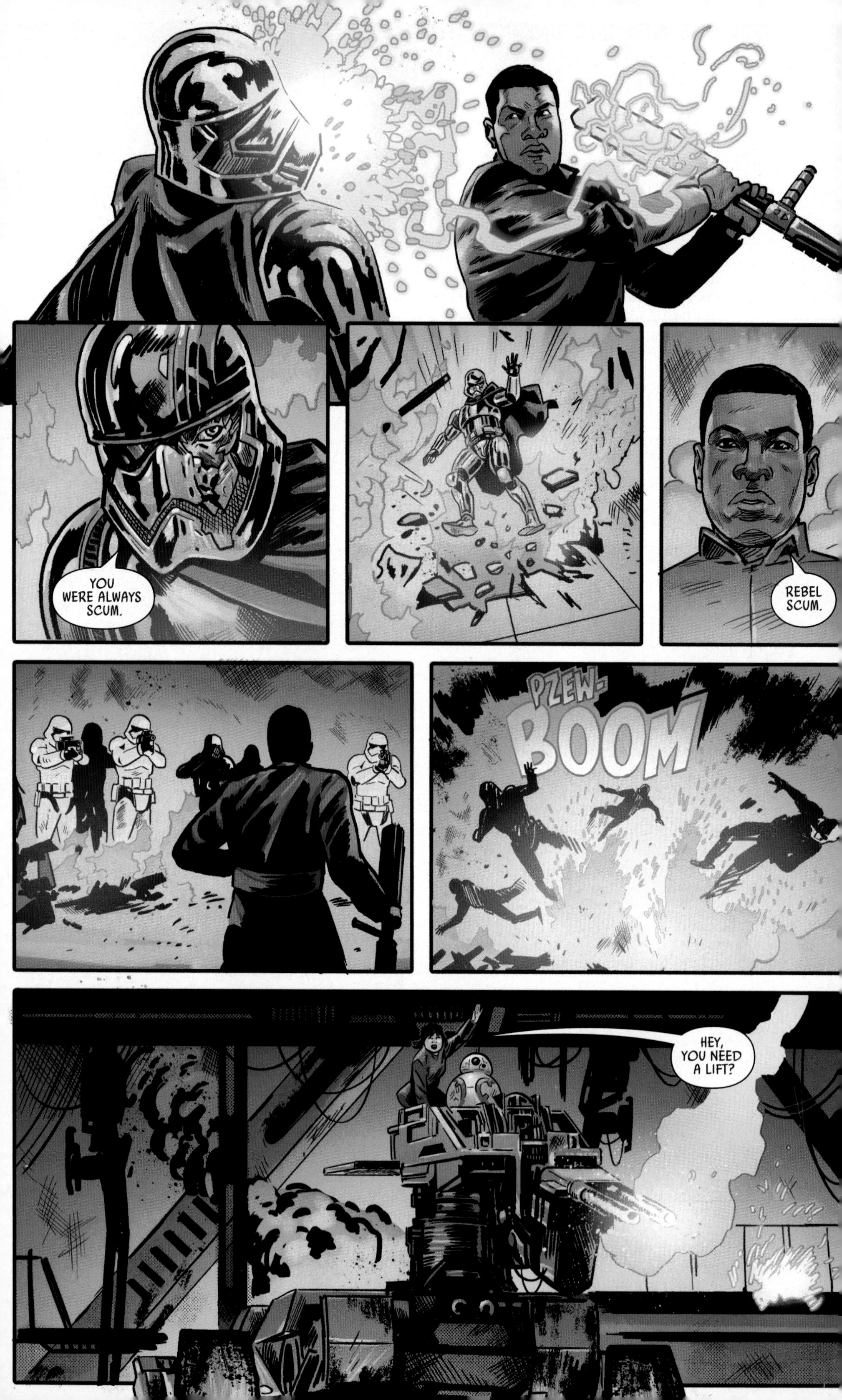
YOU WERE ALWAYS SCUM.
REBEL SCUM.
PZEW-BOOM
HEY, YOU NEED A LIFT?

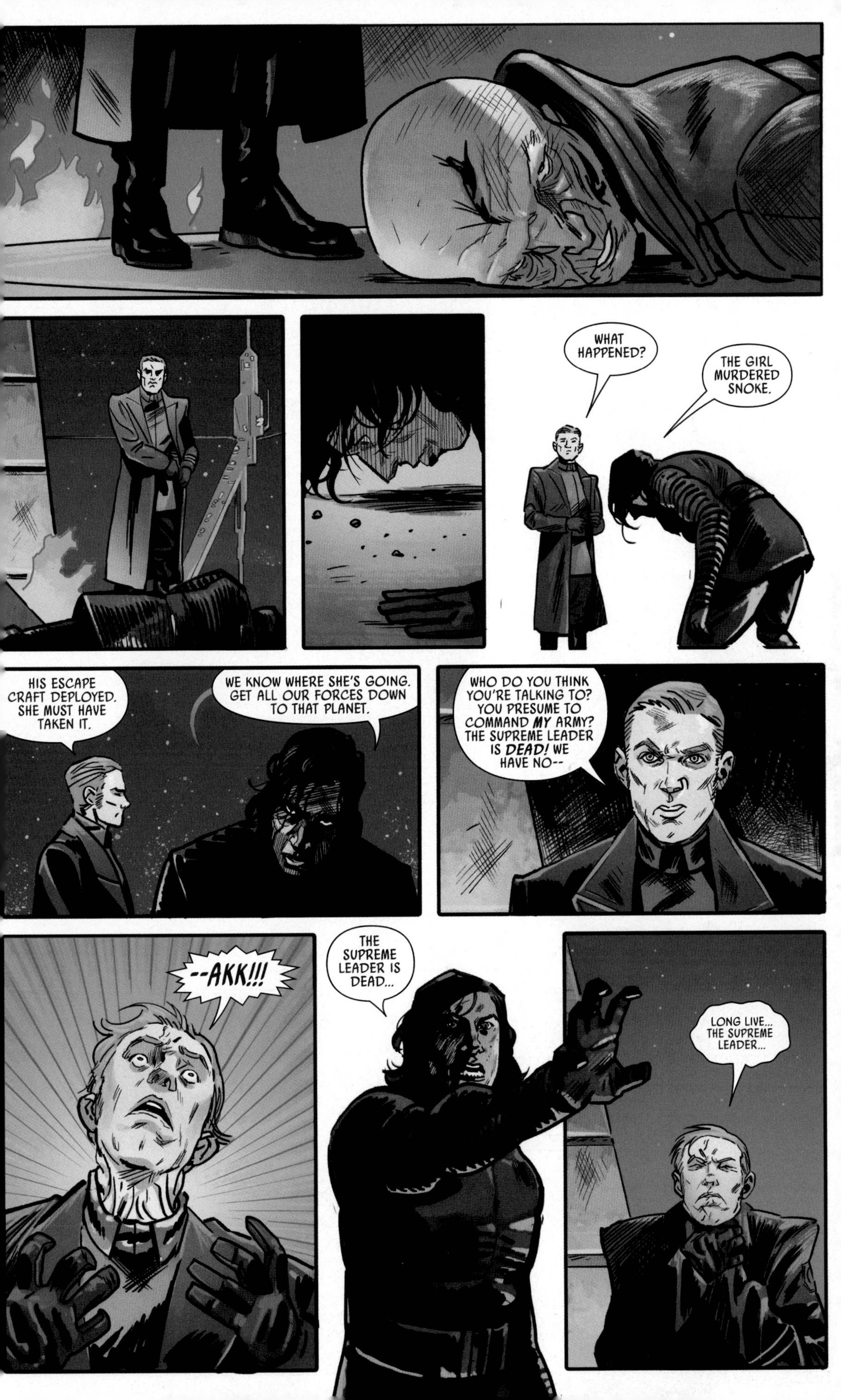
WHAT HAPPENED?
THE GIRL MURDERED SNOKE.
HIS ESCAPE CRAFT DEPLOYED. SHE MUST HAVE TAKEN IT.
WE KNOW WHERE SHE'S GOING. GET ALL OUR FORCES DOWN TO THAT PLANET.
WHO DO YOU THINK YOU'RE TALKING TO? YOU PRESUME TO COMMAND MY ARMY? THE SUPREME LEADER IS DEAD! WE HAVE NO--
--AKK!!!
THE SUPREME LEADER IS DEAD...
LONG LIVE... THE SUPREME LEADER...

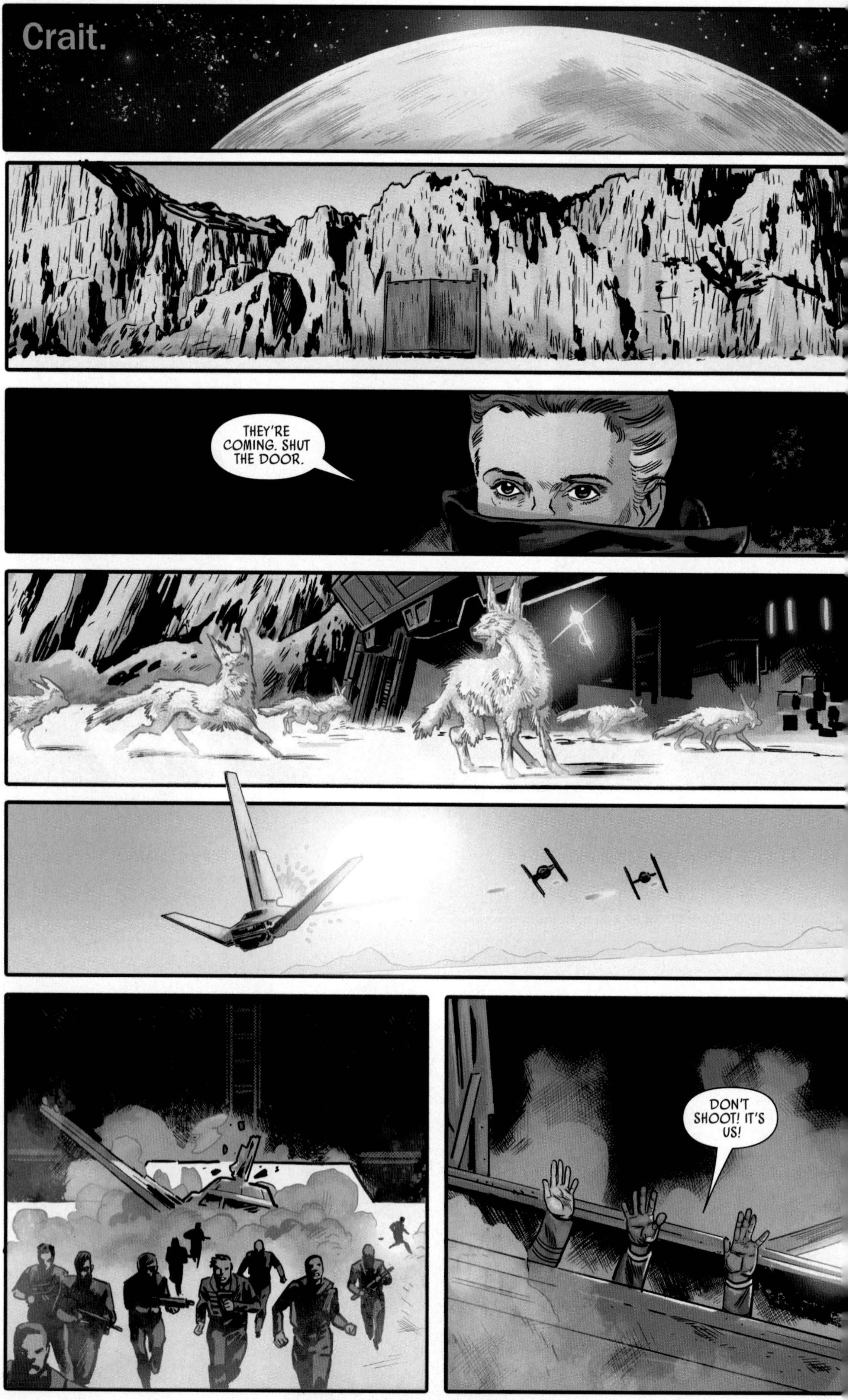
Crait.
THEY'RE COMING. SHUT THE DOOR.
DON'T SHOOT! IT'S US!

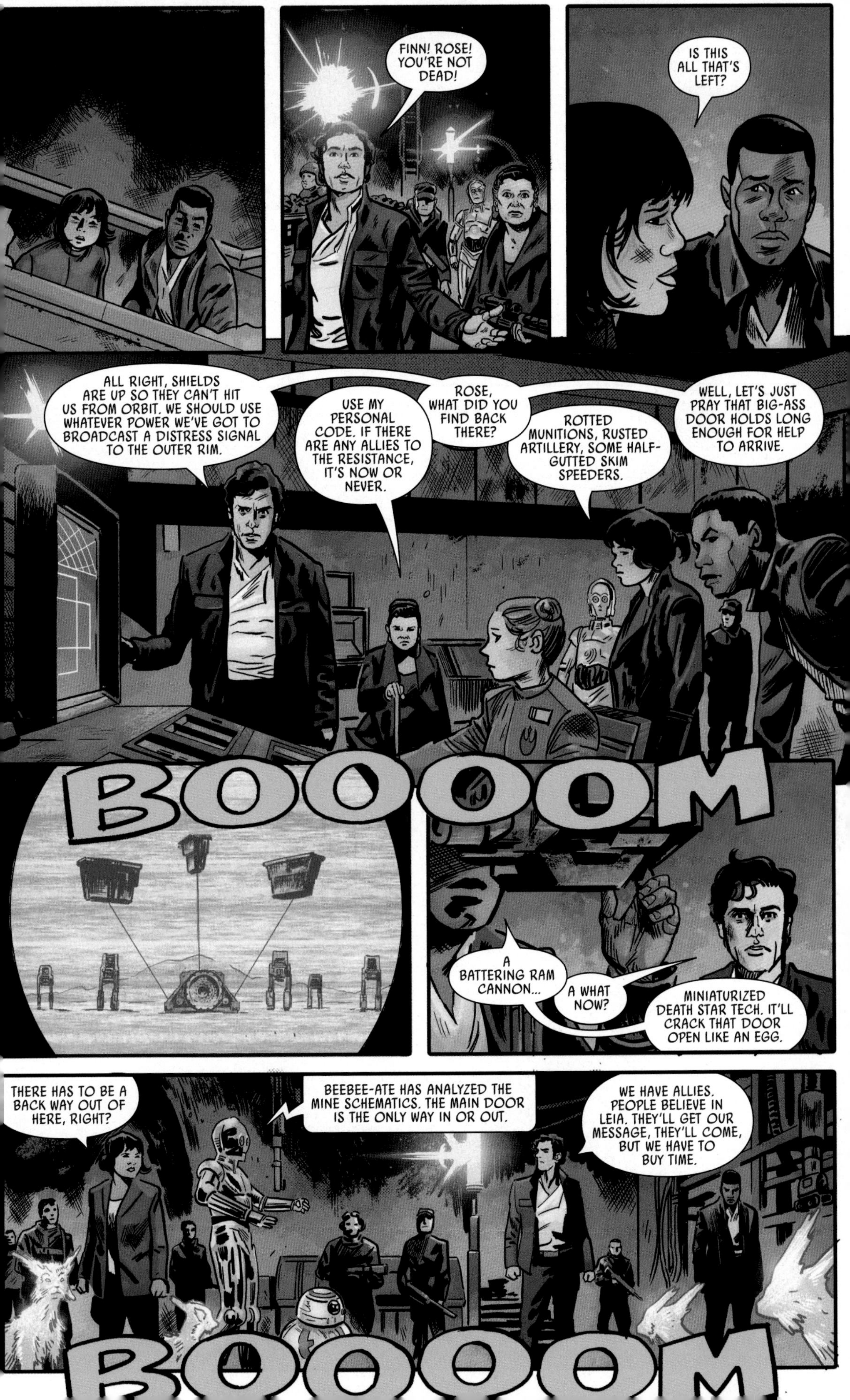

FINN! ROSE! YOU'RE NOT DEAD!
IS THIS ALL THAT'S LEFT?
ALL RIGHT, SHIELDS ARE UP SO THEY CAN'T HIT US FROM ORBIT. WE SHOULD USE WHATEVER POWER WE'VE GOT TO BROADCAST A DISTRESS SIGNAL TO THE OUTER RIM.
USE MY PERSONAL CODE. IF THERE ARE ANY ALLIES TO THE RESISTANCE, IT'S NOW OR NEVER.
ROSE, WHAT DID YOU FIND BACK THERE?
ROTTED MUNITIONS, RUSTED ARTILLERY, SOME HALF-GUTTED SKIM SPEEDERS.
WELL, LET'S JUST PRAY THAT BIG-ASS DOOR HOLDS LONG ENOUGH FOR HELP TO ARRIVE.
BOOOOM
A BATTERING RAM CANNON...
A WHAT NOW?
MINIATURIZED DEATH STAR TECH. IT'LL CRACK THAT DOOR OPEN LIKE AN EGG.
THERE HAS TO BE A BACK WAY OUT OF HERE, RIGHT?
BEEBEE-ATE HAS ANALYZED THE MINE SCHEMATICS. THE MAIN DOOR IS THE ONLY WAY IN OR OUT.
WE HAVE ALLIES. PEOPLE BELIEVE IN LEIA. THEY'LL GET OUR MESSAGE, THEY'LL COME, BUT WE HAVE TO BUY TIME.
BOOOOM

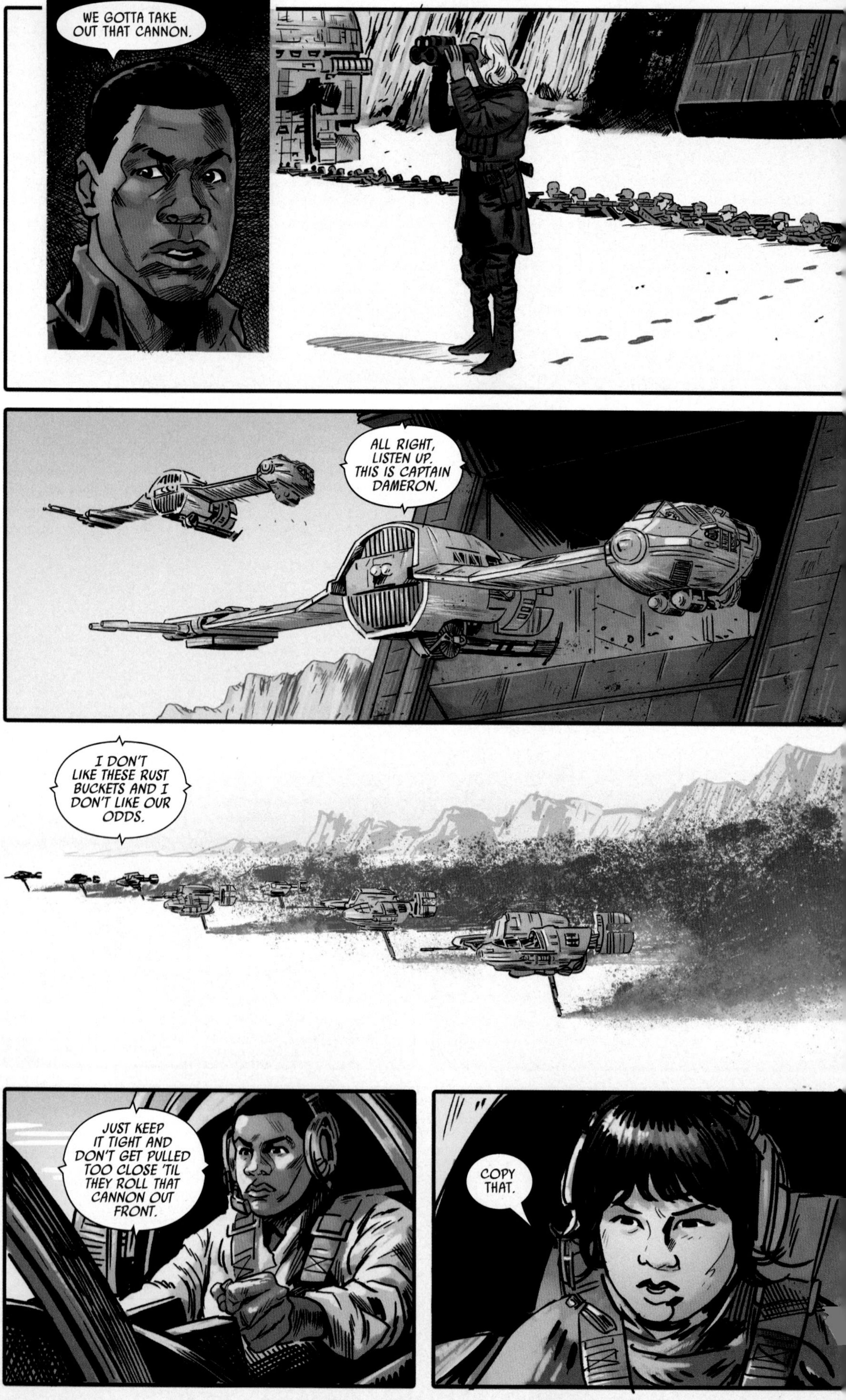

WE GOTTA TAKE OUT THAT CANNON.
ALL RIGHT, LISTEN UP. THIS IS CAPTAIN DAMERON.
I DON'T LIKE THESE RUST BUCKETS AND I DON'T LIKE OUR ODDS.
JUST KEEP IT TIGHT AND DON'T GET PULLED TOO CLOSE 'TIL THEY ROLL THAT CANNON OUT FRONT.
COPY THAT.

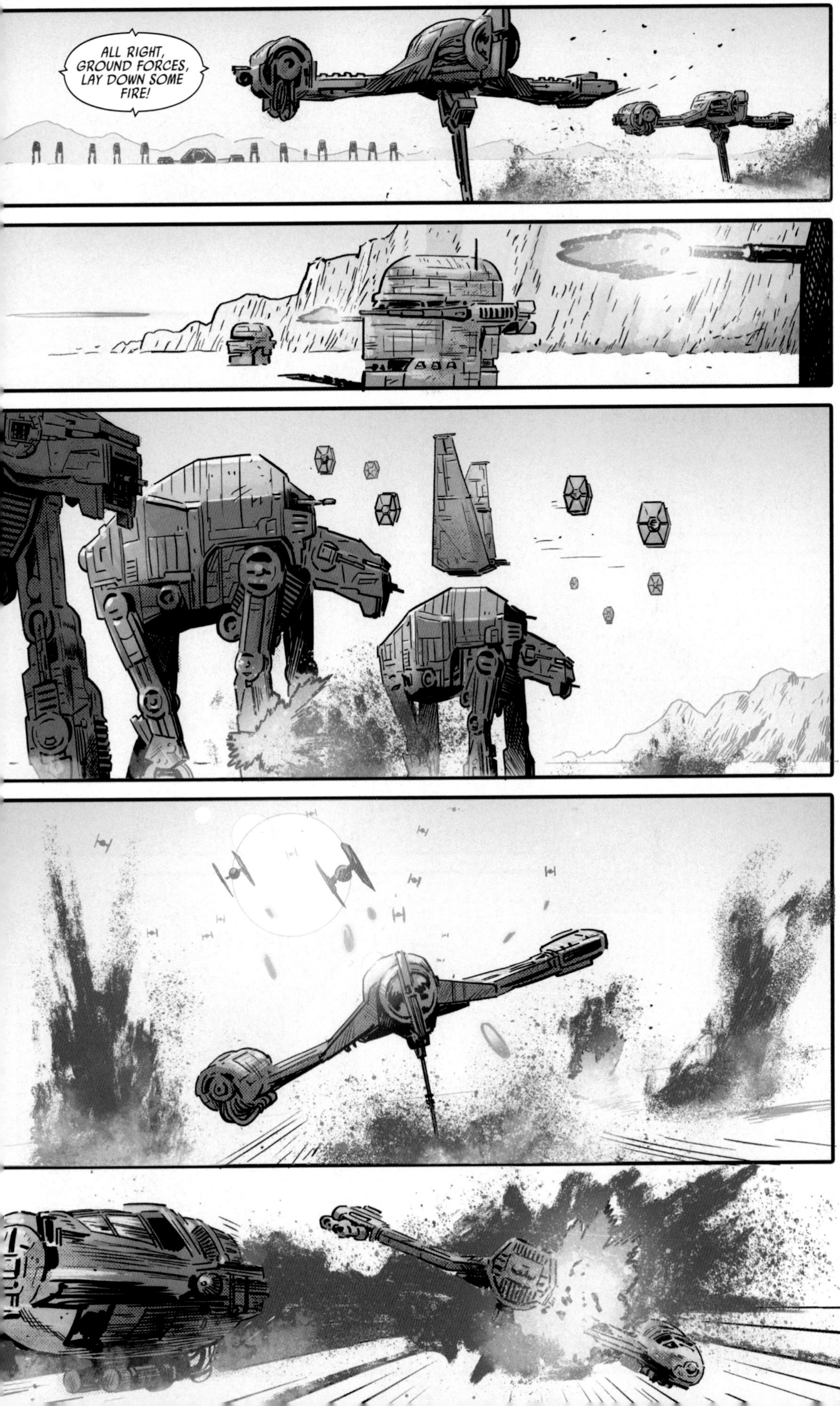
ALL RIGHT, GROUND FORCES, LAY DOWN SOME FIRE!

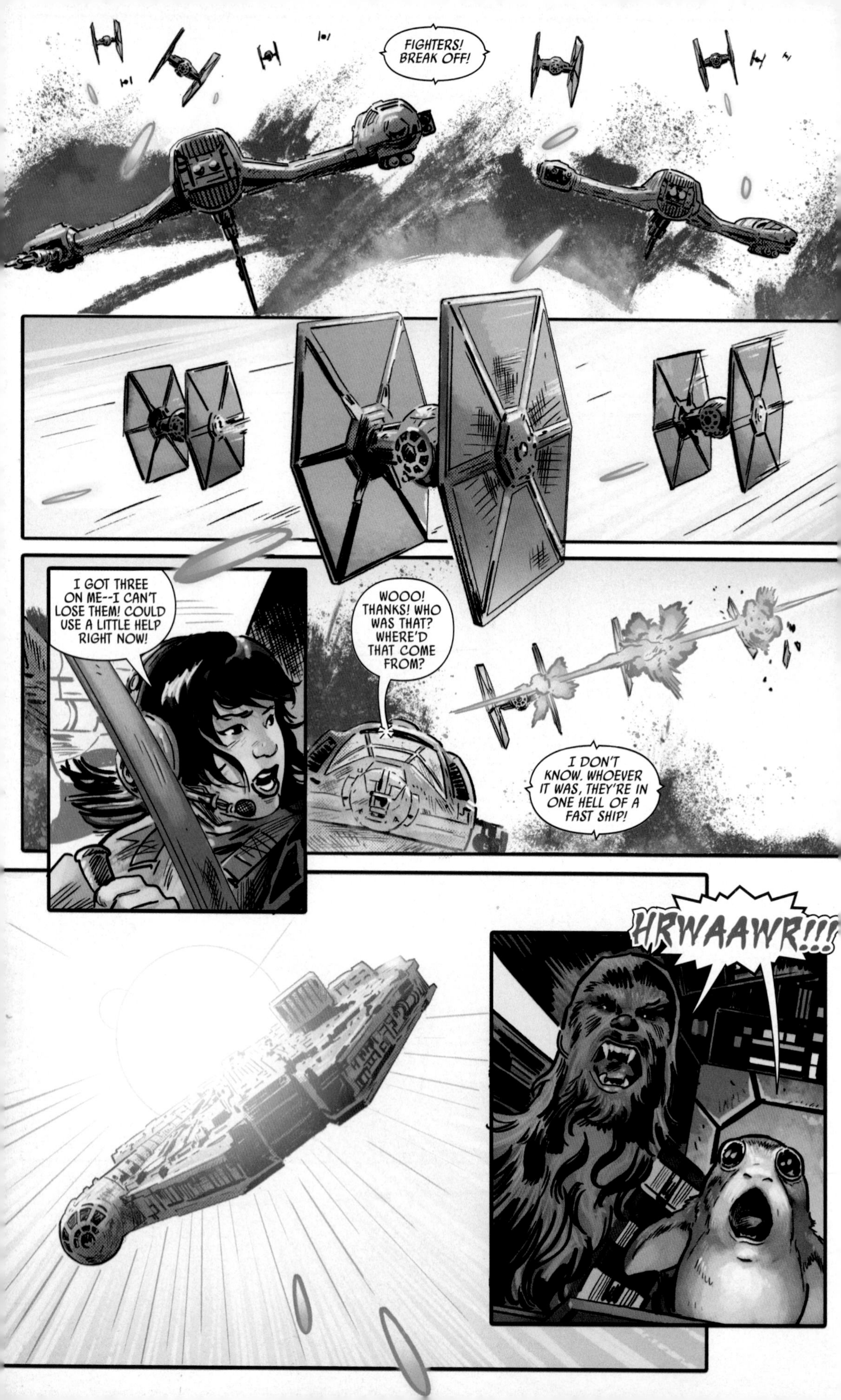
FIGHTERS! BREAK OFF!
I GOT THREE ON ME--I CAN'T LOSE THEM! COULD USE A LITTLE HELP RIGHT NOW!
WOOO! THANKS! WHO WAS THAT? WHERE'D THAT COME FROM?
I DON'T KNOW. WHOEVER IT WAS, THEY'RE IN ONE HELL OF A FAST SHIP!
HRWAAWR!!!

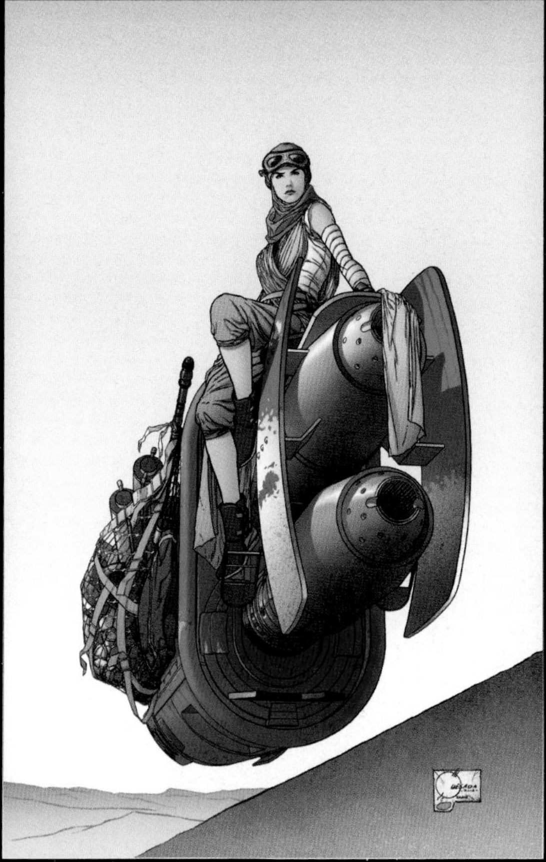

Issue #1 variant by Joe Quesada & Richard Isanove

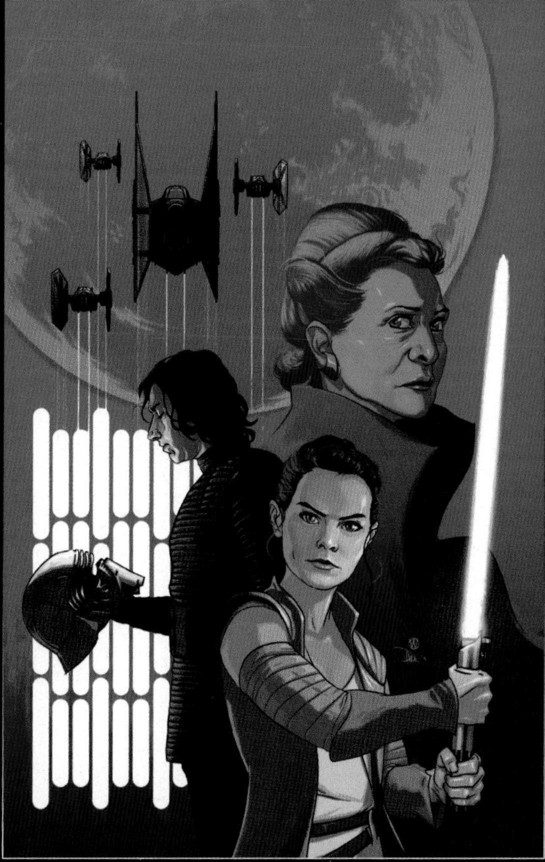

Issue #2 variant by Michael Walsh & Dave McCaig

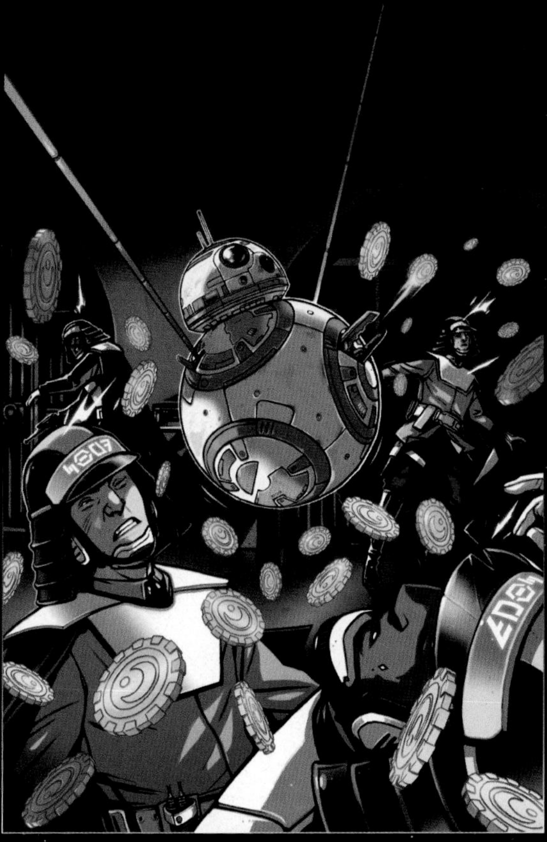

Issue #3 variant by Caspar Wijngaard

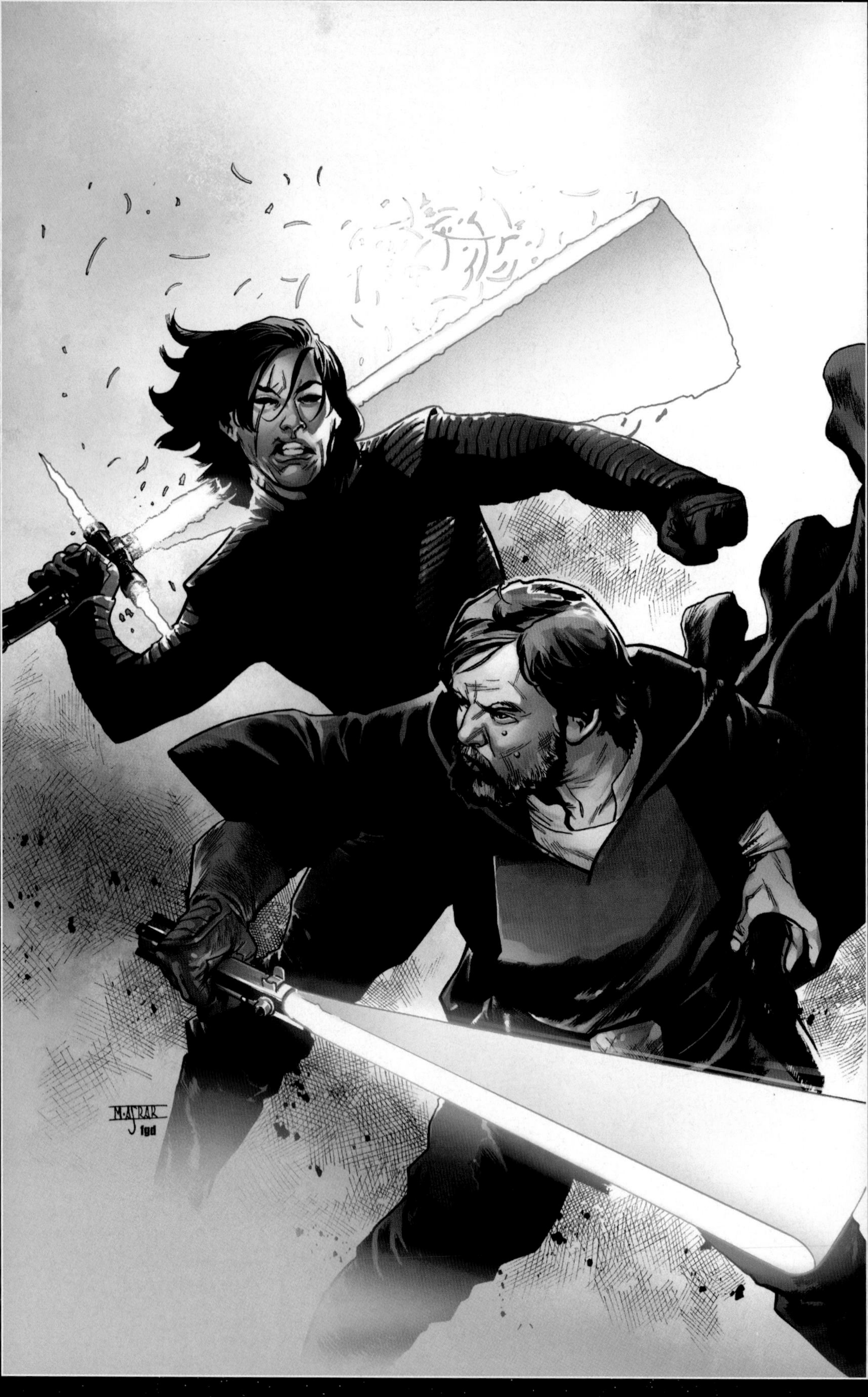
M.ASRAR
fgd

THE LAST JEDI #6

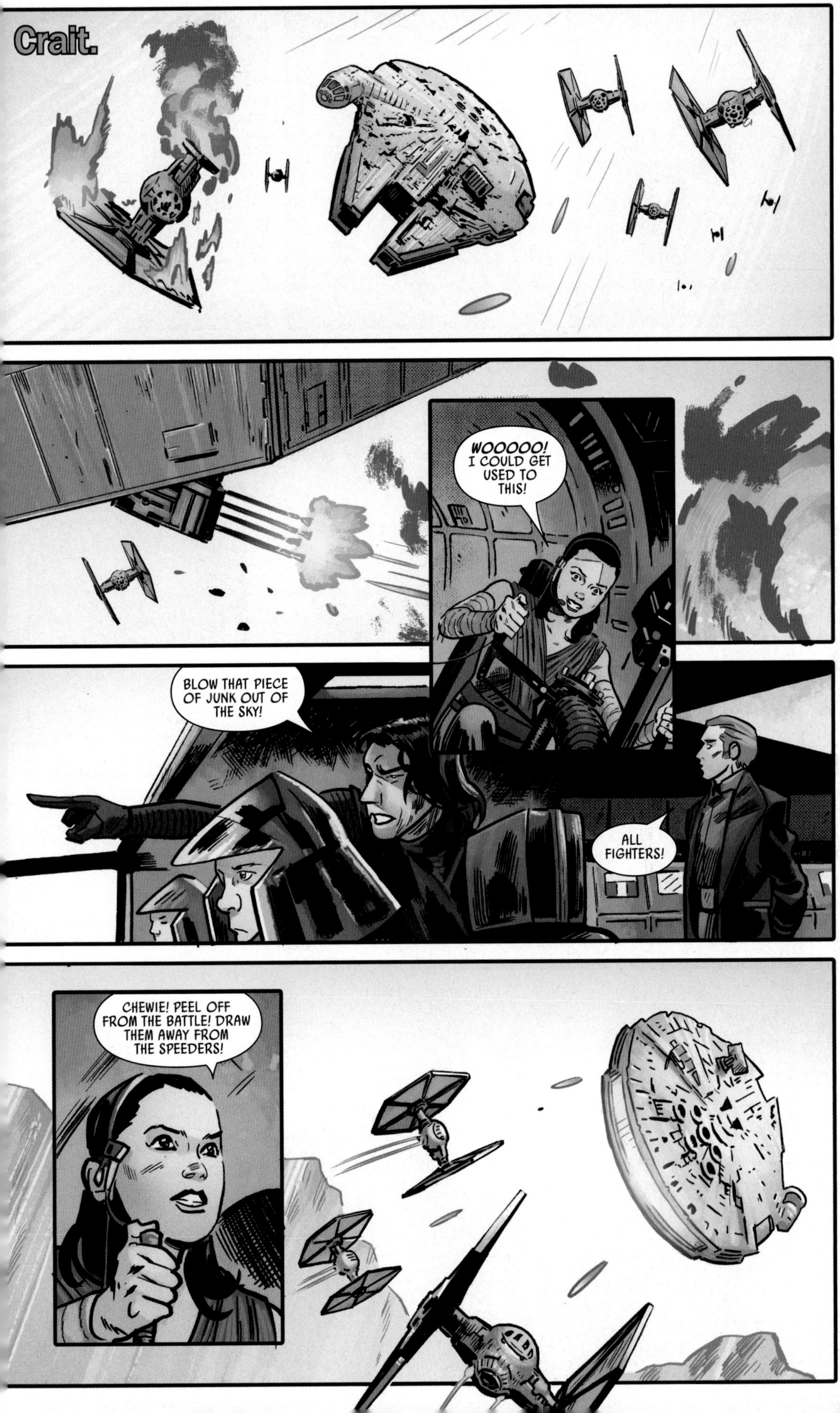
Crait.
WOOOOO! I COULD GET USED TO THIS!
BLOW THAT PIECE OF JUNK OUT OF THE SKY!
ALL FIGHTERS!
CHEWIE! PEEL OFF FROM THE BATTLE! DRAW THEM AWAY FROM THE SPEEDERS!

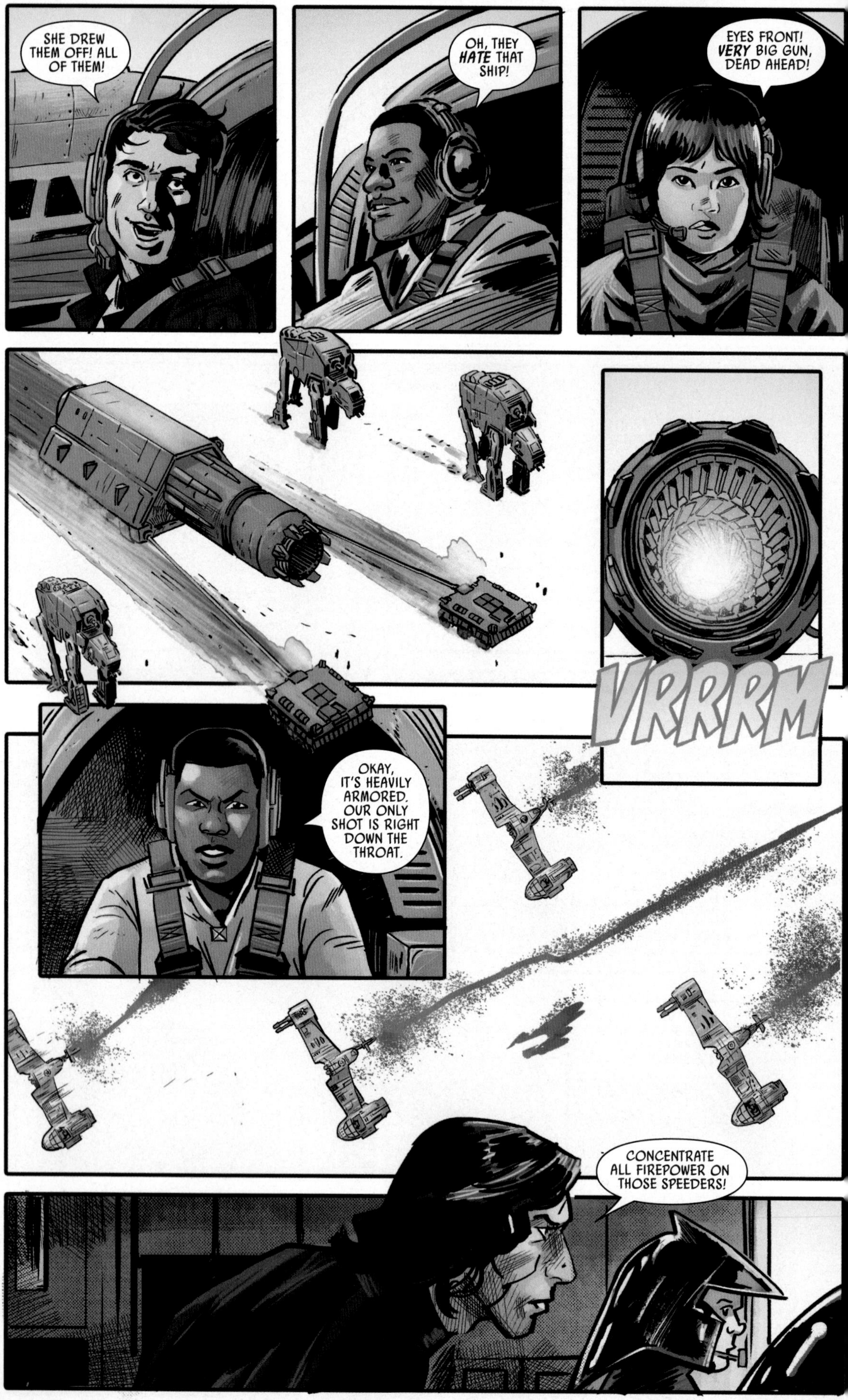
SHE DREW THEM OFF! ALL OF THEM!
OH, THEY HATE THAT SHIP!
EYES FRONT! VERY BIG GUN, DEAD AHEAD!
VRRRM
OKAY, IT'S HEAVILY ARMORED. OUR ONLY SHOT IS RIGHT DOWN THE THROAT.
CONCENTRATE ALL FIREPOWER ON THOSE SPEEDERS!

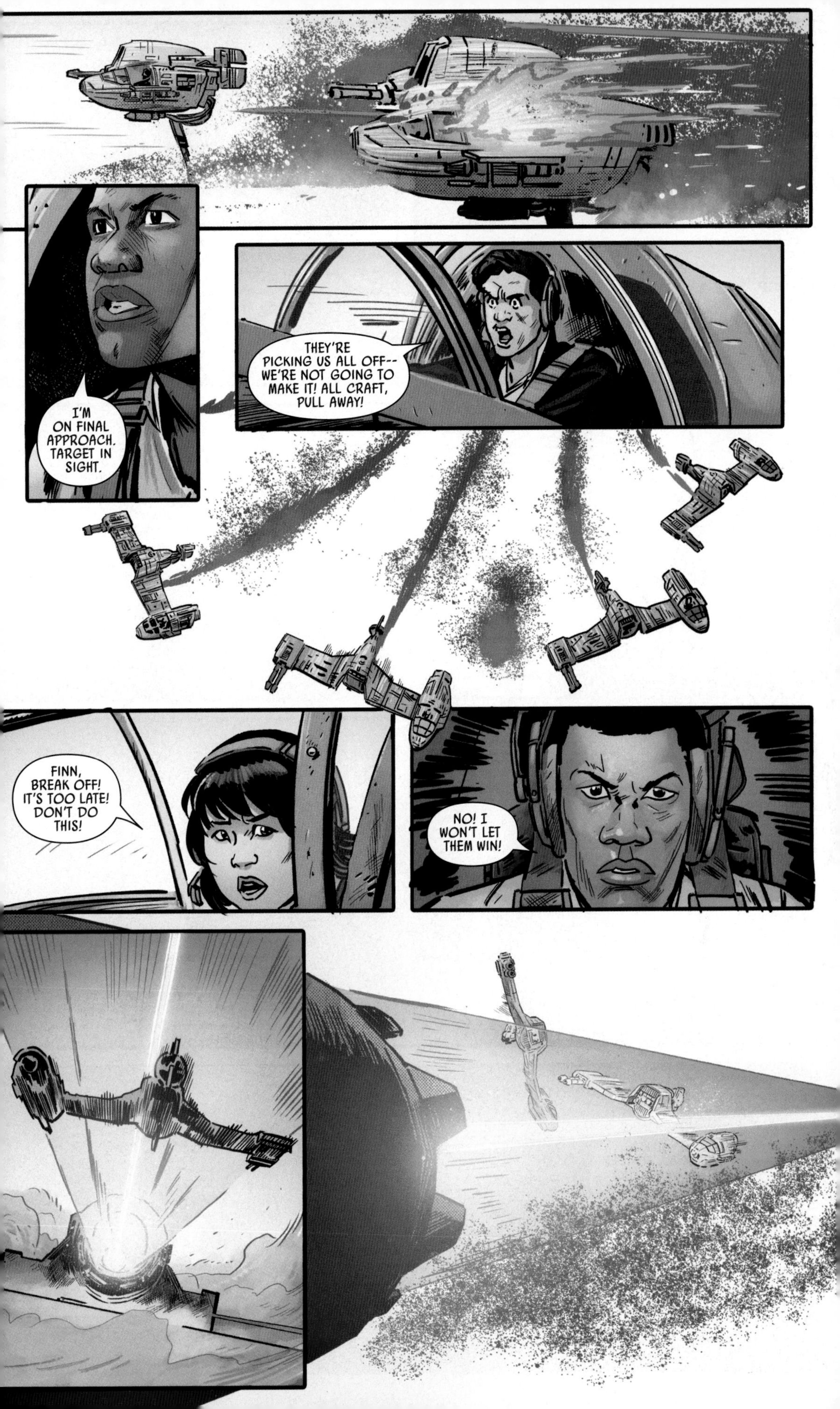
I'M ON FINAL APPROACH. TARGET IN SIGHT.
THEY'RE PICKING US ALL OFF-- WE'RE NOT GOING TO MAKE IT! ALL CRAFT, PULL AWAY!
FINN, BREAK OFF! IT'S TOO LATE! DON'T DO THIS!
NO! I WON'T LET THEM WIN!

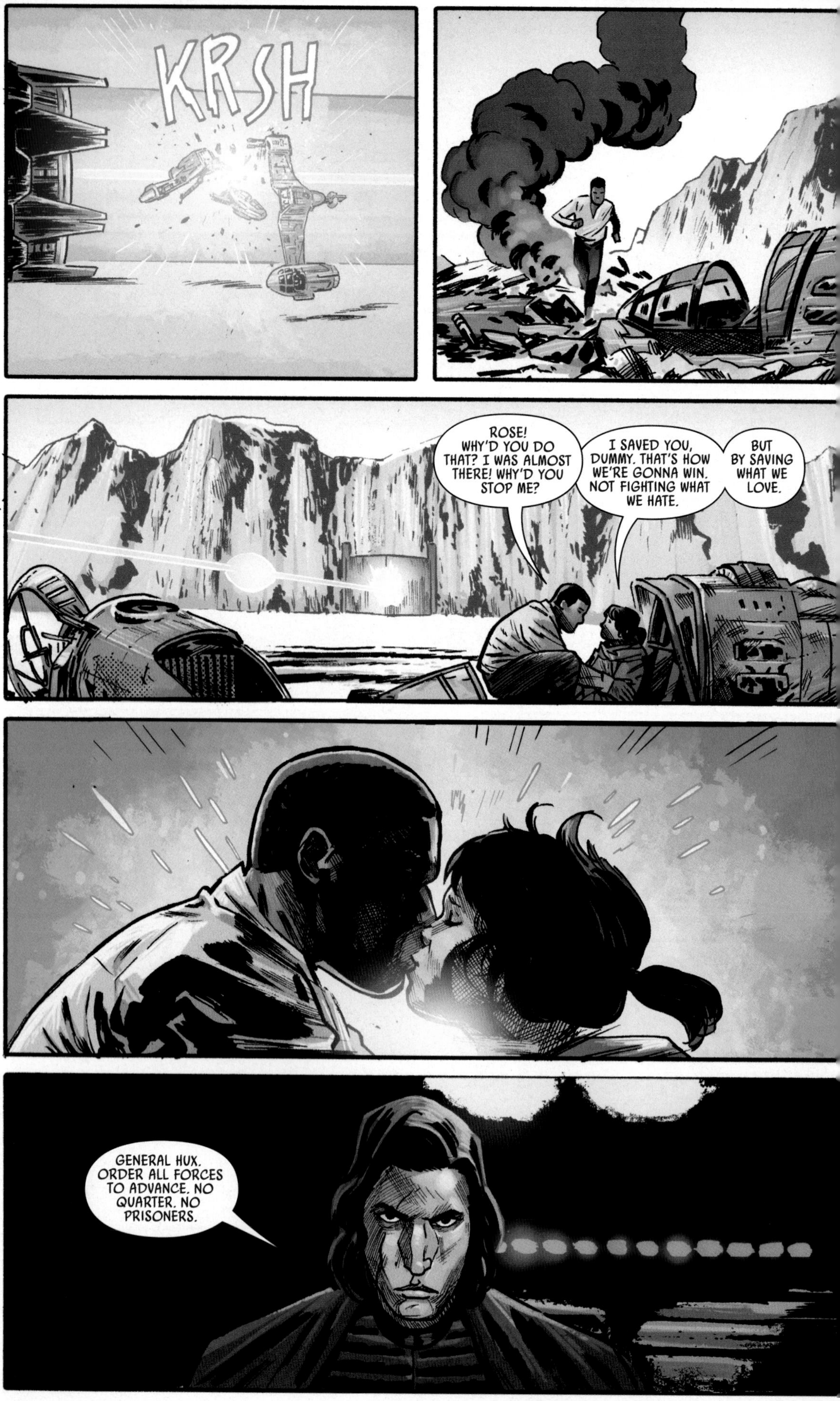
KRSH
ROSE! WHY'D YOU DO THAT? I WAS ALMOST THERE! WHY'D YOU STOP ME?
I SAVED YOU, DUMMY. THAT'S HOW WE'RE GONNA WIN. NOT FIGHTING WHAT WE HATE.
BUT BY SAVING WHAT WE LOVE.
GENERAL HUX. ORDER ALL FORCES TO ADVANCE. NO QUARTER. NO PRISONERS.

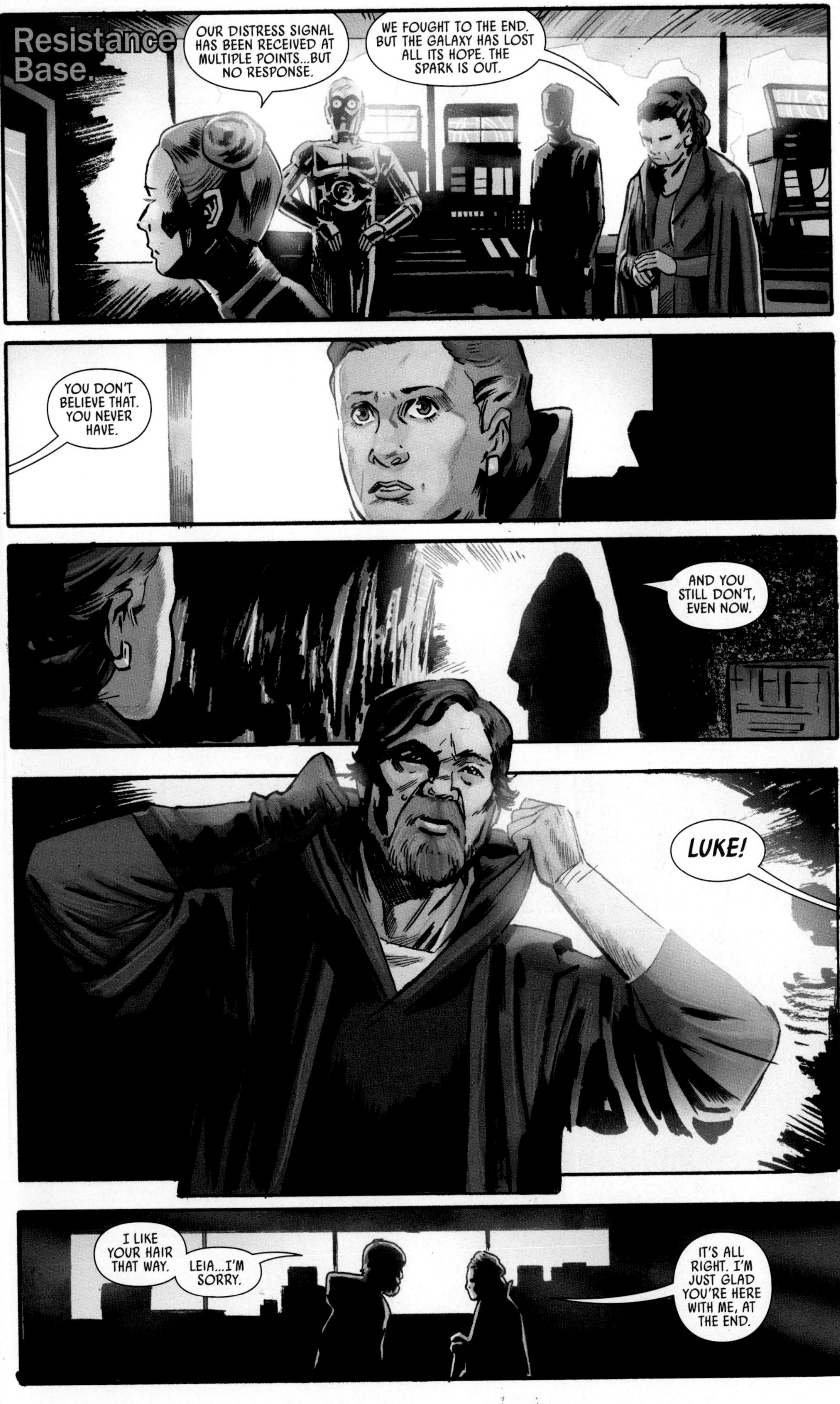
Resistance Base.
OUR DISTRESS SIGNAL HAS BEEN RECEIVED AT MULTIPLE POINTS...BUT NO RESPONSE.
WE FOUGHT TO THE END. BUT THE GALAXY HAS LOST ALL ITS HOPE. THE SPARK IS OUT.
YOU DON'T BELIEVE THAT. YOU NEVER HAVE.
AND YOU STILL DON'T, EVEN NOW.
LUKE!
I LIKE YOUR HAIR THAT WAY.
LEIA...I'M SORRY.
IT'S ALL RIGHT. I'M JUST GLAD YOU'RE HERE WITH ME, AT THE END.

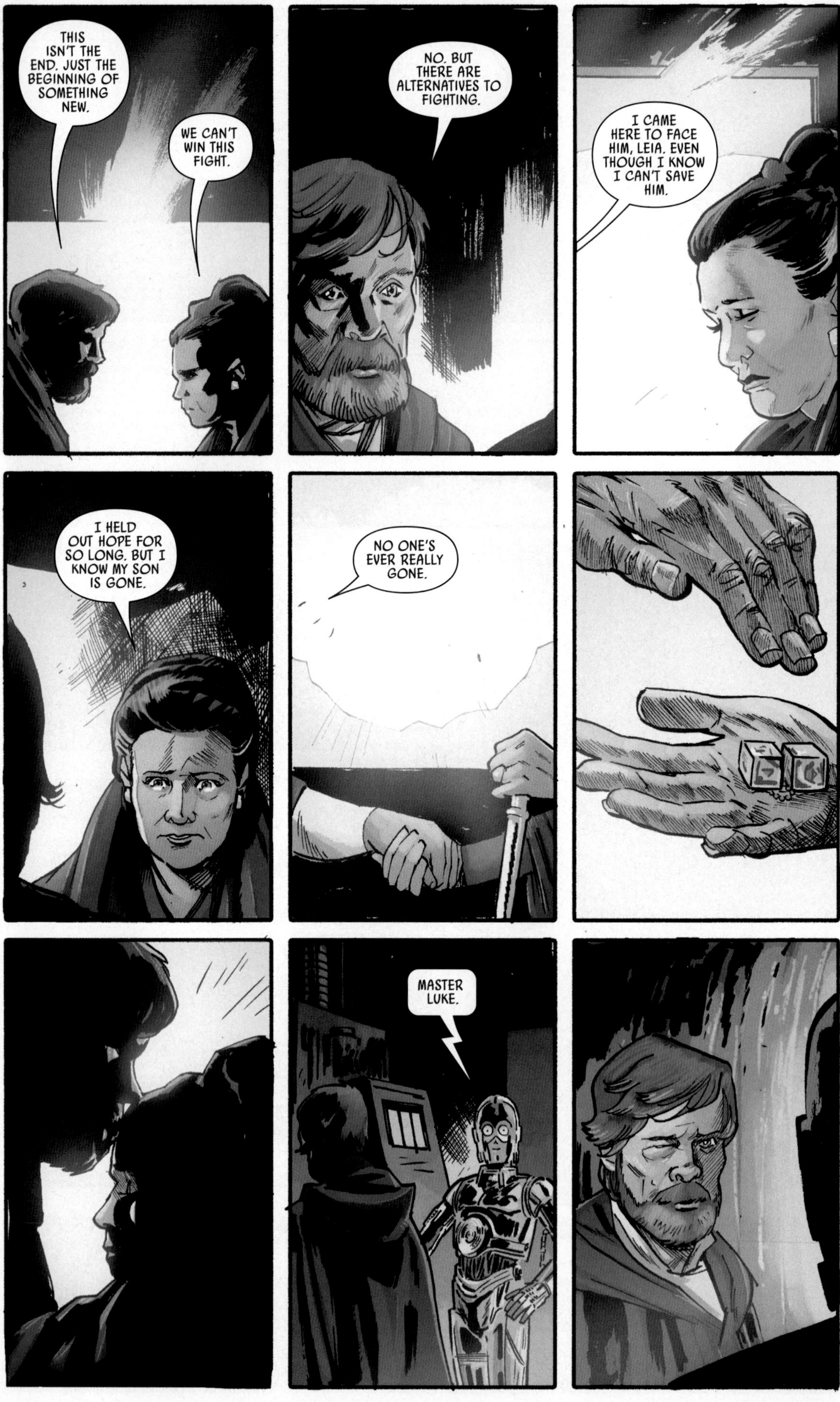
THIS ISN'T THE END. JUST THE BEGINNING OF SOMETHING NEW.
WE CAN'T WIN THIS FIGHT.
NO. BUT THERE ARE ALTERNATIVES TO FIGHTING.
I CAME HERE TO FACE HIM, LEIA. EVEN THOUGH I KNOW I CAN'T SAVE HIM.
I HELD OUT HOPE FOR SO LONG, BUT I KNOW MY SON IS GONE.
NO ONE'S EVER REALLY GONE.
MASTER LUKE.

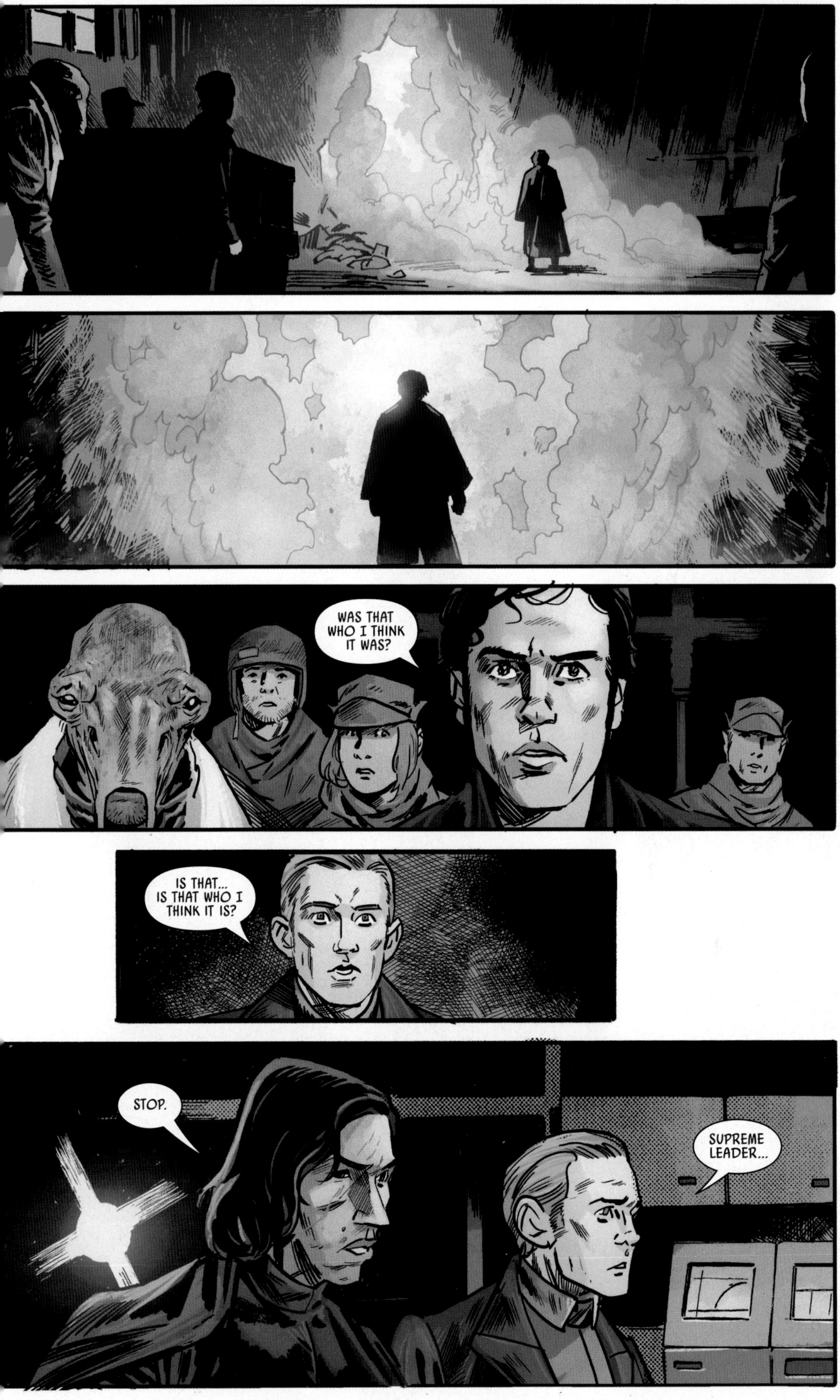
WAS THAT WHO I THINK IT WAS?
IS THAT... IS THAT WHO I THINK IT IS?
STOP.
SUPREME LEADER...

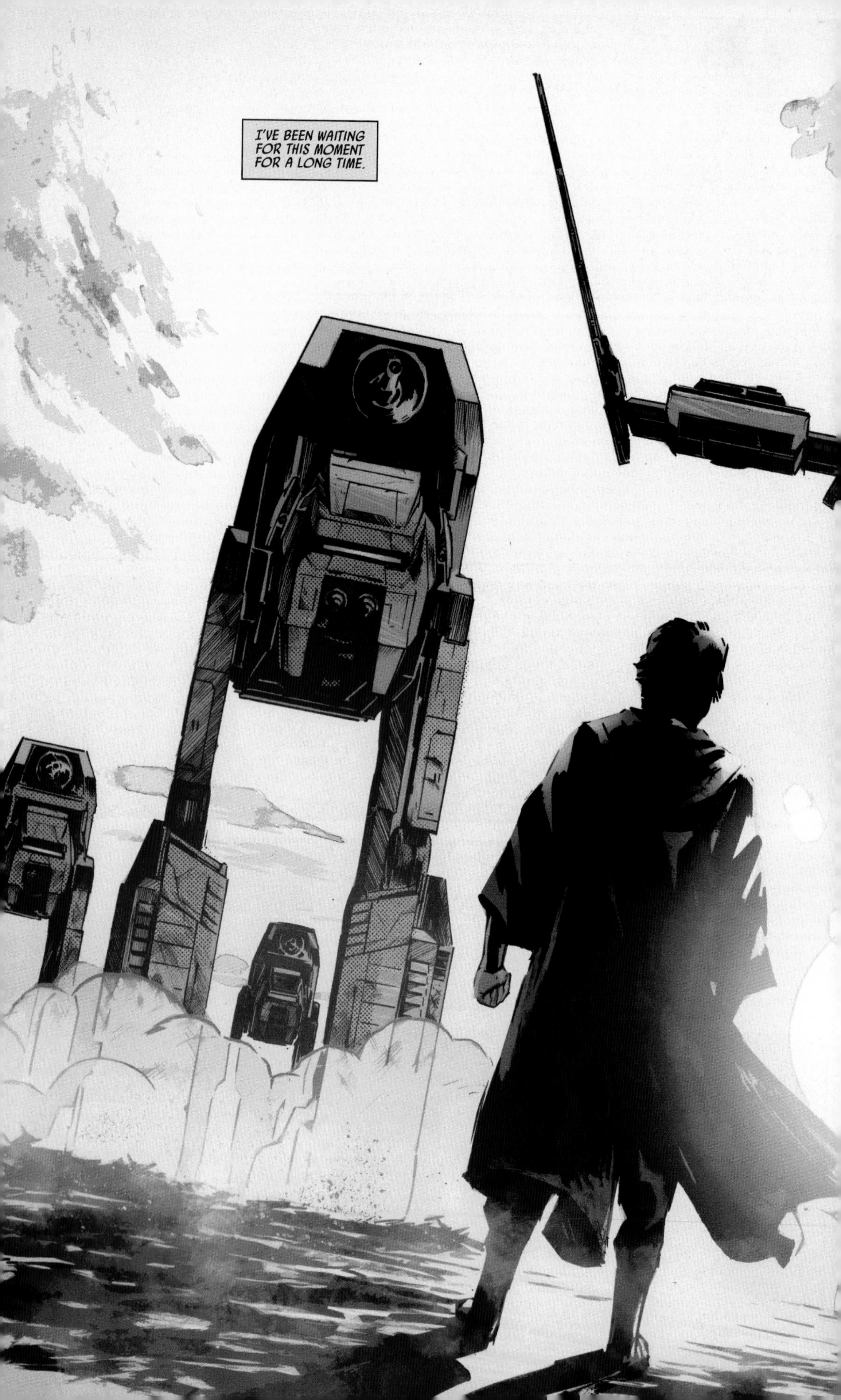
I'VE BEEN WAITING FOR THIS MOMENT FOR A LONG TIME.

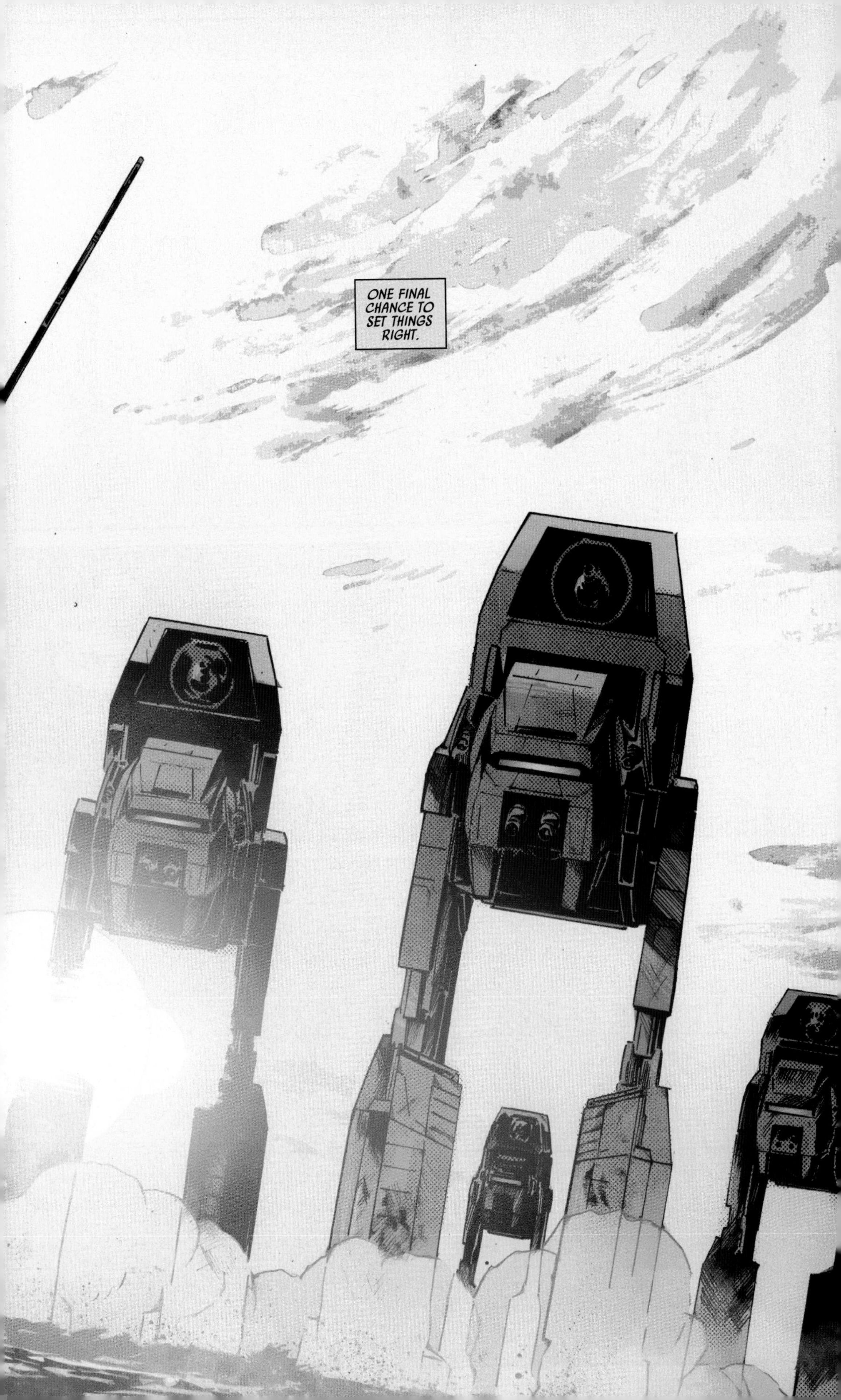
ONE FINAL CHANCE TO SET THINGS RIGHT.

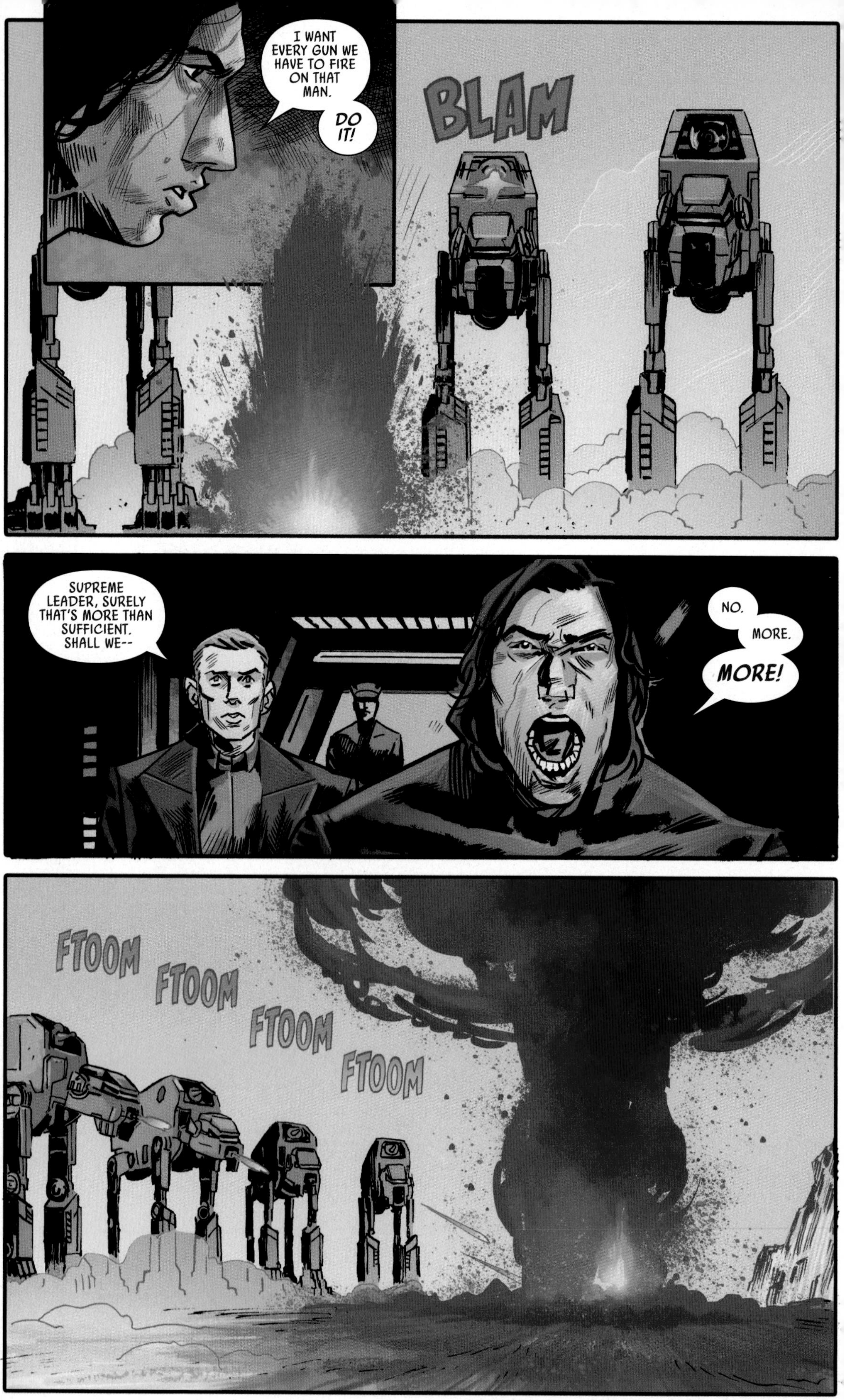
I WANT EVERY GUN WE HAVE TO FIRE ON THAT MAN.
DO IT!
BLAM
SUPREME LEADER, SURELY THAT'S MORE THAN SUFFICIENT. SHALL WE--
NO.
MORE.
MORE!
FTOOM
FTOOM
FTOOM
FTOOM

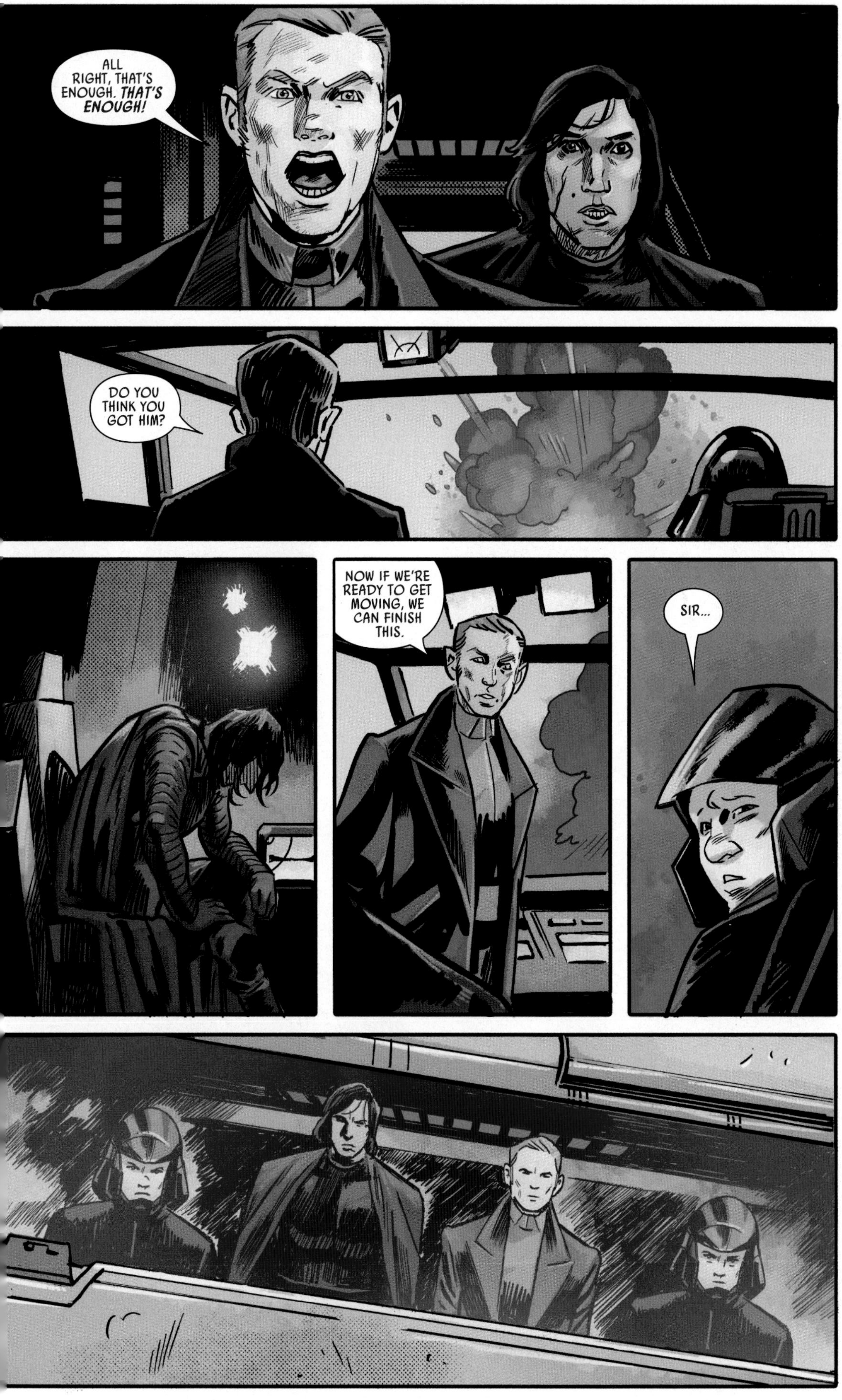
ALL RIGHT, THAT'S ENOUGH. *THAT'S ENOUGH!*
DO YOU THINK YOU GOT HIM?
NOW IF WE'RE READY TO GET MOVING, WE CAN FINISH THIS.
SIR...

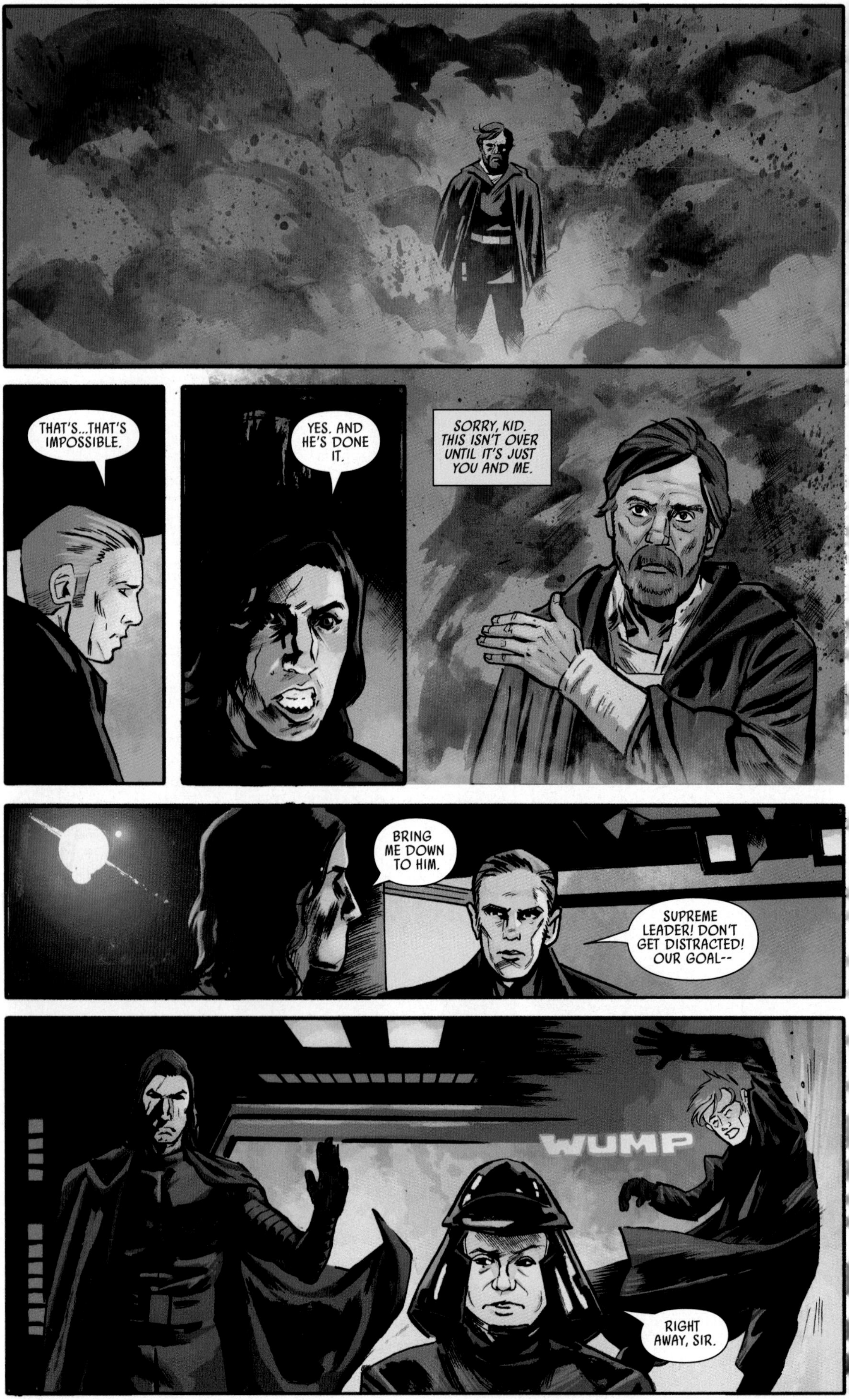
THAT'S...THAT'S IMPOSSIBLE.
YES. AND HE'S DONE IT.
SORRY, KID. THIS ISN'T OVER UNTIL IT'S JUST YOU AND ME.
BRING ME DOWN TO HIM.
SUPREME LEADER! DON'T GET DISTRACTED! OUR GOAL--
WUMP
RIGHT AWAY, SIR.

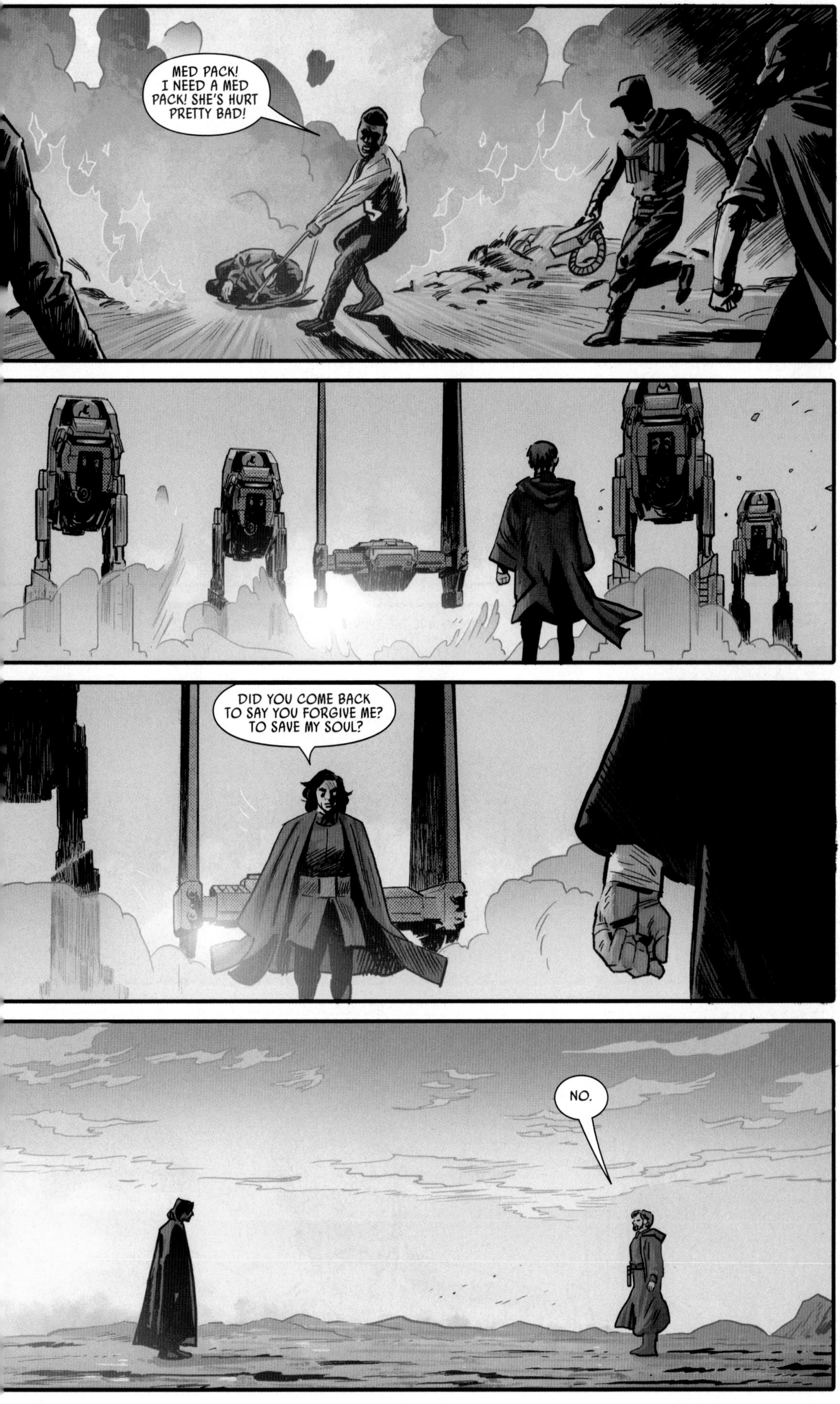
MED PACK! I NEED A MED PACK! SHE'S HURT PRETTY BAD!
DID YOU COME BACK TO SAY YOU FORGIVE ME? TO SAVE MY SOUL?
NO.

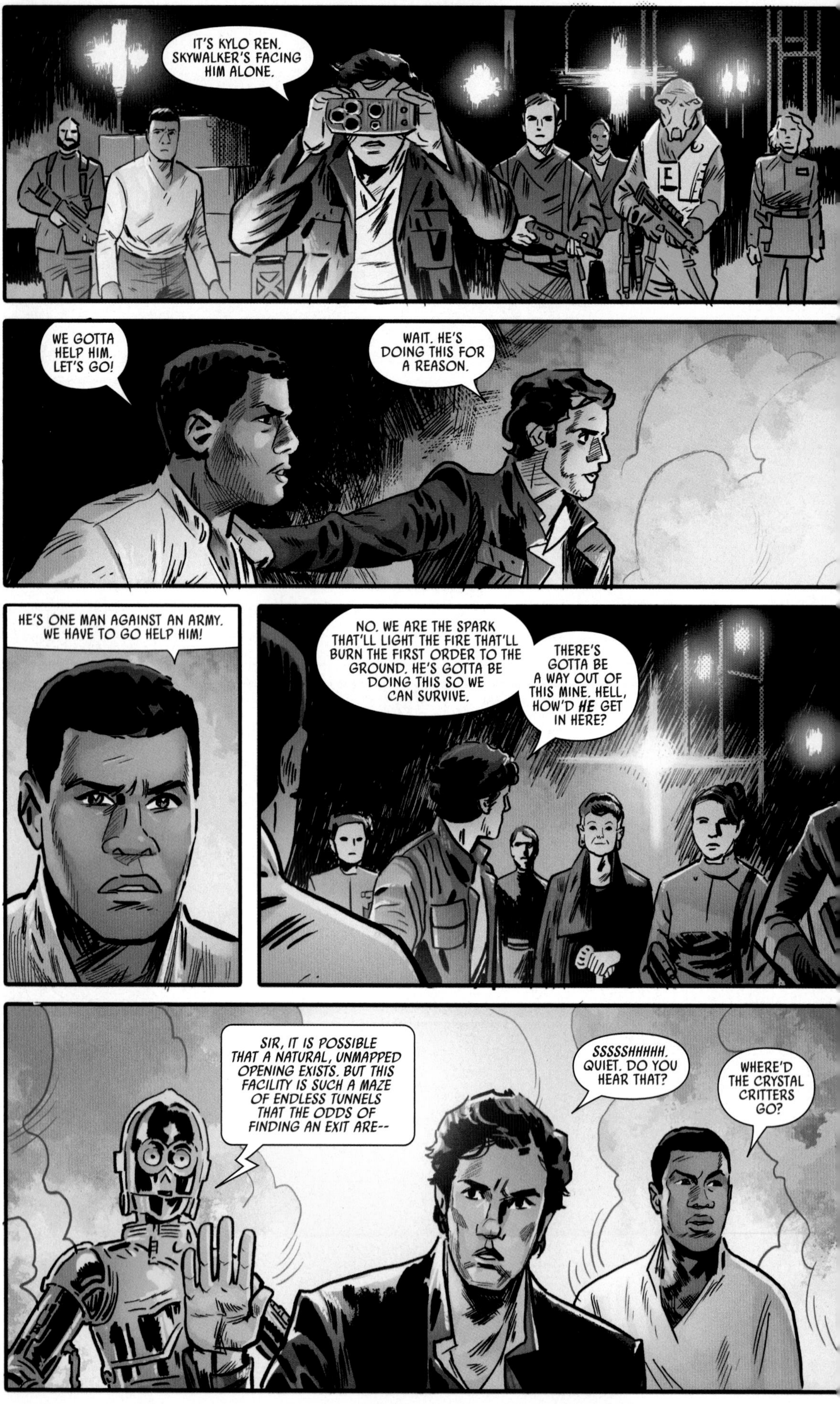

IT'S KYLO REN. SKYWALKER'S FACING HIM ALONE.
WE GOTTA HELP HIM. LET'S GO!
WAIT. HE'S DOING THIS FOR A REASON.
HE'S ONE MAN AGAINST AN ARMY. WE HAVE TO GO HELP HIM!
NO. WE ARE THE SPARK THAT'LL LIGHT THE FIRE THAT'LL BURN THE FIRST ORDER TO THE GROUND. HE'S GOTTA BE DOING THIS SO WE CAN SURVIVE.
THERE'S GOTTA BE A WAY OUT OF THIS MINE. HELL, HOW'D HE GET IN HERE?
SIR, IT IS POSSIBLE THAT A NATURAL, UNMAPPED OPENING EXISTS. BUT THIS FACILITY IS SUCH A MAZE OF ENDLESS TUNNELS THAT THE ODDS OF FINDING AN EXIT ARE--
SSSSSHHHHH. QUIET. DO YOU HEAR THAT?
WHERE'D THE CRYSTAL CRITTERS GO?

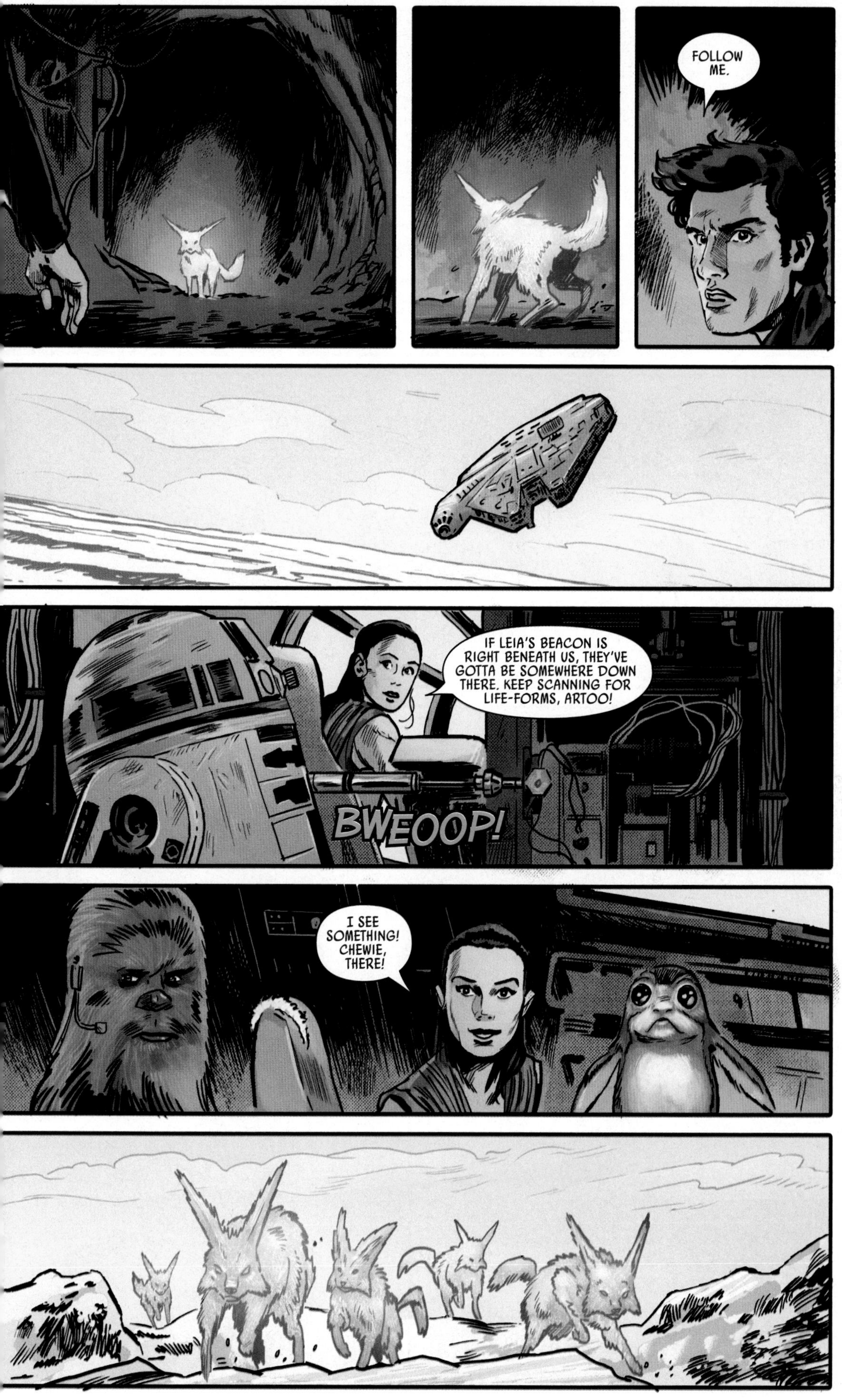
FOLLOW ME.
IF LEIA'S BEACON IS RIGHT BENEATH US, THEY'VE GOTTA BE SOMEWHERE DOWN THERE. KEEP SCANNING FOR LIFE-FORMS, ARTOO!
BWEOOP!
I SEE SOMETHING! CHEWIE, THERE!

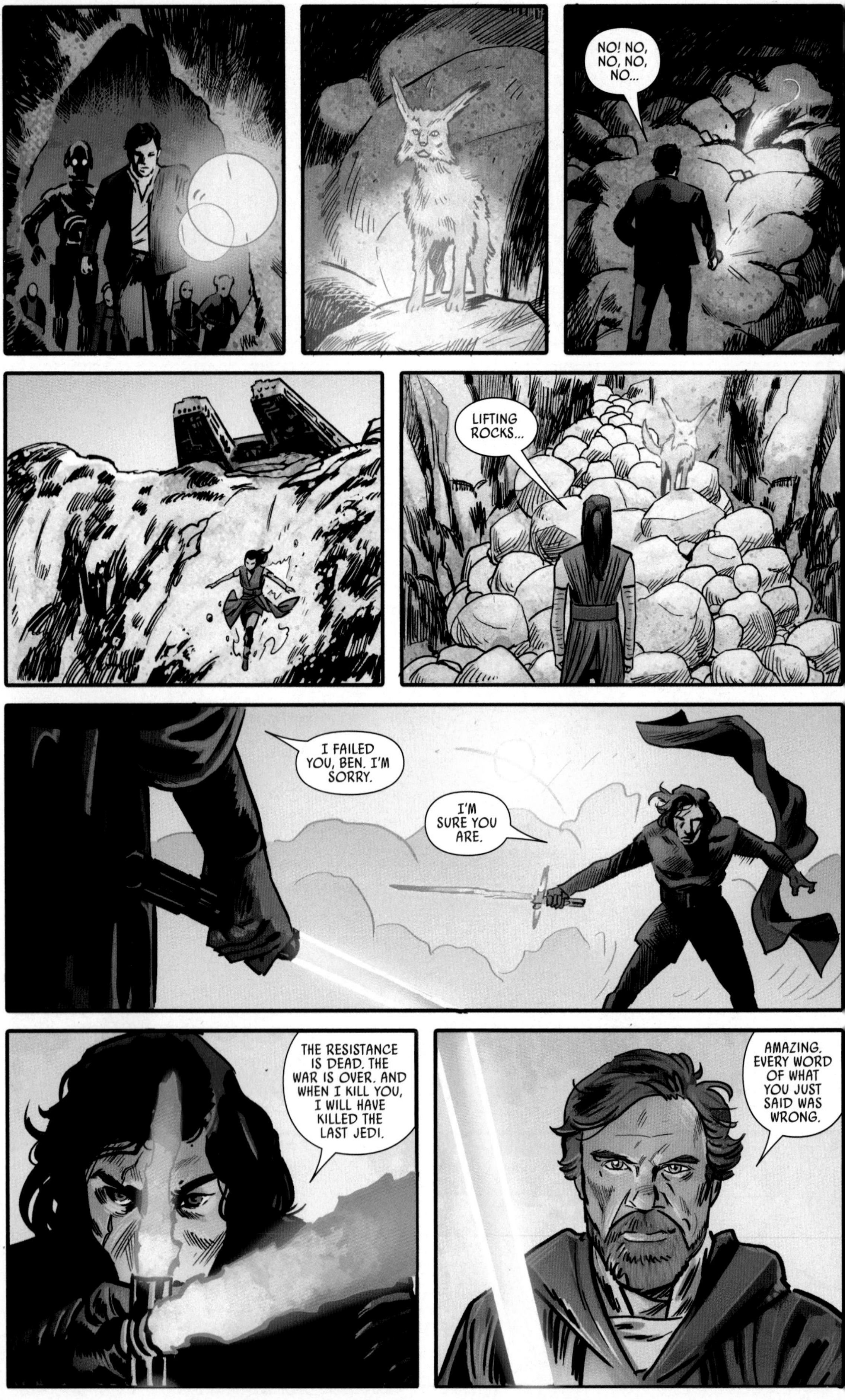
NO! NO, NO, NO, NO...
LIFTING ROCKS...
I FAILED YOU, BEN. I'M SORRY.
I'M SURE YOU ARE.
THE RESISTANCE IS DEAD. THE WAR IS OVER. AND WHEN I KILL YOU, I WILL HAVE KILLED THE LAST JEDI.
AMAZING. EVERY WORD OF WHAT YOU JUST SAID WAS WRONG.

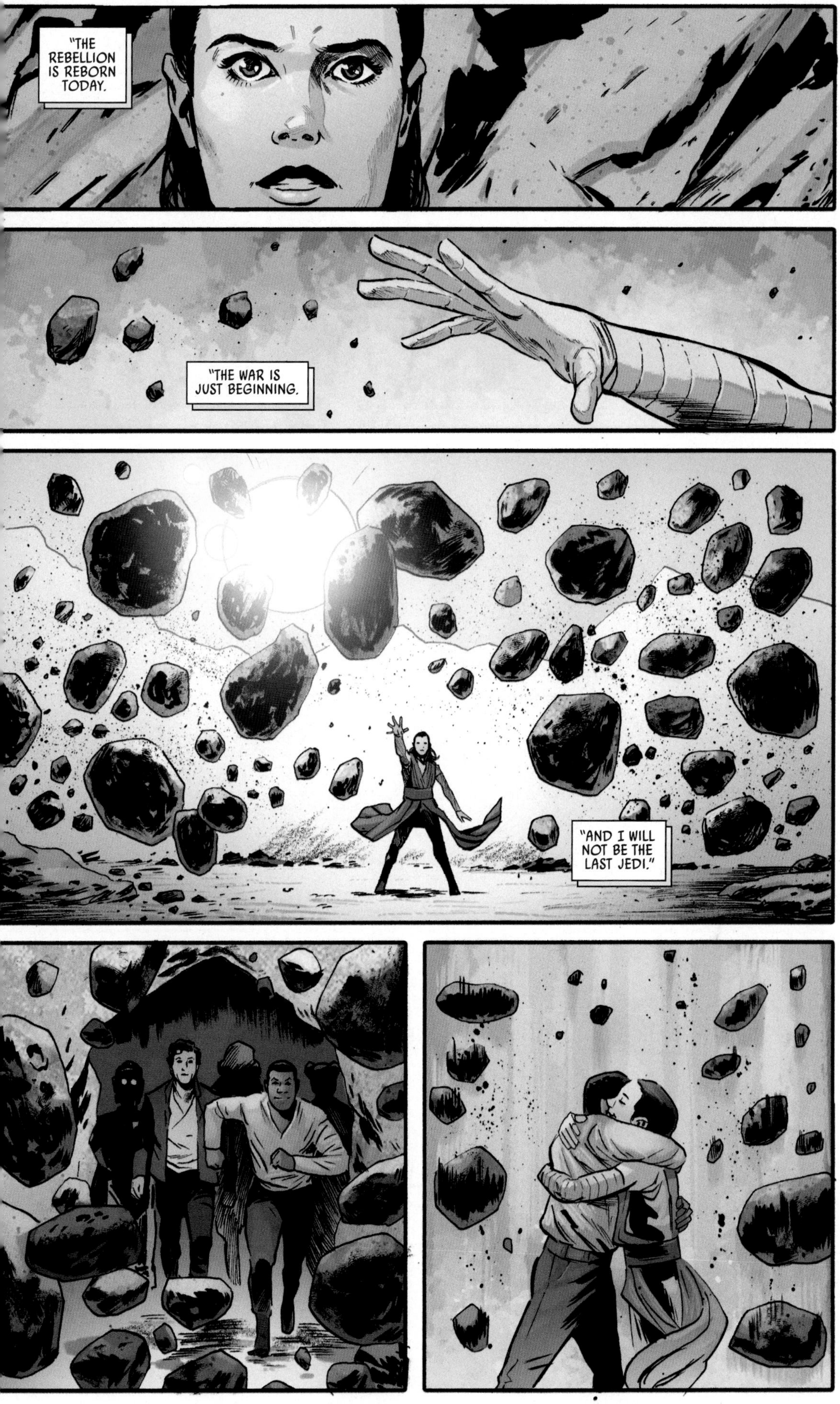
"THE REBELLION IS REBORN TODAY.
"THE WAR IS JUST BEGINNING.
"AND I WILL NOT BE THE LAST JEDI."

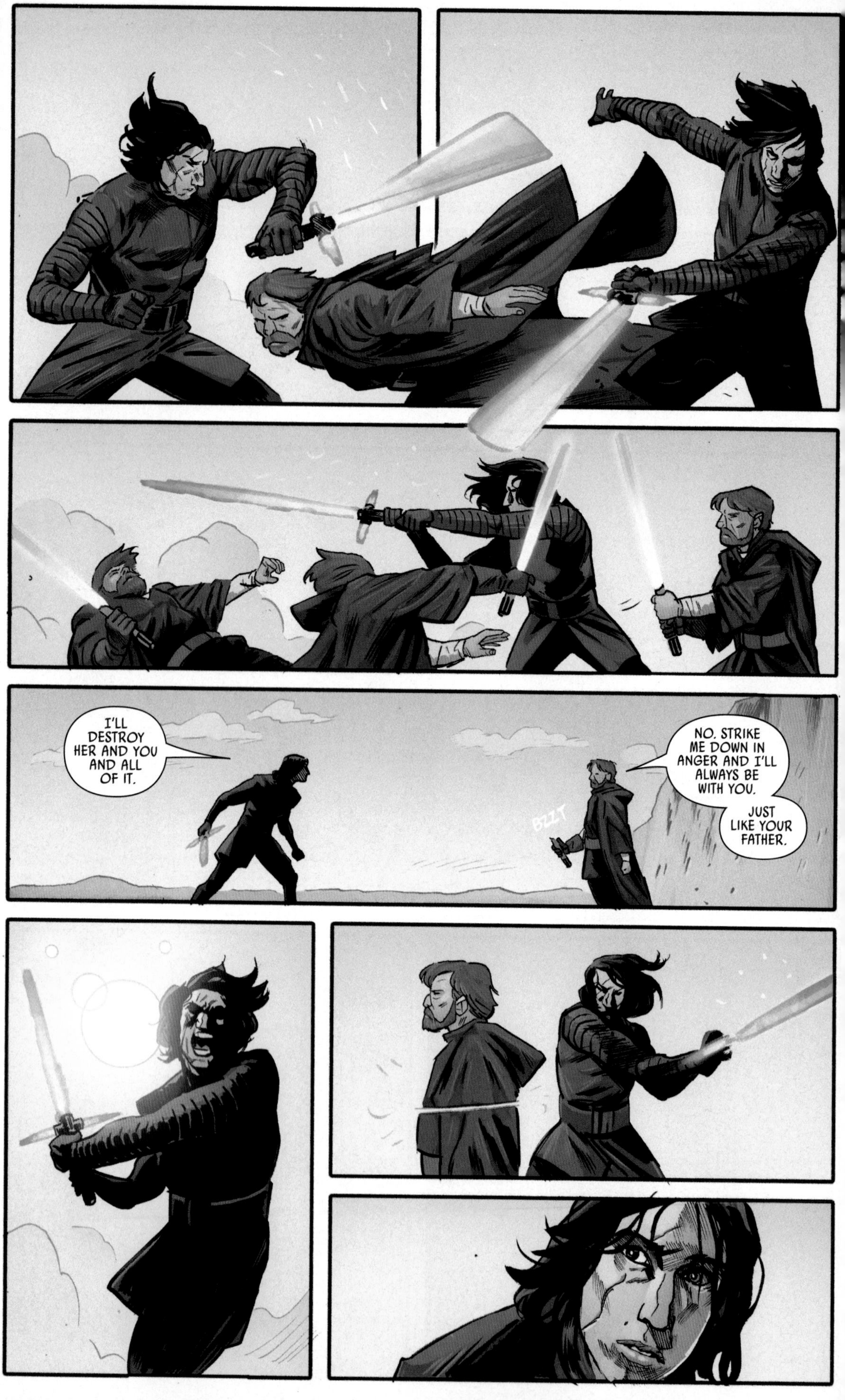
I'LL DESTROY HER AND YOU AND ALL OF IT.
NO. STRIKE ME DOWN IN ANGER AND I'LL ALWAYS BE WITH YOU.
JUST LIKE YOUR FATHER.
BZZT

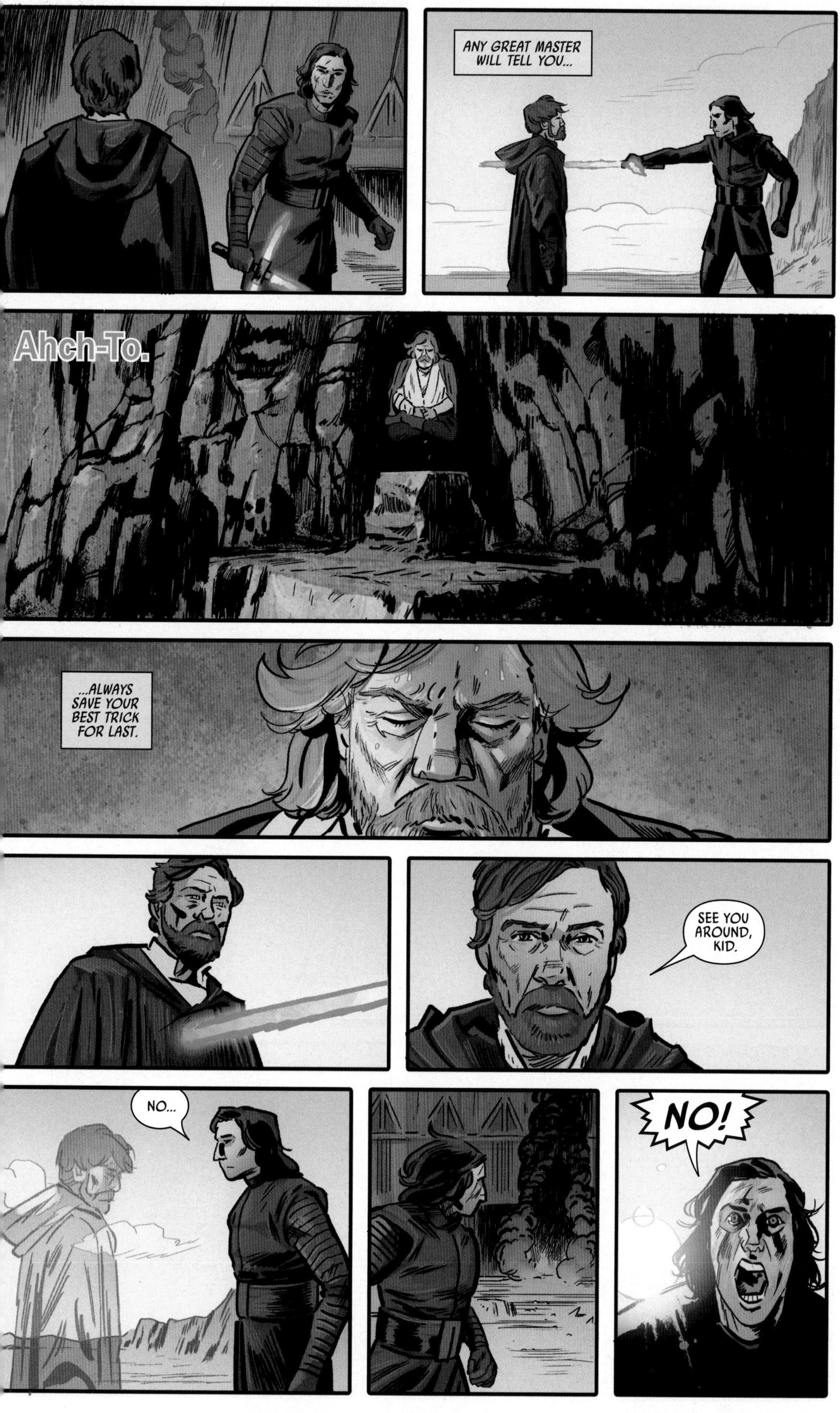

ANY GREAT MASTER WILL TELL YOU...
Ahch-To.
...ALWAYS SAVE YOUR BEST TRICK FOR LAST.
SEE YOU AROUND, KID.
NO...
NO!

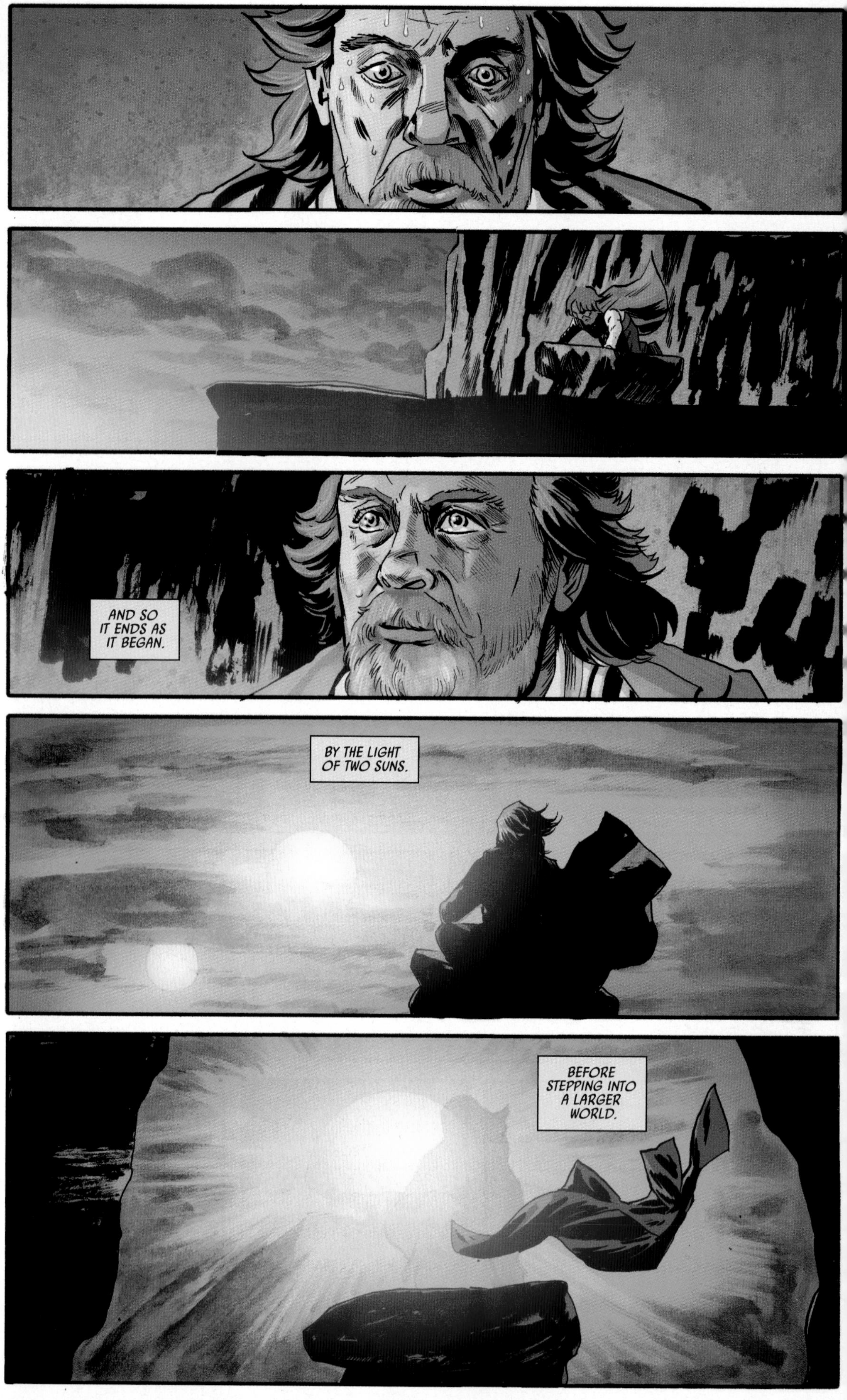
AND SO IT ENDS AS IT BEGAN.
BY THE LIGHT OF TWO SUNS.
BEFORE STEPPING INTO A LARGER WORLD.

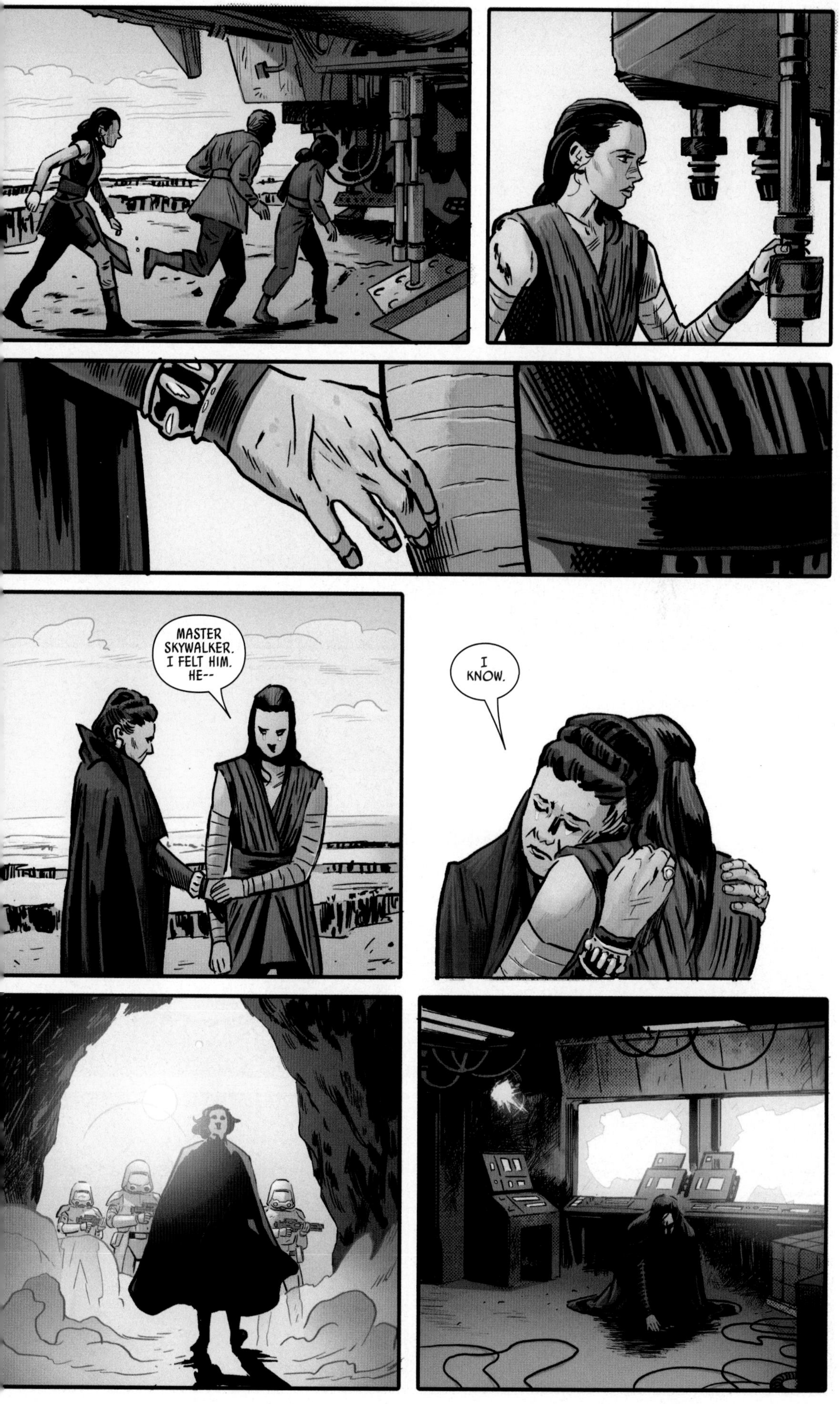
MASTER SKYWALKER. I FELT HIM. HE--
I KNOW.

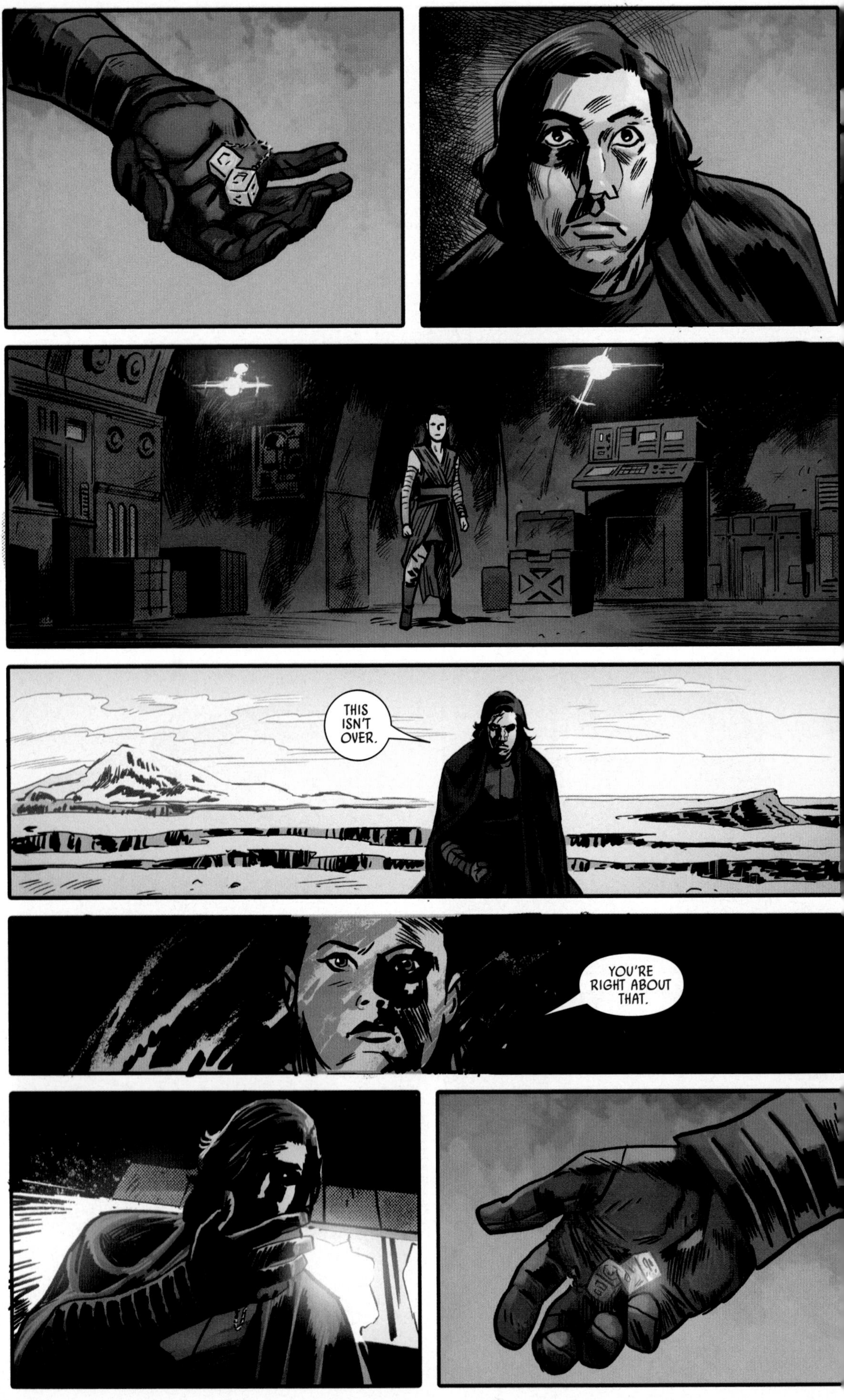
THIS ISN'T OVER.
YOU'RE RIGHT ABOUT THAT.

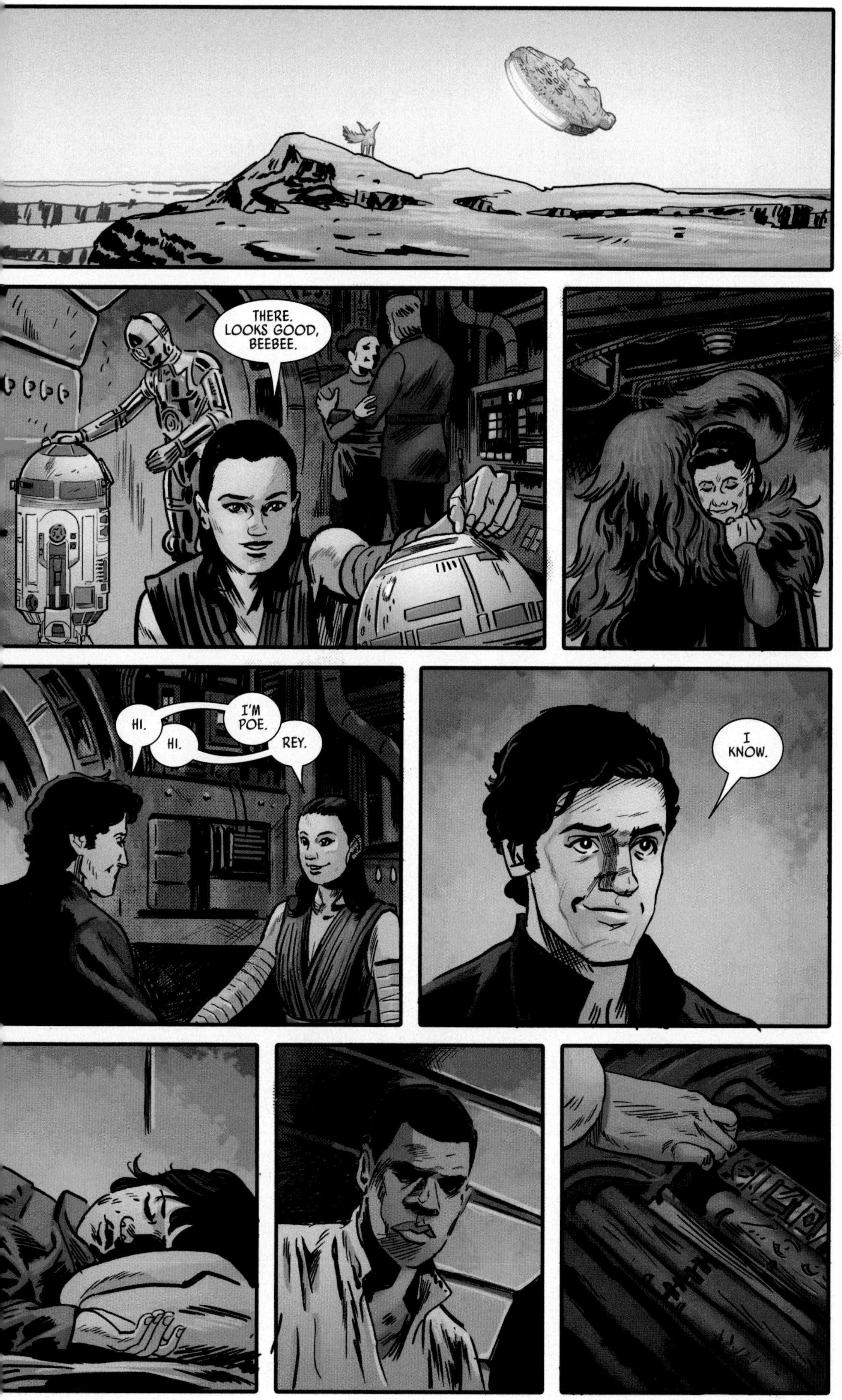
THERE. LOOKS GOOD, BEEBEE.
HI.
HI.
I'M POE.
REY.
I KNOW.

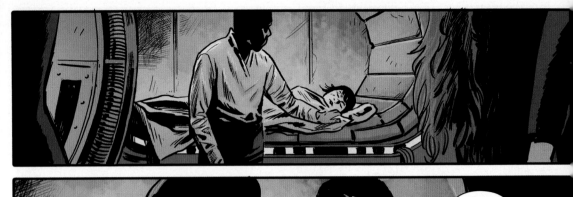

WHEN HE DIED...WHAT I FELT WASN'T SADNESS OR PAIN...IT WAS PEACE. AND PURPOSE.

I KNOW.

I FELT IT TOO.

HOW DO WE BUILD A REBELLION FROM THIS?

WHEN THE FIRST REBELLION BEGAN, THERE WERE EVEN FEWER.

"WE HAVE EVERYTHING WE NEED."

<AND THEN THE GREAT *JEDI MASTER LUKE SKYWALKER*, BRAVELY STANDING ALONE AGAINST THE FIRST ORDER-->

<BACK TO WORK! LAZY LITTLE WRETCHES!>

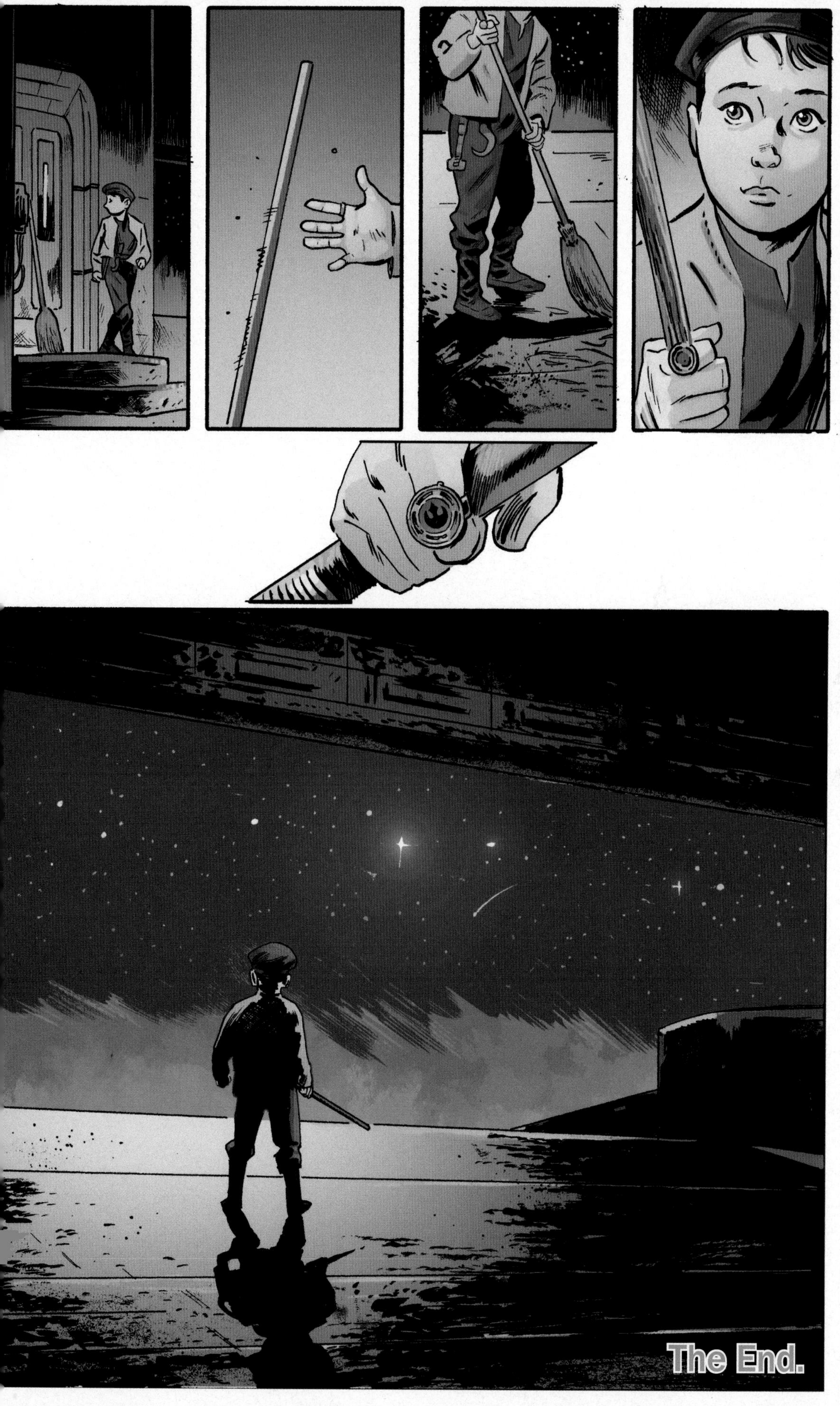
The End.

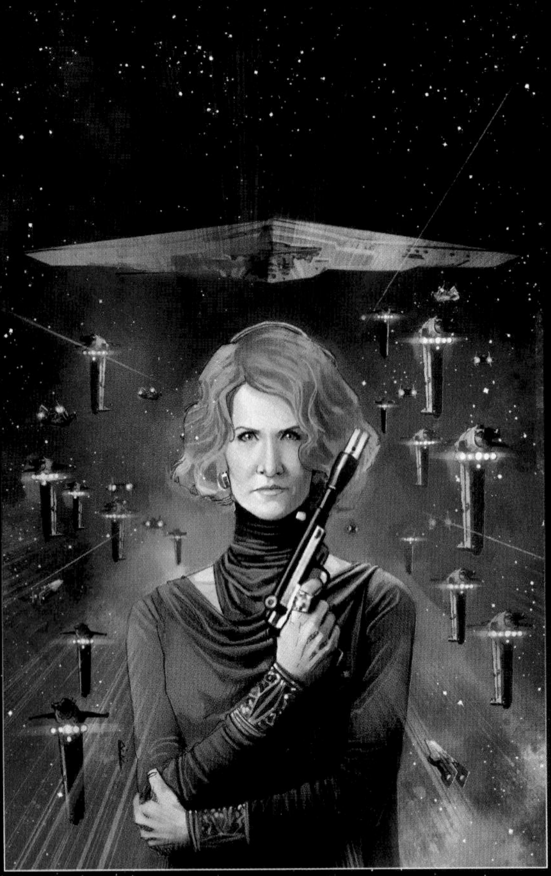

Issue #4 variant by Rod Reis

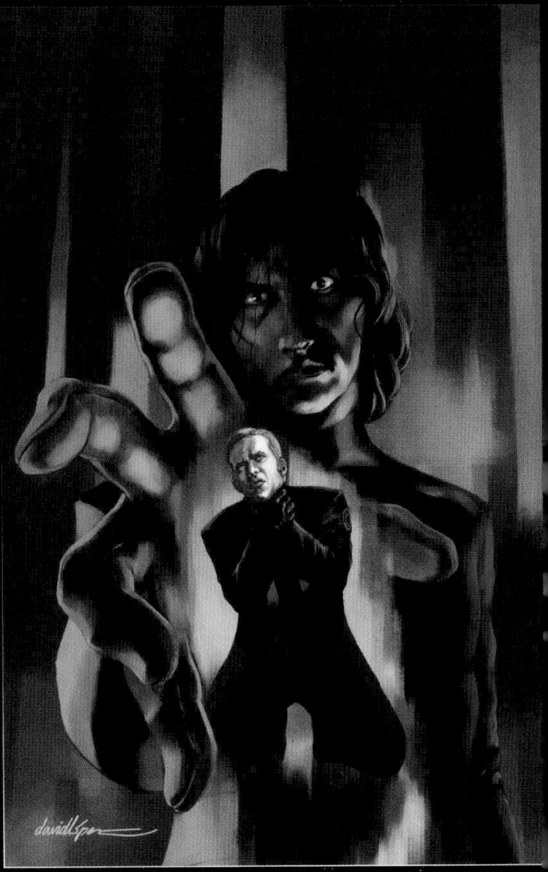

Issue #5 variant by David Lopez

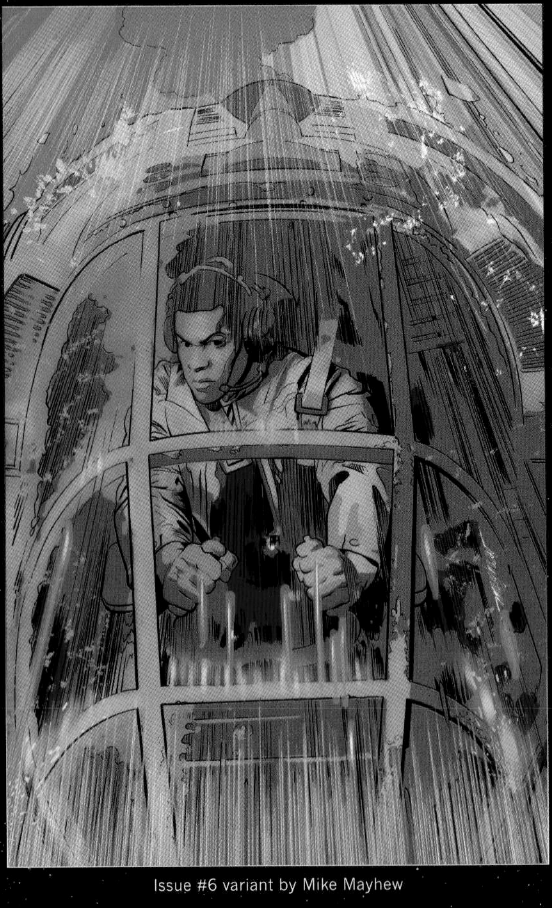

Issue #6 variant by Mike Mayhew

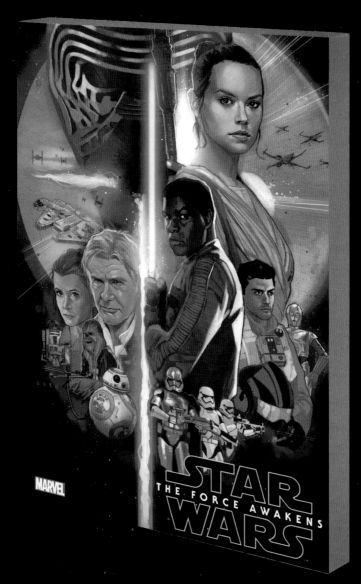

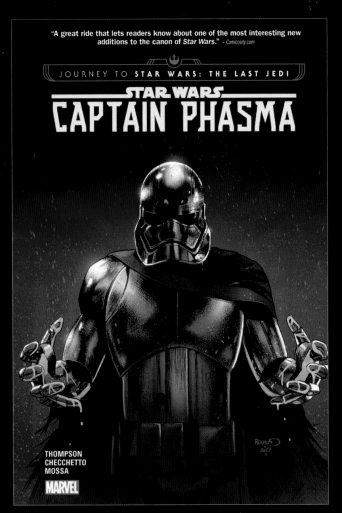

SENSATIONAL *STAR WARS* ARTWORK RETELLING THE STORY OF *A NEW HOPE!*

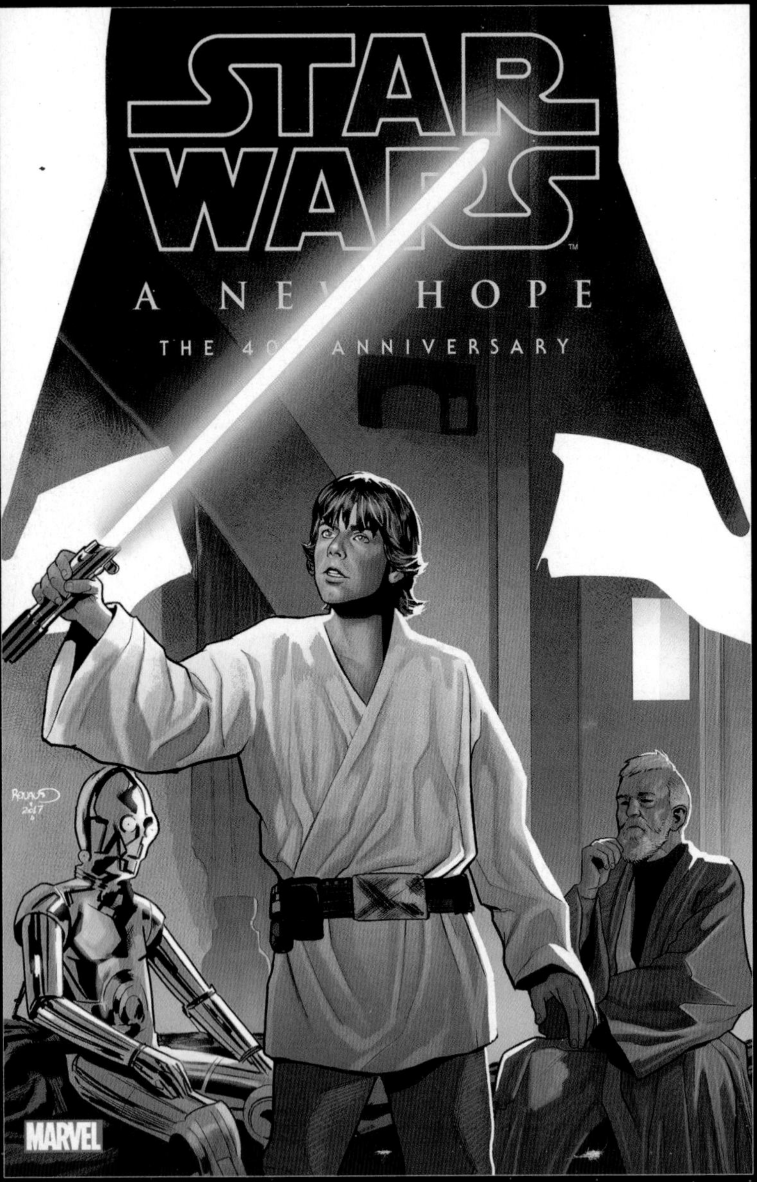
STAR WARS
MARVEL

***STAR WARS: A NEW HOPE* — THE 40TH ANNIVERSARY HC**

978-1302911287

ON SALE NOW

AVAILABLE IN PRINT AND DIGITAL WHEREVER BOOKS ARE SOLD

TO FIND A COMIC SHOP NEAR YOU, VISIT COMICSHOPLOCATOR.COM

MARVEL Disney LUCASFILM